# Salads for Small Gardens

JOY LARKCOM

# Salads for Small Gardens

ILLUSTRATED BY

ELIZABETH DOUGLASS

HAMLYN

## ACKNOWLEDGEMENTS

For this second edition, once again thanks to all those we met on our *Grand Vegetable Tour* in 1976 and 1977, who taught me so much about salads. In the intervening years thanks to Robert Hart for inspiration, to John and Caroline Stevens, founders of Suffolk Herbs, for making so many salad seeds available in this country, and to the Henry Doubleday Research Association, Malcolm Burrows and Richard Lovick for technical help. Thank you also to many friends in the USA and Canada for a host of new ideas gathered during my visit in 1987: especially all of you at the Glorious Garnish and Seasonal Salads Company, Mark Musick, Rene Shepherd of Shepherd Seeds and Alice Waters. Once again, a very warm thank you to Elizabeth Douglass for her fine work on the illustrations, to John Matthissen for sorting out the computer problems with such patience, and to my husband Don, who has shared so much of the work and experimenting over the years. Lastly, thank you to the team at Reed Illustrated Books, especially Anna Mumford for her support, and Selina Higgins, for her constructive and kindly editing.

## METRICATION

Measurements are given in metric, with approximate imperial equivalents given in brackets. Where conversions are not strictly consistent, they will be found accurate enough for all practical purposes.

First published in 1995

© Reed International Books Limited 1995
Text © Joy Larkcom 1995
Design © Reed Consumer Books 1995

Printed in Finland

ISBN 0 600 58509 3

A CIP catalogue entry for this book is available from the British Library

# Contents

# Introduction

I feel I should start by confessing that I am a vegetable kleptomaniac –
more precisely, a *raw* vegetable kleptomaniac. I find it almost impossible
to walk around a kitchen garden without nibbling a leaf here, snapping
off a pea pod there, savouring a fragment of parsley or chervil. I can only
suppose it is this habit which has led to my appreciation of the wonderful
variety of flavours and textures which can be produced in an English garden, and above all, to a passionate interest in salads.

For years I had a limited, conventional view of salads. They came with
summer (how one longed for the first fresh salad of the year), and they
were mainly lettuce, with radish, spring onion, cucumber and tomato in
supporting roles. Only gradually did I realize that it is perfectly feasible to
pick salads from your garden all-year-round and, moreover, that an
almost infinite number of plants can be used in salads: cultivated and wild
plants; roots, leaves, seed pods and flowers; sprouted seeds and seedlings.

Looking back, it seems to me that the somewhat meandering road to
these discoveries was marked with several milestones. It began in 1969
when we moved to our present home in East Anglia. With little money,
plenty of space, and a family on the way, there was every incentive to
grow vegetables. I started systematically to try out the 'unusual' vegetables in seed catalogues, and found that a great many of them were salads;
in particular, salads which could be used in late autumn, winter and early
spring, when it is so hard to grow a good lettuce. Within a few years I had
discovered celeriac, land cress and corn salad, the enormous long red
Chinese winter radish, Welsh onions which stay green all winter,
Chinese cabbage for a quick autumn crop, succulent 'Sugar Loaf' chicory
and endive.

Winter salads became one of the specialities of the house. I loved to go
out into the apparently bare garden in winter to collect a salad, digging
up roots protected with straw, and wheedling corn salad out from under
a covering of bracken. The leaves of land cress and corn salad would
be used whole, the Chinese cabbage (which survived until heavy frost)
and the various chicories would be chopped up, while the celeriac and
radish would be grated: the end result was a lovely blend of fresh flavours,

doubly welcome in mid-winter. I wallowed unashamedly in visitors' praise, and surprise: 'Not all from the garden at this time of year? – but what's this? – and this?'

The next milestone was being commissioned to write a book on growing vegetables in small gardens, during one of those periods of economic crisis when people were digging up their lawns to plant potatoes and the queues for allotments were lengthening. I began experimenting with intensive techniques such as intercropping and undercropping and growing dwarf varieties. But the most fascinating idea I came upon was the 'cut-and-come-again' technique. I knew that you could chop off an old cabbage, cut a cross in the stalk, and with luck get four or five more young cabbages growing from the cut; but I did not realize you could cut off lettuce, turnip tops, kale and spinach at different stages of growth and that they would resprout once, twice or even three times.

On a visit to some allotments in Manchester 'the Italian's' plot was pointed out to me. He was not there, unfortunately, but his fellow allotment holders told me that he grew many unusual vegetables and in most unusual ways – including 'cut-and-come-again'. My curiosity was aroused. At about the same time I heard of experiments being carried out at Horticulture Research International at Wellesbourne, with what they called 'leaf lettuce'. They were growing cos varieties of lettuce very closely, so that instead of forming hearts, they developed a cluster of loose leaves that simply fell apart when cut. This made life very simple for the catering trade, ensuring a demand for this type of lettuce. Moreover the young plants were being cut then left to resprout for a second cut making the crop doubly productive. Coupling this with successive sowings over several months, leaf lettuce could be picked continuously from spring through to late autumn, the technique enabling twice the normal weight of lettuce to be harvested from any piece of ground during the growing season.

By now I had a hunch that there was a lot to be learned about both vegetables and techniques from the Continent, particularly from the peasant farmers. I was also becoming interested in the need to collect and preserve the seed of old and local varieties which, under modern pressure for conformity and economy, and subsequently Economic Community legislation, were being squeezed out of use and were in danger of disappearing forever. Apart from their intrinsic interest and value, these old and local varieties often prove of value to plant breeders, harbouring useful genetic characteristics such as hardiness, resistance to disease, and adaptation to particular climatic conditions.

These ideas gave my husband and I an excuse to realize a long-cherished dream, to take a year off and travel. He gave up his teaching job, we rented out the house, bought a second-hand van and caravan and with our two children, then aged five and seven, set off on a year's wandering around Europe to investigate vegetable growing. We called it *The Grand Vegetable Tour*, and were fortunate enough to get a grant towards the cost from the Stanley Smith Horticultural Trust. Before our departure we had collected a mass of advice, names of people to contact, requests to look for certain species and varieties and so on. But perhaps ringing loudest in my ears as we left were the words: 'Don't forget to look out for those lovely red Italian chicories.'

As far as knowledge of salads was concerned, what a milestone that year proved to be. The first influx of new ideas came from Belgium, where in the remarkable kitchen garden attached to the de Belders' arboretum at Kalmhout I first saw little patches of gold-leaved purslane, salad rocket, ordinary cress, chervil and the oak-leaved 'Salad Bowl' lettuce – all grown for salads. Sometimes these plants took up no more than a square metre each, and were resown and cut-over several times during the year to keep a large household in supply. From Mme de Belder, who is Yugoslav, we first learnt of the Yugoslavian 'bottoms-up' phenomenon – the countryside in spring full of people, heads down, bottoms up, collecting the first young leaves of dandelion and other wild plants for salads. We were soon to be doing this ourselves in Northern Italy! It was a cold and wet late summer before we reached France. Camping in the 'Cheminot', the French Railway Workers' gardens (perhaps the nearest equivalent to our allotments), I was introduced to a whole range of curled- and broad-leaved endives, the latter all colours – reddish brown, green, yellow, striped – grown mainly for autumn and winter use and later blanched to sweeten them.

It was also in France, on the seed firm Clause's trial grounds, that I got my first glimpse into the world of Italian chicories. Being early autumn most of the red varieties had still not acquired the intense red colouring which comes with the cold weather, but I was astounded at the variety: coarse serrated-leaved wild chicories, closely resembling and closely related to dandelion; the sweet 'Sugar Loaf' types, sometimes eaten when seedlings, but also when they have developed crisp hearts; the round- and loose-headed coloured types; the green ground-hugging rosettes of the 'Grumolos' and the blade-leaved 'Spadona'; and the curious asparagus or 'Catalogna' chicories, with bitter leaves but throwing up delicious asparagus-like shoots, the *puntarelle* in spring.

Five months later we had worked our way, via Portugal and Spain, to Italy. It was early spring and on the advice of a knowledgeable friend we immediately headed north to catch the tail end of the winter salads. Our first stop, due to nightfall overtaking us, was Cuneo in the Piedmontese plain. Shopping the next morning in a local store, we encountered our first crate of mixed Italian salad, and bought half a kilo (1½ pounds). What a salad that was – both for the eye and for the palate. It was a mixture like my salads at home, but almost all the ingredients were unfamiliar. There was crinkly red-leaved lettuce of the Salad Bowl type, beautiful red, green and variegated chicories, a miniature lettuce (the exceptionally hardy 'Parella'), the contrasting lime and dark green rosettes of different varieties of 'Grumolo' chicory, mild lamb's lettuce and pungent rocket.

The next two weeks were undoubtedly our Salad Days. From Turin, we visited wholesale and local markets, market gardens and amateur gardens, seed stalls and seed houses in an attempt to unravel and identify this host of new salad plants. The task of identifying them was complicated by the fact that the common names used can vary, literally, from village to village. I discovered nine local names for 'Grumolo' chicory alone.

Apart from the immense variety of cultivated plants, the markets were full of baskets of wild plants and herbs, gathered from the Italian country-side by the peasants. Among them were dandelion, salad rocket, valeri-anella (corn salad), chicory, poppy, thistle, sorrel – and others I never identified. Yet another category were the *insalatine*, tiny seedling leaves and thinnings, mainly chicories and lettuce, for mixing into salads for extra flavour. At home, these would have been thrown away. (I misheard 'insalatine' as 'saladini', and was only corrected by our Italian seedsman friend Mario Menella after the first edition of this book had been pub-lished. By then, thinking it was rather a nice word, we had adopted it for the bags of mixed salads we were selling in London. Now, several years later, 'Saladini' has become fairly widely used in the English speaking world to describe mixed salads.)

We also learnt something about the ways of growing *insalatine*. In many cases seeds were broadcast on to long, narrow beds and thinned out in stages, the thinnings being sold. There was a great deal of clever inter-cropping, every spare piece of ground being used intensively.

On one peasant farm we came across an interesting system of inter-cropping chicory, clover and wheat. The farmer's wife had a market stall where she sold mostly wild salad plants, and I had asked if she would show us how she gathered them. She willingly agreed, and we wandered with her across the field, as with her razor-like knife she cut young growths of poppies, thistles, dandelions, saying as she went 'this one you can eat', 'this one is bitter' and so on. There was a great deal of the by now familiar 'Grumolo' chicory growing among the grass and this, she explained, had been sown the previous spring. They mixed the chicory seed with clover seed, and broadcast the two together between the rows of young wheat. First the wheat was harvested, then the clover matured and was cut and fed to livestock, and finally the chicory, unharmed by the summer cutting, struggled through the surrounding weeds to be cut in its turn in spring, two or three times. The more you cut it, said the farmer's wife, the more it grows.

We returned from our *Grand Vegetable Tour* in late summer, armed with ideas and packets of foreign seed, all of which we were longing to try in British conditions. Our own neglected kitchen garden, apart from the inevitable weeds, was almost bare of vegetables. Not quite bare, however, for some of the 'Sugar Loaf' chicories, endive and corn salad left in the ground the previous year had gone to seed and sown themselves. And this brought home to me another of the merits of these old, rustic salad crops; they have been grown for centuries simply because they are so endurable, so easy to raise from seed, and so often seed themselves.

I learnt something else from our homecoming. There were little cress-like seedlings all over the garden, and mistaking them for land cress, I transplanted them into orderly rows in useful places. But they did not behave like land cress; they were indeed the wild hairy bitter cress, and what a useful little plant it is. It disappears in hot weather but reappears in early autumn, continuing to grow in any mild spells in winter and spring, fresh and green long before even the first aconites appear. The tiny leaves can be cut off with scissors and are a lovely addition to a salad.

In the testing, long winter of 1978/79 we tried out many varieties of red chicory and found that several were truly hardy. Some we left unprotected and others we covered with a layer of straw. In mid-winter I absentmindedly put a miniature plastic cloche over one of the plants, and one bleak day in late winter found a beautiful rose-red nugget of a red chicory snuggled in the straw beneath – what a cheering sight!

We started growing our own version of the Italian mixed salads to sell to wholefood shops, blending together fifteen or twenty ingredients which varied with the seasons – and calling them 'Saladini'. The main ingredient was 'Little Gem' lettuce. To add the colour, so essential in a mixed salad, we used edible flowers: elderflowers, borage, cucumber, nasturtium and rose petals. We incorporated finely-shredded white and red cabbage, oriental vegetables such as chrysanthemum greens (also known as 'shungiku' or 'chop suey' greens) and the serrated-leaved Japanese greens 'Mizuna' – another very hardy species. We also tried various edible weeds and found chickweed, when grown in the shade, to be wonderfully succulent. I began to cultivate little patches of it, not least because, like hairy bitter cress, it is at its best in early and mid-winter. For further variety we would add a few finely-chopped herbs. I must admit I was proud of our saladini. The mixture of ingredients looked and tasted lovely. I thought we were doing something really original, which brings me to the last of the milestones.

1979 was the 'Year of the Garden', and as part of the celebrations, the Victoria and Albert Museum mounted a historical exhibition, 'The Garden', covering ten centuries of British gardening. I was invited to suggest material for the vegetable section. It was a daunting task; what did I know of vegetable growing in the past ten centuries? The answer was very little, but in attempting to discover more, I delved for the first time into the works of the great classical writers: John Parkinson, John Evelyn, Leonard Meager and J. Worlidge of the seventeenth century; Stephen Switzer, Richard Bradley and Batty Langley of the eighteenth century. And to my amazement I discovered that during these two centuries salads were considered to be of immense importance and the art of growing them was highly developed.

An astonishing range of plants, many of which have since gone out of common usage, were grown for salads. They also used wild plants, weeds, garden flowers, seeds and seedlings, and even cooked roots. Some of their lists of salads could have been our own lists of saladini. For example, Batty Langley's 'Raw Sallets for July, August and September' from *New Principles of Gardening* (1728), included: 'borage flowers, chervil, corn sallet, garden cresses, cucumber, lettice, mustard, melons, nasturtium flowers, young onions, purslane, horse radish, sorrel, tarragon'. Almost all of these had, at one time or another, gone into our saladini. We were not, it seemed, doing anything original after all; we had merely stumbled upon forgotten skills of the past. But there was no reason why we should not learn from the past and transplant some of their ideas to our twentieth-century garden; and this we have tried to do. Indeed, through following suggestions in these old books, my seed order that year contained a number of new items which I hoped to try out: skirret, violets, primroses and Jenny stonecrop for example.

One of the most authoritative of the early writers was the diarist John Evelyn, who devoted an entire book to the subject: *Acetaria, a Discourse on Salads*. He summarized his gardening ideas in 1669 in a short book of directions for his gardener at Sayes Court, which is a mine of information on the cultivation and use of salad herbs, as they were then known, in the seventeenth century. First he lists those salads which were blanched, in other words kept in the dark or grown with light excluded to render them sweeter and whiter. He goes on to describe the many plants which could be used green, stating precisely the stage at which the leaves should be picked: another sphere in which we can learn from the past, for we tend to overlook the fact that it is the young leaves which are often the tastiest, the most tender, and the most nutritious.

Here are a few examples from Evelyn's *Directions*: with lettuce use leaves 'of a fine middling size'; with the broad- and curled-leaved cresses and spinach use 'just the leaves next the seed leaves and the next to them'; with sorrel 'take only the first young leaves of spring'; with sweet chervil, burnet, Spanish rocket and parsley 'the young leaves after the seed leaves'. He then advises his gardener to select the flowers and flower buds of nasturtium; the tender young leaves of shallot, chives and young onion; the seed leaves and young tops of rampion and Trip Madam (the stonecrop *Sedum reflexum*); seed leaves of turnip, mustard, and the weed scurvy grass; the young tender leaves and shoots of sampier (or samphire, collected from cliffs), balm and red sage . . . and so on. Evelyn even suggests using the first seedling leaves of oranges and lemons. Growing these exotic fruits was the height of fashion in his day.

The early gardening writers took pains to advise the cook, and one often saw suggestions that salads 'should be judiciously mixed'. Perhaps to help the less experienced cooks they would break down the salads into 'the hot and biting' and 'the more cool and insipid'. Batty Langley graded all his plants by degrees: onion almost in the 4th degree, garden rocket 3rd degree and broom buds (a common favourite) 2nd degree. To me this was another link with saladini. In preparing it we would often have a bucket of mixed 'mild' plants and another of 'strong', to balance the final mixture. (Go steady on the broom buds as they may be mildly toxic.)

Research into the past also shows how salads have gone in and out of fashion in England over the centuries. It seems that it was the Romans who first introduced them. In Rome they were known as 'vinegar diets' and were highly valued, not least because they needed no cooking, so economizing on fuel. Pliny remarked that 'They were found to be easy of digestion, by no means apt to overload the senses, and to create but little craving for bread as an accompaniment.' This was of some economic significance, for wheat was imported from North Africa, and the price of bread was normally subsidized to bring down the cost of living.

The Romans may well have been the earliest to force salads. Emperor Tiberius, who lived from 42 BC to AD 37, was advised for medical reasons to eat cucumber all-year-round, so he devised a system of making cucumber beds on frames, mounted on wheels. These could be moved out into the sun in summer and brought indoors in winter, to be protected under frames glazed with the mica *Lapis specularia*.

So when the Romans invaded Britain, they brought with them the art of cultivating lettuce, endive, radish, cucumber and many other salad plants. As far as we can tell from the scant records that remain, most of these died out of cultivation in the centuries following the Roman withdrawal, in many cases not to be revived until Tudor times. In spite of Britain's amenable climate, we were remarkably uninterested in the use of any vegetables other than for their medicinal properties, for seasoning or for soups. When Catherine of Aragon wanted a salad she had, says Holinshed, to despatch a messenger to Flanders to procure it.

The Renaissance on the continent of Europe saw a revival of interest in vegetable growing, which eventually spread to Britain, so by the seventeenth and eighteenth centuries appreciation of salads was at its peak in this country. It apparently ebbed away slowly in favour of more substantial cooked vegetables in the middle of the nineteenth century. For some reason, as we discovered while touring Europe, interest in and knowledge of the diversity of European salad plants was never lost on the Continent, where it remained in the safe hands of the peasant classes.

Nearly fifteen years have passed since the first edition of *Salads the Year Round* was published – and a great deal has happened since then. Colourful, varied, flavoursome salads are now far easier to come by in restaurants, supermarkets, and greengrocers. Even more important for gardeners, seed of a wide selection of unusual salad varieties is offered by mail order seed companies, spear-headed in the British Isles by the pioneering company, Suffolk Herbs, and by others further afield.

In our own garden at Montrose Farm we have continued to experiment with old and new varieties – constantly extending our knowledge of what can be grown and how. Oriental vegetables have had the lion's share of our attention – especially the versatile greens, which are at their best in the winter months. Most can be used at every stage, from young cut-and-come-again seedlings to mature plants to flowering shoots – adding a wonderful range of new flavours, textures and in the case of the purple mustards – colour to our salads.

In 1985 I was able to fulfil a long held dream and spend six weeks in China, Taiwan and Japan studying vegetables. This was followed by a trip to the United States and Canada, to see what oriental vegetables were being grown there by ethnic groups. The full story is told in *Oriental Vegetables – the complete guide for garden and kitchen* but the salad discoveries are included here. . . pea shoots, garlic stems, the delicate Japanese herb mitsuba and the curiously flavoured perilla or shiso, and most exciting of all, the stunning, deep red, sweet and crispy 'Beauty Heart' radish from North China.

The design and layout of our garden at Montrose Farm has undergone many changes in the last fifteen years – not least because we have fallen in love with the concept of the *decorative* vegetable garden. This has become known as the *potager* in Europe and 'edible landscaping' in the US. Whatever the name, the essence is to grow vegetables to show off their beautiful qualities. This can be done by planting them in prettily designed or patterned beds, or grouping them so they make striking splashes of texture and colour, or selecting varieties with decorative qualities. Suitable varieties can even be planted in flower beds.

Many salad vegetables are ideal subjects for the decorative garden. Take the red frilled 'Lollo' lettuce or the many improved 'Lollo' varieties appearing on the market. They make perfect edges for flower beds, but when grouped can be woven into beautiful patches, offset perhaps by the cool green tints of their counterpart, 'Green Lollo', or the gleaming gold of summer purslane. Many of the oriental salad greens, notably mizuna, mibuna, 'rosette pak choi' and the loose-headed creamy centred Chinese cabbages, are exceptionally beautiful when growing. So in this revised edition, the decorative potential of any salad plants will be pointed out.

One of the most important changes that has taken place in our garden is that it is now completely 'organic' in the sense that we use no artificial fertilizers, chemical weedkillers or toxic sprays other than the few approved by the organic standards authorities in this country. These break down rapidly without leaving any poisonous residues in the soil. Organic gardening probably demands more skill and a little more effort than gardening with chemicals – but is infinitely more rewarding. As for salads, in most cases eaten raw straight from the garden, it seems to me the case for growing them organically is unanswerable. Moreover our own experience, reinforced by that of friends who grow organically on a commercial scale, indicates that organic vegetables keep fresh noticeably longer than their chemically raised brethren. And we all maintain they taste much better! So this revised edition of *Salads for Small Gardens* is confined to organic methods of gardening.

# Chapter 1
# Soil Fertility

If anyone were to ask me what are the most important factors in growing vegetables successfully, especially salads, I would reply without hesitation: soil fertility and shelter. So soil fertility is a good starting point, for the key to good plant growth is a good root system, and the key to a good root system is fertile soil.

## THE NATURE OF THE SOIL

What exactly is soil? It looks solid, but in an average garden slightly less than half the volume of soil is solid matter; the rest is air and water, essential for both the animal and plant life that lives in the soil. All organisms need water, and plants absorb much of their food – including elements such as nitrogen, phosphorus, potassium, calcium, magnesium and sulphur and half a dozen others known as trace elements – in water which they draw in through their roots. Roots also take in oxygen from the soil as part of the plant's breathing process. Indeed, in waterlogged airless soils plants cannot survive because they cannot breathe.

The solid part of the soil is made up of mineral particles of sand, silt and clay, which have been formed over the centuries by the gradual breakdown of rocks. Some of the nutrients required by plants are found in these particles of rock, particularly in the clays. An important five per cent of the solid material in the soil is organic matter. This organic matter is a mixture of the remains of plants and animals, decomposing vegetation and humus, and the tiny micro-organisms living in the soil. The organic matter can be looked upon as the main storehouse of the essential nutrients which plants need to feed on and, thereby, survive. But before the nutrients can be used by plants, or 'made available' to use the technical jargon, the organic matter has to be broken down into humus. This is one of the most important processes continually taking place in the soil, and is carried out by micro-organisms such as bacteria. Soil fertility largely depends on creating the optimum conditions for the micro-organisms to work productively, that is ensuring they have adequate moisture and oxygen, that the soil is not too acid or too alkaline for them, and that there is an adequate supply of organic matter for them to work on. A key factor here is soil structure.

**Soil Structure**
The mineral and organic particles in the soil join together to form small lumps or *crumbs* of varying sizes. In good soil these are stable. Around them a network of spaces or pores is built up, and the crumbs and pores together make up the soil structure. The spaces between the crumbs form channels which are the aeration and drainage system of the soil. When it rains, the surplus water drains off through the channels preventing the soil from becoming waterlogged; but the rest of the water remains in the smallest pores, forming a reservoir of moisture for roots and soil organisms. The large spaces between the crumbs are filled with air. Plant roots grow well in the conditions created by a well-structured soil.

**Soil Types**
The essential difference between the principle types of soil – clay, silt and sand – is in the size of the mineral particles. Sandy soils have very large particles, clay soils tiny particles, silt soils particles of an intermediate size. In practice most soils are a mixture of different types, the ideal gardener's 'loam' being a soil in which the different types are mixed in more or less equal proportions. 'Clay', 'silt' and 'sandy' soils are soils in which clay, silt or sand particles predominate. To get some idea of your soil type, rub it between the fingers and thumb. Sandy soil feels gritty, a silt feels silky, while clay feels sticky.

What is important is that the size of the soil particles determines the characteristics of the soil and its ability to form soil crumbs. The large particles of sandy soils are very reluctant to stick together. So the spaces between the particles are large, water drains away easily and the soil contains plenty of air. These types of soil therefore warm up quickly in spring, but dry out rapidly in summer. They are often, but not always, poor in nutrients, which are washed out in the drainage water. Sandy soils are easily worked and considered 'light'.

A clay soil is at the other extreme. Because of its chemistry the particles have a tendency to stick together and form clods. Pure clay is so sticky that there are very few spaces for both air and water to drain through it easily. When it does dry out it is apt to form hard, impenetrable lumps. It is, however, very rich in nutrients. Clay soils are hard to dig and considered 'heavy'.

In a good loam – a balanced mixture of sand, silt and clay – the sandy elements make for good drainage and aeration, and the clay for richness, retention of water in summer, and the cohesion essential for the formation of crumbs.

## The Role of Humus

The crumbs of a well-structured soil are formed by contrasting actions: by particles of sand and silt being bound together and by clods of clay being broken apart. In both cases the main agent is humus. Humus not only has the ability to coat particles of sand and silt so that they cohere, but it plays a vital intermediary role in the breakdown of large clay clods, initially into small clods, and then into crumbs.

Humus also has great water-holding capacity. This is particularly important in sandy soil, as it helps prevent nutrients being washed out so rapidly. In addition humus is a source of nutrients in itself. So clearly in the long term the structure and fertility of almost all soils can be improved by the addition of 'organic matter' which will be converted by natural processes into humus. Organic matter can be defined as any material of animal or vegetable origin – manure and compost being the commonest forms used by gardeners.

## OTHER INFLUENCES ON SOIL FERTILITY

### Earthworms

Earthworms are beneficial in many ways. For a start they pull leaves and debris on the soil surface down into the soil, increasing the organic matter in the soil. In ploughing through the earth (they almost literally eat their way through it) soil and organic matter pass through their bodies. In the process they are mixed together and enriched with gums and lime from the worm's intestines. This is the first stage in the conversion of organic matter into humus.

The burrowing types of worm create channels in the soil which help to improve drainage and enable roots to penetrate. Some types of worm form soil-like casts from the materials passed through their bodies. These worm casts are pockets of concentrated fertility – very rich in minerals, plant nutrients and micro-organisms, but also very stable and a key agent in forming soil crumbs. When deposited on the surface they increase the topsoil, while those deposited within the soil increase its fertility. Worms also help control some plant diseases by removing the debris on which the disease spores over-winter. And to complete this catalogue of virtues, when worms die their protein rich bodies eventually return very appreciable quantities of nitrogen to the soil.

So everything possible must be done in order to encourage earthworms. The principal method of doing this is by supplying their food – organic matter – to the soil. Experiments have shown that worms prefer dung to anything else, followed by lush green leaves, followed by dry vegetation. Hence the value of manure. Half-rotted compost actually supplies more food for earthworms than well-rotted compost! Worms thrive in cool conditions, and keeping the ground cool by mulching – with manure, cut vegetation, even carpets put down to suppress weeds – will encourage worms.

## Plant Roots

The ramification of plant roots through the soil helps to build up crumbs in sandy or silty soils, and to break down clods in clay soil. This is one reason why soil seems to improve simply with use. It also explains why the best soil structure is found in fields which have been grassed for many years. The agricultural practice of improving soil by sowing leys of grass or grass and clover, left for a year or more before ploughing them in, could be adopted, on a small scale, in gardens where ground can be spared. (See Green Manuring pp.34-5.)

## Soil Acidity

Soil acidity is another factor with a bearing on soil fertility. It is measured on the pH scale on a range of 0-14, the neutral point being 7, the pH of pure water. Soil with a pH below 7 is acid and with a pH above 7 is alkaline, the change from one pH level to the next indicating a tenfold increase or decrease in acidity or alkalinity. Acidity can be measured fairly simply with amateur soil-testing kits, which, if used carefully, are accurate enough for practical purposes.

Broadly speaking, the acidity of a soil reflects the amount of calcium (lime or chalk) in it: the higher the calcium level the more alkaline the soil. In humid climates, such as in the British Isles, rain is continually washing calcium out of the soil, so it tends to become more acid all the time. This is most apparent in regions with very high rainfall, in cities and industrialized areas where the acid in the atmosphere accelerates the loss of calcium, and on fast-draining light sandy soils. Heavy soils such as clays are less likely to become very acid. Most soils in the British Isles are slightly acid – and fortunately most vegetables do best on slightly acid soils, with a pH of about 6-6.5.

Where soils are too acid or too alkaline nutrients either become 'locked up' and unavailable to plants, or are so concentrated that they become toxic. In addition the micro-organisms which break down humus cease to function, and earthworms move out of the soil.

The most common pH problem in the British Isles is over-acidity, which is corrected by liming. As over-liming is harmful, liming should only be carried out if it seems to be really necessary. If plants are doing well and there is a large worm population, assume everything is all right. Where plenty of organic matter is worked into the soil regularly, acidity problems are less likely to develop.

Indications that a soil is too acid and needs liming are a sour look – moss growing on the surface, weeds such as sorrel and docks, and vegetation on the surface which is not rotting.

Liming needs time to take effect, and it is inadvisable to apply more than 300g per sq m (8oz per sq yd) in one season. It may take several dressings over the course of two or three years to raise the pH of very acid soil to a slightly acid level.

Organic gardeners are advised to use slow acting ground limestone or dolomite, rather than quick acting gardener's lime. The amount required depends on the soil type. The following are the National Centre for Organic Gardening recommendations:

Applications of ground limestone required to raise soil pH from 6.0 to 6.5 are shown below. These quantities would be roughly doubled to raise the pH from 5.5 to 6.5.

| Soil type | gms per sq metre | ozs per sq yard |
| --- | --- | --- |
| Sandy | 146 | 4 1/4 |
| Loamy | 187 | 5 1/2 |
| Clay or peaty | 238 | 7 |

Liming is best done in the autumn, working it well into the soil. Never apply it at the same time as fertilizers or manure, as undesirable chemical actions will occur: allow at least a month to elapse. Where practical, lime six months before sowing or planting. Lime can also be added indirectly to the soil by using spent mushroom compost (which has chalk in it) or by working ground limestone into a compost heap.

## Drainage

Poor drainage is a common cause of soil infertility. In a waterlogged soil animal and plant life is starved of oxygen with dire consequences: soil structure deteriorates, and the soil is cold. Improved drainage often produces almost miraculous results in a 'difficult' garden. Signs of poor drainage include water still lying on the soil surface several days after heavy rain; water encountered when digging 30cm (1ft) or less deep;

poor vegetation (plants with a mass of small shallow roots rather than deep roots); lack of worms; and soil that is greyish, bluish, blackish or mottled rather than brown. Various factors can be responsible for bad drainage: very heavy topsoil (usually clay) with little humus in it; an impenetrable layer or 'hard pan' in the soil; topsoil lying over impervious rock or impervious subsoil; and low-lying land.

Where heavy topsoil is the problem, working in plenty of bulky organic matter can be a very effective remedy. If this fails to have an appreciable effect within a year or so, artificial drains will be needed to remove water lying near the surface.

The same applies where there is an impermeable layer or on low-lying land. Simple trench drains are often sufficient, laid either across the lower end of the slope, or down the sides of a level area. Dig them about 30cm (1ft) wide and 60-90cm (2-3ft) deep, fill the bottom third with clinkers, stones, broken brick or rubble before replacing the soil in the top layer. A 'hard pan', a very hard layer occasionally found at varying depths in the soil, may be caused by a natural deposit of mineral salts, or by compaction of the soil by heavy machinery.

It has to be broken up physically with a spade or pickaxe. Where drainage is a problem it may be advisable to grow plants in raised beds (see below).

### IMPROVING AND MAINTAINING FERTILITY
If you are unlucky enough to be faced with gardening on poor, infertile soil the main steps for improvement can be summarized as follows:
* Improve drainage if necessary.
* Work in plenty of bulky organic matter.
* Check acidity, especially in city gardens. If necessary, correct by liming.

In poor soils it is worth concentrating initially on creating pockets of fertility, by working any available compost or manure into small concentrated areas. Salad crops are ideal for the first sowings as most are shallow rooting, have a short life cycle, and give quick returns. At the other end of the scale potatoes and Jerusalem artichokes are useful crops to plant at the outset in a below-par garden, especially where the problem is heavy soil. Their root systems break up soil remarkably well, and get the whole process of improving fertility underway.

Good soil structure is a precious, but fragile commodity. It can be destroyed by cultivating soil when it is very wet or very dry, by heavy rain beating on the bare surface, or by walking on the surface frequently. The best way to preserve the soil structure is to keep the soil surface permanently covered. This can be done by growing crops, by mulching the soil, or simply by allowing weeds to grow – provided they are dug in before they go to seed. Adopting the bed system is a measure that goes a long way towards preserving soil structure.

## THE BED SYSTEM

In the bed system vegetables are grown in relatively narrow permanent beds separated by paths. They are worked entirely from the paths, and plants are generally evenly spaced across the bed. This is in contrast to the more common system of extensive vegetable plots, with vegetables grown in widely spaced rows across the plot. In this case the whole plot is dug and manured (a waste of resources and energy), much of the soil is trodden in the course of cultivation and harvesting (destroying the soil structure), and weeds spring up in the spaces between plants.

### Advantages of the Bed System

* All work is done from the paths separating the beds, eliminating the need to tread on the soil.
* All manure is concentrated where plants will be grown, and not wasted on ground that will become paths.
* These factors, coupled with the permanent nature of the beds, increase soil fertility appreciably.
* As a result plant roots penetrate more deeply and plants can withstand drought better, plants can be grown more closely, and overall yields and productivity are higher than otherwise.
* Equidistant spacing ensures minimum competition between plants.
* When mature most vegetables will form a leafy canopy covering the soil, which largely prevents the germination of weed seeds. An exception is narrow-leaved plants, such as onions. Mulching between plants is all that is necessary to keep down weeds completely.
* Narrow beds are easily covered with long low tunnels for protective cropping. (See Protected Cropping pp.115-17.)
* The well-trodden paths between the beds encourage worm activity.
* It is easier to work out a rotation system with a number of narrow beds rather than one large plot.

### Types of Bed

*Standard Narrow Bed* – The bed is made at ground level, normally 90cm-1.5m (3-5ft) wide. Choose a width where the centre can be reached comfortably from the path.

*Soil Raised Bed* – Here the soil is raised anything up to 30cm (12in) above ground level. For stability the beds are usually wider at the base than the top, typically 1.2m (4ft) at the base tapering to 90cm (3ft) at the top. The top can be level, or the bed can be rounded, which effectively increases the growing area. A bed with a rounded top needs to be about 1.2m (4ft) wide. Raised beds have good drainage, but being more exposed at the sides, they dry out faster in hot weather. They may not therefore be suitable in dry climates unless there is irrigation. As the structure and shape of a raised bed makes it awkward to dig deeply, fertility is usually maintained by applying thick layers of mulch to the surface. This also helps to prevent soil being eroded from the sides.

*Built-Up Raised Bed* – These beds enable people with disabilities to work at a convenient height without bending, or from a wheelchair. The bed is made within a concrete, brick or wooden frame, generally about 60cm (2ft) high, but the height must be chosen to suit the gardener concerned. The lower 30cm (12in) or so is filled with rubble or drainage material, while the top 30cm (12in) is filled with good soil. This type of bed can also be used to overcome intractable soil conditions in gardens where plants will not grow successfully.

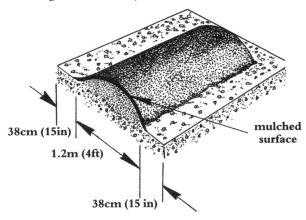

*Raised bed with a rounded top to increase the surface area*

*Deep Beds / Intensive Beds* – These are beds made with exceptionally deep and thorough digging, using very large quantities of organic matter.

*Variable Beds* – Gardeners tend to make their vegetable beds one standard size, but there is no reason why this should be so. If you want to create a decorative vegetable garden or 'potager' consider having beds of varying

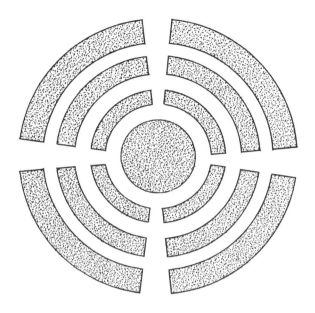

*Semi-circular vegetable beds arranged in a striking pattern*

shapes and sizes – square, crescent shaped or round as well as rectangular. They can be arranged in patterns. Salad vegetables, with their contrasting textures and colours, lend themselves to being grown decoratively.

## Paths

Bare soil paths, unless they are very compacted, tend to splash up on to plants that may be growing close by and invite weeds. Covering the paths between the beds is therefore to be recommended. There are many options: they can be grassed down and mown,

*Typical narrow beds with paths mulched with carpet*

**carpet mulch path**

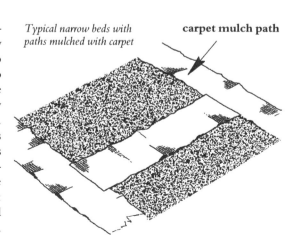

23

laid permanently with concrete, weathered brick, or stone, or kept mulched with bark or wood chippings, old carpets (avoid foam backed carpets) or the plastic ground-cover materials used by commercial growers. These both suppress weeds and allow for drainage.

For practical purposes, the minimum width for paths is approximately 30-38cm (12-15in). It is worth making every third or fourth path wider, say 45-60cm (18-24in) wide, to allow easier access to the beds.

## Edges

To neaten beds and to help retain soil, beds can be edged with for example tiles, brick or timber. These materials can be laid on the surface or embedded in the soil as appropriate. The most common edging for vegetable beds is wood, laid on the surface but held in place with upright wooden pegs.

*Beds edged with timber (above), and bricks (below)*

## SOIL CULTIVATION
## Digging

Digging the soil is normally the first step in improving soil fertility. Digging has two main functions. The first is to make the soil workable or 'friable', so it is easy to sow or plant into it. The second is as a means of working in manure or compost – the basis for making it fertile.

When breaking in new ground or tackling a garden with low fertility, it is recommended to double dig it initially (see opposite). Once this has been done thoroughly, single digging, forking over the top spit of soil only, should be all that is required in future. Digging can be done between harvesting one crop and sowing and planting the next, or when the ground is empty in the autumn or spring. As a general rule, heavy soils are best dug over in autumn, as exposing heavy clods to frost helps to break them down. Light sandy soils, on the other hand, are best left undisturbed until the spring. Both benefit by being protected with a mulch of organic matter during the winter months. This also helps to prevent nutrients and nitrates being washed out of the soil.

## Double Digging

Double digging is undertaken to improve the soil drainage and incorporate manure or compost by working the soil two spits deep. It involves moving the top layer of soil, then forking over the layer beneath to create better drainage, prior to working in the nutrient-rich manure. If laying out a vegetable garden in narrow beds the ground should be double dug initially as outlined below. Essentially the same method is used for digging a large vegetable plot.

### Making a Narrow Bed

* Mark out the boundaries of the bed with string.
* Working across the bed, remove a spade width, to the depth of a spade, across the bed. Put the soil in a barrow and wheel it to the far end of the bed. Do the same with the adjacent strip of soil to give a wide working space.
* Fork over the lower spit in the first strip, breaking up any hard pan with the fork as you go.
* Turn the soil from the adjacent top spit into the first row. At the same time work in some bulky organic matter, trying to distribute it evenly through the soil.
* Continue to the far end of the bed in this way, filling the last rows with the soil collected from the first rows.

### Making a Raised Bed

There are various ways of making a raised bed, but it is important to make it when the soil is in good condition, neither too wet nor too dry. This is one basic method. (For Further Reading see p.251.)
* Start by digging the whole area to a depth of 15-20cm (6-8in). Alternatively it can be double dug.
* Mark out the beds.
* Spade soil from the paths on to the bed area to raise it to the required level (that most convenient to the gardener).
* Standing on the path, first on one side, then the other, rake up the soil from the sides to the middle to shape the bed.
* Firm the sides with the back of a spade.

### Winter Ridging

Heavy soil benefits from being ridged up in winter. This keeps the bed well-drained (level soil can become very waterlogged in winter, even if mulched), and exposes a greater area to the action of winter frost, which helps to break up clods. If the ridged bed is then covered with manure or compost, most of this will be worked into the ground by earthworms during the winter.

It is then a simple matter to rake down the ridge in spring, just before the ground is required for sowing or planting. There is no doubt that the very heavy clay soil in our narrow beds has improved enormously since we adopted this practice. We try to do it every autumn. We first fork down the centre of the bed, along its full length. Then the soil from each side is spaded onto the forked area, making a ridge about 30cm (12in) high. This is covered with manure or compost.

### 'No-Digging' Systems

'No-digging' systems rely entirely on mulching the surface with manure or compost to keep the soil fertile. The mulch is drawn aside carefully for sowing and planting. No-digging is often used on raised beds, where digging is more awkward. If fertility in a 'no-dig' raised bed seems to be declining, it may be necessary to dismantle the bed every four or five years and double dig thoroughly, before reverting again to a less time-consuming 'no-digging' system.

'No digging' only succeeds where the soil is well-drained. For this reason it is more widely adopted on light, well-drained soils than on heavy soils. However in gardens where soil fertility is continually being improved and regular mulching is practised, the need to dig certainly lessens with time – to the point where it almost becomes unnecessary. One benefit of digging which should not be overlooked is that it exposes soil pests to birds.

# Chapter 2
# Manures and Fertilizers

Manures and fertilizers are used to improve soil fertility and supply plants with the necessary nutrients. There is no clear-cut division between them. Roughly speaking, manures are bulky organic products. They are primarily used to improve the soil, increasing its fertility, but also contain some plant foods. Fertilizers are concentrated liquid or solid substances, essentially a source of plant nutrients and not necessarily improving soil fertility.

One of the fundamental principles of organic gardening is *feed the soil, not the plants*. This puts the emphasis firmly on the use of bulky organic manures to build up soil fertility. Fertilizers have a useful but supplementary role in stimulating plant growth, and compensating for any nutrient deficiencies in the soil.

## BULKY ORGANIC MANURES
Finding bulky organic manure, and getting it transported to your garden, is one of the main problems facing the modern gardener. The problem is most acute in urban areas, though with initiative sources such as riding stables and street markets can be tracked down. In practice most gardeners have to supplement available supplies by making their own compost and by the use of green manuring (see p.33).

A variety of things, of animal or vegetable origin, can be used as bulky manures. For improving the soil structure, it is probably true to say that the bulkier the better.

### Some Bulky Manures
Animal Manure
Fresh animal manure is best stacked in a covered heap for about six months before use. Animal manure is usually mixed with stable litter. Where this is wood shavings it should ideally be stacked for at least a year, to enable the wood to break down. Otherwise nitrogen is 'robbed' from the soil in its decomposition.

Bird and Rabbit Manure
These manures are more concentrated than most animal manures, so are best worked in small quantities into a compost heap.

Spent Mushroom Compost
An excellent manure. The chalk fragments in spent mushroom compost help to break down very heavy clay soils. It is advisable to rotate it around the garden to avoid a build up of lime. It has usually been sterilized so is free of weed seed.

Seaweed
Another excellent manure, containing about the same amount of organic matter and nitrogen as farmyard manure, as well as numerous trace elements. It can be used fresh, dried or composted. If it is spread on the ground in summer it may attract flies; if this is the case cover with a thin sprinkling of soil.

Recycled Urban Waste and Treated Sewage Sludge
These products are increasingly available. Make sure they are guaranteed free of heavy metals.

Straw and Hay
Both are very beneficial to the soil. They are best stacked for about six months in a heap, in layers about 15cm (6in) deep. Water each layer well. Sprinklings of poultry manure and lawn mowings can be added to each layer, to enrich it and hasten decomposition.

Pond Mud
The layers of mud which accumulate at the bottom of ponds are very fertile. Where feasible, dredge it up and work it into the top of your beds.

**A Note on Leaves**
These rot very slowly into almost nothing, so can hardly be termed 'bulky'. Where large quantities are available collect them in bins (see diagram p.30) or in plastic bags. They will take about a year to rot into leaf mould, and are probably best used in potting compost or as a mulch. Small quantities can be worked into a compost heap. They are an excellent soil conditioner.

**A Note on Peat**
Peat is no longer recommended in organic gardening as its extraction involves the depletion of peat reserves and the destruction of the natural habitats of peat bogs. In the past it was used as a soil conditioner, particularly on heavy soils. It is very low in plant nutrients.

## MAKING COMPOST
### Garden Compost
Compost is twentieth-century man's answer to the disappearance of bulky animal manures from our daily lives. It is made from vegetable and animal waste, and every gardener should consider making a compost heap – preferably several heaps – a top priority.

The heat generated in a well-made heap destroys weed seed as well as disease organisms. Research has indicated that a temperature over 70°C (158°F) needs to be maintained for atleast 30 minutes to kill most of the weed seed and disease organisms. In cold and wet climates, and where only small quantities of waste are available, this is not always easy. The larger and better insulated the heap, the higher the temperature that can be obtained.

Thoroughly decomposed compost looks like soil – blackish brown, crumbly, uniform in texture and with no half-decayed vegetable stalks in it. It is pleasant to handle. But don't worry if your compost is not like this. The important thing is to be returning some kind of organic matter to the soil – and as mentioned earlier, half-decayed compost provides more immediate food for earthworms. The drawback is that partially rotted compost may contain weed seed and disease spores. Depending on conditions, compost in a well-made bin can be well decomposed in three to four months in summer, but will take on average six to eight months in winter. A simple compost heap (see p.30) will take at least a year, perhaps longer, to rot thoroughly.

What to Use
A fair amount of raw material is needed to build up a heap quickly. This can be a problem in a small household or garden. If so, scrounge wastes from friends, neighbours, shops, restaurants, parks, and so on. A great deal of priceless organic material is wasted in our society.

Almost anything of animal or vegetable origin is suitable for composting. Possibilities include: kitchen waste; garden waste – lawn mowings (allow them to dry off before composting them); weeds, provided they haven't seeded; vegetable remains (bruise or chop solid material such as old cabbage stalks); bonfire ash; small quantities of autumn leaves (even pine needles), shredded woody prunings, shredded newspaper and animal manures can be worked into a compost heap.

Materials to avoid include: diseased plant material (burn it); roots of perennial weeds such as couch grass, bindweed and ground elder (unless killed first by drying in the sun); woody material and tough evergreen material (unless shredded or cut very small); and non-rotting material such as plastics and man-made fibres. (In my bitter experience hand trowels, hand forks, and garden knives, all of which have a great affinity for compost heaps, only rust, never rot, during their incarceration.) Grass turves are best made into a heap (see Heap Method p.32). For health reasons cat and dog manures should not be composted.

The decomposition of waste in a compost heap is brought about by bacteria. To operate effectively they need a combination of air, moisture, warmth, and a source of nitrogen. In the summer months the nitrogen is supplied by fresh green leafy material; in the winter months it can be supplemented by animal manure (poultry is very good), concentrated organic fertilizers such as seaweed extracts or blood, fish and bone, or a commercial compost activator. The composting guidelines below aim to create the optimum conditions for the bacteria to work.

Composting Guidelines

★ Make the bin as large as possible or heat will not be generated. A minimum size is 1m sq (3½ ft sq). It should be very strong as a full bin is bulky and weighty. Strong corner posts or a rigid frame are advisable. The sides should be well insulated: brick, wood, concrete, breeze blocks, straw bales are good materials to use. It is convenient to make the front of removable boards or panels, so compost is easily put in or removed. (Pairs of upright metal pipes can be put in at the corners, and the boards slipped between them.)

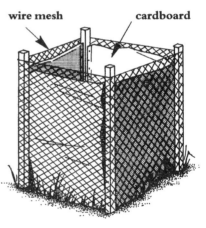

*Simple wire mesh compost bin*

A cheap bin can be made from wire mesh, lined with cardboard or carpeting to increase insulation.

★ Make the heap on a soil base, then worms can move in when the compost has cooled down. Never make it on concrete which will impede drainage. Start with a drainage layer about 8-10cm (3½ -4in) thick of clinkers, stones, rubble, tile drains or brushwood.

★ If possible, make several bins side by side. This allows for one to be built up while another is in use. Moreover a bin can sometimes be turned into an empty adjacent bin to reactivate it.

★ Premix materials together thoroughly, with a good balance between the fibrous, drier material and the leafy material. Too much leafy material, such as a mass of lawn mowings, can become compacted and airless, while too little will mean a shortage of nitrogen. Ideally material should be collected beforehand

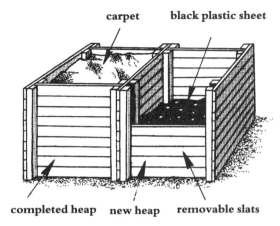

**carpet**    **black plastic sheet**

**completed heap**    **new heap**    **removable slats**

*Well insulated pair of compost bins, built side by side for maximum convenience and efficiency*

and the bin filled in one go. If this is impractical build it up in layers 15–23cm (6-9in) deep at a time. Shred very coarse material or decomposition will be extremely slow. Add a nitrogen source (see opposite) if there is insufficient fresh green material. Recommended levels are: animal manure, 1 bucket per sq m (sq yd); dried blood, fish and bone, 300g per sq m (8oz per sq yd); seaweed extracts, following the manufacturers' recommendations.

★ If the compost is very dry it should be watered when the layers are being built up. Otherwise the heap should be kept covered to keep out the rain. A sheet of heavy plastic film with 2.5cm (1in) holes cut every 30cm (12in) or so can be used as a covering.

★ When the heap reaches the top of the bin, cover it with an insulating layer of say 5cm (2in) of soil, or a heavy duty sheet of polythene with ventilation holes. Finally cover it with a layer of permeable insulating material such as straw or carpet.

★ When a heap is completed the temperature initially rises, then after a few weeks it falls again. (Measure the temperature with a compost thermometer.) If the heap is 'turned' at this point more oxygen is introduced and it is reactivated, so decomposition is speeded up. Ideally turn it into an adjacent box; alternatively turn it 'sides to middle' as the outer layers tend to dry out and decompose more slowly. Don't worry unduly if you are unable to turn your heap. Stalks that have not decomposed can easily be put back into the next heap.

### Heap Method

Compost *can* be made simply by piling wastes in a heap, covered with a couple of inches of soil and an old carpet or heavy duty polythene. It is a useful means of rotting chopped-up woody material, evergreens and grass turves. (Turves can be stacked on their own, grass side down. They rot into lovely friable material, which can be used in potting or to improve poor soil.) The drawback to heaps is that temperatures are unlikely to rise high enough to kill disease spores and weed seeds, and they may take at least a year to decompose. For this reason you may want to try out alternative methods of making a good compost.

### Pit and Trench Methods

Compost is sometimes made in pits. They conserve heat well, but run the risk of becoming waterlogged unless the underlying soil is properly drained so that water can escape.

Trenches can be dug on well-drained ground and filled with various household wastes during the winter. They are then ready for planting with hungry crops such as runner beans in spring. The National Centre for Organic Gardening suggests making trenches 30cm (12in) deep and wide, and covering each bucket of wastes with a layer of soil and, in places where the soil is very acid, also with a handful of lime. The trench is covered with soil when full and left a couple of months to settle before planting commences.

### Worm Compost

An excellent system for making compost in small households has been developed by the American biologist, Mary Appelhof (see Further Reading p.251). Garden and domestic waste is put into a box or bin and fed to small redworms or brandling worms. The worms convert it into a very rich material, of peaty consistency, which can be used either as a fertilizer or made into a potting compost.

Worm compost can be made in a wooden box 45 x 60cm (18 x 24in) and 23cm (9in) deep. Fill it with about 1.5kg (3 ¼ lb) of shredded newspaper as bedding, moistened with 4.5l (1 gal) water. Put in a handful of worms, and cover the box to keep it moist. The bin can be kept in a kitchen as there is no odour, and the worms will not escape. Feed them regularly with small quantities of domestic wastes. When the food supply is exhausted the worms die, but before that point is reached, the box can be emptied and filled with fresh bedding, transferring a few worms into it to keep the system going.

## Applying Manure

Manures and compost can either be spread on the surface or dug in when the soil is being prepared (see Soil Fertility, p.24). Fairly raw manure or compost is probably best spread on the soil in the autumn. Although excessive amounts of manure can lead to sappy, disease prone growth, in practice it is difficult to put on too much manure or compost. It disappears surprisingly fast. Think in terms of a layer at least 5-10cm (2-4in) thick, applied to the vegetable beds every year.

## GREEN MANURES

Green manures are crops which are grown and then dug in to improve soil fertility. They are an excellent way of supplementing the organic matter and/or nitrogen in the soil and improving its fertility. In dry areas they improve the moisture holding capacity of the soil noticeably. If even a small piece of ground looks like being vacant for a few weeks or several months, it is worth sowing it with a green manure.

## Types of Green Manure

Green manures can be divided into three broad categories.

Fast Growing Crops
These quickly make a leafy canopy, which, when it is dug in, gives an almost immediate release of nitrogen. Mustard, rape (a rich source of nitrogen and phosphorus), fodder radish and the blue flowered *Phacelia tanacetifolia* are examples. Note that all these, except for *Phacelia*, are brassicas (crucifers) in the cabbage family, so avoid growing in soil where there is clubroot.

Leguminous Crops
These members of the pea and bean family have nodules on their roots, which fix the atmospheric nitrogen in the soil, releasing it slowly to following crops. Their leaves also produce nitrogen when they rot. Examples are various types of clover, alfalfa, lupins, winter field beans, field peas, winter tares, and fenugreek (though this will not fix nitrogen in cool climates). Alfalfa and some of the clovers are perennial, so can be sown on surplus pieces of ground and left for a year or so.

Fibrous Rooted Crops
These develop dense fibrous root systems. While growing they ramify through the soil so improving its structure. When dug in they increase

the organic matter in the soil. Grazing rye grass and buckwheat are useful green manures in this category.

**When to Sow**
The main alternatives are as summer 'catch crops' or for over-wintering.

Summer Catch Crops
Fast growing green manures are sown as 'catch crops' between one crop being lifted and another sown, whenever a piece of ground becomes vacant. They are dug in a few weeks or months later, as appropriate. Buckwheat, mustard, *Phacelia* and fenugreek are typical.

Over-wintering
These are generally sown from summer to autumn and dug in the following spring. In cold areas they must be winter hardy. Over-wintering green manures not only protect the soil surface during the winter, but they take up nitrogen and other nutrients, preventing them from being washed out of the soil. The nutrients are returned to the soil when the crop is dug in spring. Grazing rye grass, winter tares, field beans and red clover are examples of winter green manures. Grazing rye and field beans are particularly useful as they can be sown in late autumn.

**Cultivation and Management**
Green manures can be broadcast, sown in narrow or wide drills, or, in the case of field beans, sown individually (see Seed, Sowing Outdoors and Planting p.71). As a general rule they are dug in while still young and before they start to flower. If they are very bulky they can be awkward to dig in. In this case cut off the top growth first. Either leave it on the ground to wilt before digging it in, or put it on the compost heap, or use for mulching. The remaining roots and stems will be much easier to dig in. Turn them into the top 15cm (6in) of soil.

**Choice of Green Manure**
Many crops are used for green manuring, and it is important to choose those which suit your soil type, conditions, and the immediate purpose. For example, buckwheat tolerates poor soil, alfalfa is fairly drought tolerant, *Phacelia* can stand up to weed competition, Alsike clover performs well on wet, acid soils. If you are embarking on green manuring for the first time, I would suggest trying small patches of different green manures side by side. It soon becomes evident which do best under your soil

conditions. Consult a good seed catalogue for the choice available: organic suppliers tend to have the widest range.

The green manures I use most in my own garden are *Phacelia* and fodder radish in summer (this is cut down by the first hard frost and forms a natural mulch), and winter tares, grazing rye, crimson clover, and field beans for over-wintering. These seem to suit our slightly acid clay soil, low rainfall – about 50cm (20in) per annum – and winter temperatures dipping to -7°C (20°F) but rarely for more than a week at a time. For more on green manuring (see Further Reading p.251).

## CONCENTRATED ORGANIC FERTILIZERS
Where the soil has been brought to a high level of fertility with bulky manures, good crops can be grown normally without the use of concentrated fertilizers. However they can be useful in the following cases:
* To help to remedy fundamental soil deficiencies. If plant growth is unaccountably poor, a laboratory soil analysis will indicate if mineral deficiencies exist.
* To supply extra nutrients in poor soil. Building up soil fertility takes several years, and fertilizers can help bridge the nutrient gap in the early stages. Nitrogen is the element most likely to be in short supply, as it is rapidly washed out of the soil, and is needed in large quantities by fast-growing, leafy crops.
* To obtain higher yields. Heavy feeders such as tomatoes respond to a boost of fertilizer during growth.

### The Organic/Inorganic Argument
Organic gardeners use a limited range of natural, organic fertilizers instead of manufactured, artificial, chemical fertilizers. There are several reasons for this:
* Artificial fertilizers are soluble chemicals which are taken up rapidly by plants. This leads to soft, sappy growth which makes plants more susceptible to pest and disease attack. Excess nitrogen or potash fertilizers can inhibit germination in a seedbed. By contrast organic fertilizers have to be broken down by soil micro-organisms before they are available to plants, so they are released slowly over a longer period. This can be a drawback in spring, as the micro-organisms will not start working until soil temperatures have warmed up.
* Most artificial fertilizers only contain one or more of the main elements nitrogen (N), phosphorus (P) or potassium (K). While these feed the plant, they are of little benefit to the soil. Organic fertilizers can supply all

the principal elements, but in many cases are also a source of minor and trace elements and plant growth promoting substances. In addition they benefit the soil.

* It is easy to apply an 'overdose' of artificial fertilizers. This can damage growth or, through chemical reactions, lead to deficiencies of other nutrients. There is a strong risk of excess nitrogen being washed into the soil, especially in winter when plants are not growing and taking up nitrogen. This contributes to the problem of nitrate pollution.

### Applying Fertilizers

Fertilizers are applied as *base dressings* shortly before sowing or planting, or as *top dressings* or *foliar feeds* during growth.

There are dry and liquid forms of artificial fertilizer: the fertilizer value is the same. Dry fertilizers, usually supplied as dusts, granules, or pellets, are scattered on the soil, hoed or dug into the top 8cm (3½in), and watered in well if the soil is dry. Liquid fertilizers, normally sold in concentrated form, are diluted and then watered on the ground around the plants. Younger plants should generally be fed with more diluted solutions. Liquid feeds can be made from comfrey, nettles and manure mixtures (see pp.37-8). Liquid fertilizers are sometimes sprayed directly on the leaves as foliar feeds.

Foliar feeding

With foliar feeding nutrients are generally absorbed fairly rapidly, but it is advisable to spray in dull conditions, in early morning, or in the evening, when uptake is best. It seems that plants can only take in quite limited amounts through their leaves, so foliar spraying should not be regarded as the only method of feeding. It is very useful for supplementary feeding (seaweed extract foliar feeds seem to be particularly beneficial), for correcting trace element deficiencies with special compounds sold for the purpose, and in periods of dry weather, when solid fertilizers would need copious watering.

### Organic Fertilizers in Use

The following organic fertilizers are widely used on vegetables. Other proprietary compounds are also available, often made from chicken or animal manure.

*Fish blood and bone meal* – source of nitrogen and phosphate; used as base and top dressing.

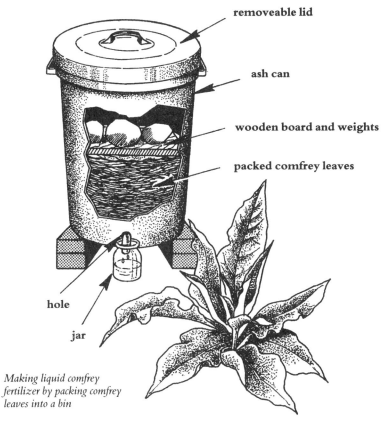

removeable lid

ash can

wooden board and weights

packed comfrey leaves

hole

jar

*Making liquid comfrey fertilizer by packing comfrey leaves into a bin*

*Hoof and horn* – mainly supplies nitrogen; recommended as top dressing for leafy crops.

*Liquid seaweed extracts* – a source of a wide range of nutrients and trace elements; seem to stimulate plant growth and disease resistance; used as both liquid and foliar feed.

*Liquid comfrey concentrate* – general purpose liquid feed; contains a high level of potash which benefits tomatoes and peppers.

*Seaweed meal* – General purpose base dressing and soil conditioner.

## Homemade Liquid Feeds

'Black Jack' or 'manure tea' – make this by suspending a sack of animal manure in a barrel of water. The animal manure can be mixed with lawn mowings, or, a common component in the past, soot. Dilute it to the colour of weak tea before application.

Comfrey Manure or Comfrey Tea

This is made from the deep rooted, perennial plant comfrey (*Symphytum officinale*). Although wild strains can be used to make the manure, the most effective is the cultivated variety 'Bocking 14'. This is easily grown in the garden. It does not set seed, and therefore must be cultivated from root cuttings or by dividing established plants. Plants and cuttings can be purchased through organic suppliers.

The simplest, and least smelly, method of making comfrey manure is in a barrel or bin. Drill a 1.3cm (½in) diameter hole in the base, or insert a tap near the bottom. Fill the barrel with leaves, and weight them down, for example by covering them with a board with stones on top. The comfrey concentrate slowly drips through. Use it diluted between 10 and 20 times with water.

Besides being made into a liquid feed, comfrey leaves also make an excellent, compact mulch. They can also be cut and used as a semi–bulky manure. We like to line our tomato trenches with comfrey leaves.

Nettle Manure

This can be made in the same way as comfrey manure and comfrey tea. Alternatively it can be made in buckets, filling the buckets half with water, half with nettles. Consider it ready for use when it starts to smell! Use it without dilution as a general feed.

Note: The basis of my own manuring policy is to work some bulky manure into the whole garden every year, rotating homemade compost, farmyard manure and spent mushroom compost. During the growing season I boost growth with seaweed extract liquid and foliar feeds, about once a month for the plants that most seem to require it.

# Chapter 3
# Shelter, Water and Weeds

## SHELTER

Shelter is one of the most undervalued factors in vegetable growing. Research has shown that shelter from even light winds can increase plant yields by as much as 20-30 per cent. All ordinary vegetables seem to benefit from increased shelter, but for salad plants, whose tender leaves are so easily toughened by any kind of exposure to the elements, protection can ensure quality. As for tender, warmth loving vegetables such as tomatoes and cucumbers – which can often be coaxed into reluctant growth in the colder climates – some shelter can spell the difference between success and failure.

Low temperatures combined with strong winds take the greatest toll on plants. So by taking the edge off a keen wind, shelter tips the balance in the plant's favour. The value of greenhouses, plastic tunnels, frames, cloches and the various polythene and fleecy film 'covers' used to protect crops lies as much in providing shelter as in the higher temperatures they generate within.

### Windbreaks

In exposed gardens consider erecting some kind of windbreak. The ideal windbreak is not, as might be imagined, a solid wall. It should be about 50 per cent permeable to the wind, such as a hedge or a closely-woven fabric fence. Wind simply jumps over a solid barrier, creating a damaging area of turbulence at some point on the far side. The effect of a windbreak lessens with distance. As a rule of thumb, it is effective up to a distance of about six times its height; so 1.8m (6ft) high barriers would need to be about 12m (40ft) apart. Theoretically, windbreaks should be sited in the path of the prevailing wind, but where the direction of the prevailing wind is variable, that is easier said than done.

Windbreaks are either living or artificial. The disadvantage of living windbreaks such as trees or hedges is that they compete with plants for nutrients, water and light, may create too much shade, and also require some maintenance. Poplar, willow, and conifers such as *Cupressocyparis leylandii*, *Chamaecyparis lawsoniana* and *Thuja plicata* are often used in temperate climates.

Within the vegetable garden, the sturdy vegetables like Jerusalem artichoke, sweet corn, sunflower and cardoon can be grown as windbreaks. With the exception of cardoons, which grow into plants with a substantial spread, grow them in rows at least two or three deep, staggering the plants. Salads, and wind-susceptible crops such as dwarf beans, can be grown in the lee of these tall plants.

Artificial windbreaks such as lath or wattle fences, or strong, manufactured windbreak nets do not, of course, compete for nutrients and water, though they will need to be replaced from time to time. Secure netting to firmly anchored posts with battens. The force of wind blowing into netting can be very strong, so corner posts may need to be reinforced to take the strain. Where it is impractical to erect or plant a large scale windbreak, strips of nylon netting or hessian sacks 30-60cm (1-2ft) high can be strung between beds of vegetables. Even ordinary wire netting has some effect in breaking the force of a wind.

In built-up areas devastating wind tunnels can be created between buildings. It is well worth planting trees or shrubs in such gaps (though *they* may need protection to start them off), or erecting fencing that extends well to either side of the gap. Wind will creep up cunningly around the edge of a windbreak.

*Even low strips of hessian can serve as windbreaks, improving the yield and quality of salad crops*

Having stressed the importance of shelter, one should mention the reverse side of the coin. Vegetables should never be grown in claustrophobic conditions, which encourage the build up of pests and diseases. Most do best in what is called an 'open site', free of deep shade created by buildings or large overhanging trees. Drips from trees can be very damaging to vegetables. However, in hot weather some cool-loving salads such as lettuce, cress and sorrel are apt to run to seed in positions exposed to full sun. They will do much better in light shade, provided the ground is reasonably moist.

## WATER

Most leafy salad plants require a reasonable amount of water, but the extent to which watering is necessary depends on climate and soil. Soils with plenty of organic matter in them hold moisture well and provide a fertile growing environment. Heavy clay and loamy soils naturally hold more water than free-draining light soils. If there is a shortage of water near the surface plant roots tend to grow deeper and spread more widely in search of it. This root spread is much easier where the soil has been deeply dug or cultivated.

### Minimizing Watering

In many areas water is an increasingly scarce resource and watering is hard work, so it makes sense to water as little as possible. Moreover frequent watering washes nutrients, especially nitrogen, out of the soil or beyond the reach of roots. It also encourages plants to develop shallow root systems near the surface of the soil, rather than a deep root system which will sustain them in periods of water shortage. Too much water diminishes the flavour of salad plants – most noticeably in tomatoes. In dry situations everything must be done to conserve the water in the soil. Besides being lost through natural drainage and transpiration via the plant leaves, a great deal of moisture is lost by evaporation from the soil surface. This is highest in hot and windy conditions. Keeping the surface mulched by covering it with a loose organic layer or solid materials such as plastic films, is the most effective way of conserving moisture (see Mulching pp.46–50). It is particularly valuable on light and shallow soils, for example a soil lying over impermeable rock, which prevents roots from penetrating deeply.

Reducing the competition between plants for the nutrients and water in the soil around them also lessens the need to water. The closer the planting, the stiffer the competition, so in dry climates planting can and should be much further apart than would otherwise be the case. Weeds of course, compete for water, which is why they must be removed. If possible, pull them up rather than hoe them up. This is because evaporation occurs rapidly from the top centimetre (half inch) or so of soil. Once the surface is dry it slows down, the dry soil layer effectively cutting off the capillary action and acting as a mulch. Hoeing will disturb this and encourage further evaporation. In dry weather disturb the surface as little as possible.

All these measures, coupled with the universal panacea of working in as much organic matter as possible, will cut water losses.

**How to Water**

Soil becomes wet layer by layer, and until the top layer is saturated, the soil beneath remains dry. It is surprising how much water it takes to wet the soil. Push your finger into the soil after a shower of rain: it is astonishing how dry it still is. The moral is that heavy, albeit infrequent watering is *far* more effective than frequent light watering. Casually sprinkling the soil is useless and only encourages roots to come to the surface.

An exception is newly planted transplants: these will need frequent, light watering until they are established and have developed a good root system. The same is true of very shallow rooted plants.

Plants should be watered as gently as possible. Water delicate young plants with a can with a very narrow spout or fine rose. The various types of perforated and porous hose, 'layflat tubing' and 'seephose' for example, are recommended, as water percolates slowly out of the holes or through the skin and there is little wastage. Attach the hose to a tap or ordinary hose and lay it between the plants. It can be laid permanently down the centre of a narrow bed for example, or moved from one part of a garden to another. Some types can be buried in the soil. In dry weather water in the evening, to minimize evaporation, but allow time for plants to dry off before nightfall.

When planting, confine watering to a small circle around the plant rather than the whole bed. This will discourage weeds from germinating between the plants. In dry areas it is advisable to mulch after planting.

**Critical Periods**

All plants require moisture to germinate and when first planted, but after these stages many have a *critical* period when lack of water is most damaging. Where water is scarce, concentrate watering on these periods. They vary with the type of plant.

Leafy Vegetables

These require moisture throughout growth, but in hot weather benefit from 11-16 litres per sq m (2-3 gal per sq yd) per week. The most critical period is 10-20 days before maturity. One very heavy watering at this stage will to some extent compensate for lack of water earlier. The more closely together leafy crops are grown, the more water they require.

Fruiting Vegetables

Vegetables grown for their 'fruits', such as peas, beans and tomatoes, need a steady supply of moisture throughout growth, but their highest water requirements are when flowering, when fruit is setting, and when the fruits start to swell. At these stages a heavy weekly watering, as much as 22 litres per sq m (4 gal per sq yd) will increase the yields considerably. At earlier stages water enough to prevent the soil drying out.

Root Vegetables
Roots such as radishes only need enough water for steady growth during the early stages: overwatering encourages leaf rather than root growth. Once the roots are starting to swell they can be watered moderately if the soil is dry. Excess watering after a dry period can cause the roots to crack.

## Miscellaneous Watering Techniques
Sowing Outdoors in Dry Conditions
* Make a wide or narrow drill (see Seed, Sowing Outdoors and Planting pp.70-1).
* Water the *bottom* of the drill only very thoroughly.
* Sow the seed on the moist soil and press it in.
* Cover the seed with *dry* soil. This acts as a mulch, and enables the seed to remain moist until it has germinated.

Watering via Clay Pots
This economical method is most suitable for large plants. Sink clay pots into the soil near the plants, the rims at soil level or a little below, and confine watering to the pot. Water gradually seeps through to the roots.

Watering when Away
This is most practical for plants in greenhouses or containers. Make wicks 1.3-2cm (½-¾in) thick from glass–fibre lagging, wool or soft string. Dangle one end in a bucket of water, the other near the plant's root or in the container. Water will seep along the wick to the plant. A 5cm (2in) deep layer of stones, as a surface mulch will help cut down evaporation.

Watering in Greenhouses
Greenhouses, polytunnels and other structures in which plants are grown heat up and dry out rapidly in sunny weather, so mulching is especially recommended. Water in the evening to minimize evaporation. In cool weather and during the winter water in the morning, so that the foliage has time to dry before nightfall. This helps to prevent disease. For the same reason, in winter it is advisable to water the soil around the plants, rather than the plants.

## WEEDS

Weeds are *persona non grata* in the vegetable garden because they compete for water, nutrients, space and light. Many weeds also harbour pests and diseases. Aphids over-winter in groundsel (*Senecio vulgaris*) and also in chickweed (*Stellaria media*), which, along with shepherd's purse (*Capsella bursa pastoris*) and fat hen (*Chenopodium album*), harbour lettuce mosaic virus in winter. This poses a dilemma for salad eaters: whether to remove the plants or let them grow. Chickweed, shepherd's purse and fat hen are worthy additions to a salad!

Weeds do have other good points. They are rich in mineral nutrients and also in organic matter, which can be recycled by putting them on the compost heap. Some weeds do an excellent job in breaking up the soil: the fibrous root systems of chickweed are particularly good in this way. And weeds such as nettles (*Urtica* sp.) can be a source of food for beneficial insects.

### Controlling Weeds

The approach to take in order to control weeds depends on whether they are annual or perennial.

Annual Weeds

These are the commonest garden weeds. They germinate, flower, seed, and die within a year, in some cases having several generations a year. They tend to be shallow rooting and are easily dug up. Most are prolific seeders, producing maybe tens of thousands of seeds in just a season. So if weeds are in residence in your garden, the top layer of soil can quickly become riddled with weed seed. Fortunately much of this is lost, due to exposure to the elements and birds, when the soil is cultivated. It really does take the proverbial seven years for one year's seed to disappear from the topsoil. The important thing is to prevent the weeds from going to seed in the first place.

Weed seed in the lower levels of the soil can remain dormant for many years, ready to germinate when exposed by cultivation to light and moisture. This explains the huge crop of weeds which appears when neglected land is first dug over.

To control annual weeds in an established garden:
\* Grow plants on the bed system at equidistant spacing, in 'blocks' rather than widely spaced rows (see Soil Fertility p.21). With the exception of narrow-leaved plants like onions, the leaves of most of the salad plants

eventually form a canopy over the soil suppressing weed development.

* Keep plants mulched wherever practical (see Mulching pp.46-50).

* Hoe or pull out weeds when necessary between narrow-leaved plants before they are mulched, and young plants before the canopy stage is reached. For vegetables sown in the ground, weed competition starts to be really serious about three weeks after the vegetable seedlings have germinated. Tackle the weeds before this.

My favourite tool for hoeing among salad crops is the swan necked onion hoe. It is small, light to use, easily controlled and shallow in action. Where hoeing is essential (but see Minimizing Watering p.41) hoe when the soil is dry so that weeds can be left on the surface to dry before being composted. In wet conditions some weeds may contrive to re-root. Don't compost weeds that have gone to seed unless you have a very efficient compost heap.

To control annual weeds in a neglected or weedy garden:

* Before sowing in spring cover the soil with clear plastic film to encourage weed seed to germinate. Allow the first flush of weeds to germinate, and hoe them off before sowing.

* During the growing season only cultivate shallowly, to avoid bringing up fresh weed seed.

* Use mulches as much as possible.

Perennial Weeds

These remain in the soil from one year to the next. Typical perennials have deep tap roots, or malevolent creeping runners which spread rapidly, or roots which can resprout from small fragments left in the soil. The most serious perennials vary from garden to garden. Mine are ground elder (*Aegopodium podagraria* ), bindweed (*Convolvulus* sp.) and couch grass (*Agropyron repens*).

Most perennials can be eliminated by digging them out, which can be hard work initially. Try to remove every piece of root from perennials with easily regenerating roots such as bindweed, ground elder and couch grass. If the weeds are still getting the better of you and you don't want to use chemical weedkillers to eliminate them, the only effective remedy is to blanket the affected area with heavy duty black polythene sheeting, old carpeting or cardboard. This may have to be left in place for as long as twelve months before the roots die off.

Don't put roots of perennial weeds on a compost heap until they have been completely killed by drying them out.

# Chapter 4
# Mulching

Mulching is such a useful technique for growing salad plants organically that it deserves a chapter to itself. A mulch is anything laid on the surface of the soil. It can be organic material such as straw or compost, which eventually rots into the soil, or inorganic material such as carpeting, polythene film, or even stone, gravel or sand.

Mulching is probably one of the most ancient gardening techniques, practised centuries ago by highly skilled gardeners such as the Arabs and Chinese. It was also used long ago in Britain: a thirteenth century accounts book for Norwich Cathedral records labourers being paid three pence a day for 'thatching' fields with straw! (Seven centuries later, 40 miles away, the basic rate for mulching at the time of writing is three pounds an hour!)

As most salads are leafy, thirsty crops, mulching is particularly relevant to salad growing, especially when in dry conditions. One of the most interesting techniques we encountered on our travels through Europe was the extensive use of mulching with sand, stone and gravel on the very hot and dry Spanish coast. Tomato and cucumber were among salad crops being mulched in this way – some in the open, some under low plastic tunnels, some in greenhouses. Here the heat absorbed by the stones during the day is radiated at night.

## BENEFITS OF MULCHING
Depending on the material used, most mulches will offer several of the following benefits:

★ Suppress weeds and prevent weed germination.
★ Conserve soil moisture by preventing evaporation.
★ Protect the soil surface during heavy rain and prevent erosion.
★ Lessen compaction when the soil is walked on.
★ Encourage earthworm activity and soil life. (Surprisingly, earthworm activity seems to increase with both organic and polythene film mulches.)
★ Lessen the need to cultivate, culminating in making a 'no–dig' system feasible (see Soil Fertility p.26).
★ Lessen the risk of fungus infection by keeping leaves, and the fruits of

sprawling cucumber and tomato plants, cleaner and drier. This may make it unnecessary to wash them before use.

★ Generally insulate the soil, keeping it cooler in summer and warmer in winter months.

★ *Organic mulches* add organic matter and nutrients to the soil.

★ *Film mulches* can deter pests. Shiny and chequered plastic mulches deter aphids and some other insects (see Pests and Diseases pp.54–5).

★ *Clear film mulches* warm up the soil (this is especially useful for early spring sowings).

**Types of Organic Mulches**
Organic mulches divide into those which are a source of nutrients and increase soil fertility (they will also keep down weeds if used thickly) and those used primarily to suppress weeds and/or conserve moisture. Most organic mulches should be applied in a fairly well-rotted state, or nitrogen is taken from the soil in the early stages of decomposition. This is particularly true of mulches derived from wood, such as sawdust and shredded bark. It is inadvisable to use them on vegetable beds until they are a couple of seasons old. Allow lawn mowings to dry out for a couple of days before using them as a mulch.

Ideally organic mulches should be loose enough in texture to allow water to penetrate through them to the soil. Straw, for example, is much more permeable than lawn mowings, which become compacted if used in a thick layer, especially when fresh.

Most of the organic mulches which increase soil fertility have already been mentioned in the chapter of manures and compost. They include garden compost, well-rotted animal manure, spent mushroom compost, wilted comfrey, well-rotted lawn mowings, well-rotted straw and hay, seaweed, and various types of waste products. In the United States the marsh plant salt grass (*Spartium patens*) is a popular garden mulch, used whole or shredded.

Organic mulches with little nutrient value, but which nevertheless control weeds and retain moisture, include newspaper (laid several layers thick), cardboard, old carpets and matting, pulverized, shredded and chipped bark, sawdust and miscellaneous manufactured materials. These are all best used on paths, waste ground, or around fruit trees and bushes.

**Types of Film Mulches**
The range of materials available to home gardeners is continually changing. These are some examples:

*Black unperforated film* keeps down weeds, helps retain moisture and any warmth in the soil, but does little to warm up the soil. It keeps out rain except where holes are cut.

*Black perforated film* keeps down weeds but allows some rainfall into the soil. It is used mainly on perennials or long term crops.

*Clear film* warms up the soil, to some extent helps retain moisture, but does little to suppress weeds.

*Opaque white film* reflects light up onto plants. In dull climates it is used to mulch fruiting vegetables such as tomatoes and peppers to accelerate ripening. Suppresses weeds by acting as a physical barrier. It is useful for mulching winter salads grown under cover, for example oriental brassicas, lettuce, endives and chicories.

*Black and white film* is a combined film with a black underside that suppresses weeds and a white upper surface that reflects light onto fruit.

*Chequered and shiny film* is used primarily to deter aphids; to some extent suppresses weeds and conserves moisture.

*Brown film* is a halfway house between black and transparent film. It warms the soil like transparent film, but suppresses weeds.

*Permeable black film* allows water and air through to the soil, but suppresses the growth of weeds. Use heavy duty films for mulching paths, and perennial plants and substantial plants; lighter films are best for mulching smaller plants.

(Fleecy films and perforated transparent films are best used to bring crops on earlier; see Protected Cropping pp.123-4.)

Disposing of Polythene Film
If possible avoid burning scrap polythene, as poisonous gases are given off in the process. It can be buried or laid beneath paths where it slowly degrades. Where available and practical, use photodegradable films, which slowly break down in sunlight.

## Mulching Guidelines
The key point about a mulch is that it maintains the *status quo* of the soil. Never mulch when it is very cold, very dry, or very wet: the soil will stay that way. The ideal time is when the soil is moist but warm. In spring wait until the soil has warmed up to at least 6°C (43°F), but mulch before it has dried out completely.

If watering becomes necessary, push organic mulches to one side. With film and other inorganic mulches water through the planting hole. Perforated or permeable hoses can be laid underneath a mulch to make watering easier. Slugs may collect under mulches, particularly cool materials such as black films, so keep an eye out for them.

Laying Organic Mulches
On the whole the best time to mulch is after planting. With spring planting, wait until the soil has had a chance to warm up. In summer, water thoroughly when planting and then mulch. This can cut down dramatically on the need to water during summer. Similarly, mulching in greenhouses can save a lot of watering. The mulch can be built up around the stems as they grow. With seedlings, it is best to wait until they are several centimetres high before mulching, or they may be swamped. Birds love to peck in a mulch and will scatter it all over young seedlings. Salad crops which will be over-wintered in the soil, winter radish or celeriac for example, can be mulched in the autumn. By protecting the soil this makes it easier to dig them up when the ground is frozen.

As a general rule, the deeper the mulch the more effective it will be: a depth of 2.5–5cm (1–2in) is a good start. To suppress weeds completely an organic mulch probably needs to be at least 10cm (4in) deep. Don't worry if this proves difficult: it is fairly easy to pull out any weeds which make their way through a more shallow mulch.

Laying Stone, Sand and Gravel Mulches
Here again it is a case of the deeper the better. The Spanish sand and stone mulches that we saw on our tour were often 10cm (4in) deep.

Laying Film Mulches
On the whole it is easiest to lay the films *before* sowing or planting. Spread the film over the bed or areas to be covered, and anchor the edges. The simplest way of doing this is to weight down the film edges with bricks, clods of soil, pieces of timber or polythene bags filled with sand or soil. Alternatively use a spade or trowel to make slits at least 7.5cm (3in) deep in the soil alongside the film. Bury the film edges in the slits, pushing the soil back to keep them in place. This makes a particularly neat edge. The same methods are used for anchoring fine, insect-proof nets laid over hoops (see diagram p.53).

Incidentally, it is easier to lay films over slightly domed beds, which have the added advantage of not puddling after rain.

To sow large seeds make holes or slits in the film with a knife or the point of a dibber at the required spacing, and sow through them. Smaller seeds are best raised separately and transplanted as young plants. To plant through the film, cut a cross, or two sides of a triangle, large enough to insert the plant. Ease the plant into the ground through the hole.

Where potatoes are grown under black films they are planted first, then covered with the film. When the leaves are seen pushing up against the film, cut a cross to allow them to come through. Where covering a planted crop roll the film over the crop, cut slits or holes in the film where appropriate to allow the plants through, and then anchor the film in either of the methods given on the previous page.

For sowing cut-and-come-again seedling crops in weedy soil in cut-out plastic strips (see Salad Techniques pp.85-6).

# Chapter 5

# Pests and Diseases

Fortunately there are not many serious pests and diseases on salad crops, but inevitably problems arise from time to time. For organic gardeners chemical spraying, even with the safer, non-lasting sprays approved by the organic authorities, should be the last resort. Instead the emphasis must be on preventive medicine.

Plants that are well grown, and thereby strong and healthy, are far less susceptible to pest and disease attack, and stand a better chance of throwing off any attacks that occur. Weak, overcrowded plants are always the first to go. So the key to success lies in the old fashioned concept 'good husbandry', coupled with non-chemical methods of protection, prevention and control where they exist.

## GOOD HUSBANDRY IN A NUTSHELL

* Make the soil as fertile as possible.
* Practise rotation to limit the development and increase of soil pests and diseases (see Siting and Planning pp.126-7).
* Grow appropriate crops for your area. Attempting semi-tropical plants outdoors in cool areas is a recipe for disaster.
* Never overcrowd plants. Overcrowding is a common cause of disease and encourages pests.
* Practise intercropping as far as is practical. This lessens the chance of a pest or disease sweeping through a crop.
* As far as possible raise plants in individual pots or modules so they develop a good strong root system (see Raising Plants 'Indoors' pp.76-84).
* Encourage rapid germination, whether outdoors or in propagators. Lingering seedlings rarely do well. Never sow or plant in very cold, very wet or very dry soil.
* Thin early to avoid overcrowded and leggy seedlings; steady growth is healthy growth.
* Where feasible adjust sowing times to avoid or minimize pest attacks. Base this on local knowledge. For example in some areas flea beetle attacks are serious in spring, but far less so in autumn.
* Don't overcoddle or overfeed plants: grow them 'hard' to increase their resistance. Harden-off well before planting outside.

* Keep greenhouses well ventilated. In hot weather 'damp them down' frequently by spraying with water. This will lower the temperature and discourage greenhouse pests such as red spider mite which thrive in hot dry conditions.

* Keep plants adequately watered. Limp plants are most vulnerable to aphid attack.

* Handle storage vegetables such as onion, garlic and potatoes with great care. Diseases often enter where they have been bruised or cut.

* Never plant diseased plants or bulbs. Remove and burn diseased leaves to prevent infection spreading. Burn plants infected with viruses, club-root or other serious diseases.

* Dig up old brassica (crucifer) stumps at the end of the season, as they harbour over-wintering pests. Bury them in the ground or deep in the compost heap.

* Keep the vegetable garden and paths free of rubbish and weeds which provide cover for over-wintering pests and slugs.

* Keep propagating equipment clean to avoid 'damping off' diseases. Wash pots and seedtrays after use. Always use sterile sowing and potting composts, stored in the dry. Keep water butts covered, as they provide breeding grounds for pests and diseases.

* Keep a constant watch for early signs of trouble from pests such as cater-pillar eggs, young caterpillars and early aphids. At this stage they are eas-ily squashed. If a young plant wilts unexpectedly dig it up carefully: perhaps it's been dislodged by a mole, or a soil pest has just started to nib-ble the stem or root. It may be possible to replant and save it.

* Avoid spraying with toxic chemicals so that natural, beneficial preda-tors are encouraged. These include lacewings, predatory beetles, hover-fly, ladybirds, frogs and toads – all of which help keep down pests and diseases. There are also beneficial insects in the soil, which can be killed by pesticides. If an unidentified creature is fast-moving the odds are that it feeds on the animal kingdom and is likely to be beneficial. The slow movers tend to be vegetarian and are therefore pests. Don't automatically squash everything!

* Plant flat open flowers, such as dwarf convolvulus, calendula (pot marigold), limnanthes (poached egg plant), nemophila (baby blue eyes) to attract hoverfly in particular. Their larvae feed on greenfly.

## NON-CHEMICAL METHODS OF PEST CONTROL
Hand Picking
Unless you are squeamish many pests can be squashed or picked off by

hand. These include caterpillars and colonies of green, black and mealy aphids. Collect night-feeding pests like slugs, snails, and the larvae of cutworms and chafer beetles at night by torchlight. Pick off celery and celeriac leaves affected with leaf miner.

Net Barriers
Very fine horticultural nets (rather like strong mosquito netting) will protect plants from a wide range of flying pests such as birds, aphids, whitefly, flea beetle, pollen beetle, cabbage and carrot root fly, butterflies and moths. The simplest way to use them is to lay the net over steel, wire, rigid plastic or rubber hoops. Anchor it at the base either by weighting it down or burying the edges in the soil (see Mulching p.49). Pests will only be kept out *if there are no gaps, holes or tears.* In some cases nets can be laid directly over the plants. The very light fleecy films also give considerable protection against flying pests, though they are less durable and are usually removed at some stage of growth (see Protected Cropping p.123-4).

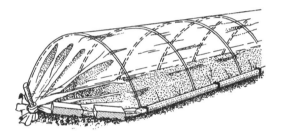

*Well anchored fine net tunnels exclude a wide range of flying pests*

Fences and Cages
For permanent protection against rabbits, deer and other large animals it may be necessary to erect sturdy wire fences or cages around the vegetable garden that will effectively keep out this type of intruder. To keep out rabbits use 4cm (1 ½in) mesh, buried at least 10cm (4in) underground with the wire turned outwards to prevent them burrowing beneath to reach the garden. Use purpose-made lightweight bird nets to cover cages for protection against birds.

Traps
Where essential use suitable humane traps to catch small rodents such as moles, mice and voles.

Bird Scarers

Birds may be scared by anything that flaps, glints or makes a noise, or by replicas of hawks or other large birds. However, they become accustomed to anything unless it is moved frequently. Keep small birds off seedlings by running a single strand of strong black cotton or button thread 5–7.5cm (2–3in) above the row, tied to a stick at each end.

Cabbage Root Fly Discs

Protect brassicas (crucifers) from cabbage root fly with 13cm (5in) diameter discs made from rubberized carpet underlay, or similar material. Make a small hole in the centre and a slit from the outer rim of the disc to the centre; this enables them to be slipped around the stem at soil level when planting. The discs prevent the adult cabbage root fly from laying her eggs at ground level, give cover to beneficial predatory beetles, and also keep the plant mulched.

Slug Barrier

Cut the bottoms off plastic bottles or pots and place the tops over young plants, pushing them well into the soil. They need to be about 10cm (4in) high. They will give protection against slugs in the most vulnerable early stages, but will need to be removed once the plant is well established. They also have some effect against cutworm and leatherjackets.

Yellow Sticky Traps

These are yellow plastic sheets, coated on both sides with sticky glue. They range in size from 8 x 25cm (3½ x 10in) to 25 x 40cm (10 x 16in). Although they will not completely control insects they catch reasonable numbers of aphids, whitefly, thrips, leaf miner flies, leaf hoppers and mites. Hang them slightly above the plants in greenhouses and among crops. To control greenhouse whitefly, hang them early in the season so they catch the first flies to appear.

Flea Beetle Traps

Catch flea beetles with a piece of wood coated with heavy grease. Hold it a couple of centimetres or so above attacked plants; the flea beetles will jump on to the board and stick in the grease.

Reflecting Mulches

Various types of shiny, reflecting films can be laid around and among plants to deter insects such as aphids and thrips. Aluminium film is an excellent deterrent for aphids; and even black films and white films have some effect. For maximum efficiency about 50 per cent of the ground should be covered with film.

## Biological Control

A biological control is a natural predator, parasite or infection which is introduced to control a pest. At present it is used mainly in greenhouses to control whitefly, red spider mites and aphids. A biological control cannot be introduced until the pest has appeared, and may itself die if temperatures fall. There is no risk of it becoming invasive as once its 'host' has been killed off, it has no more food and dies out. New biological controls are continually being developed. At the time of writing a nematode parasite is being launched for the control of slugs. Watch for news in the gardening press. Mail order seed catalogues often list suppliers. Introducing biological controls requires skill; the supplier's instructions must be followed carefully.

## Resistant Varieties

Plant breeders have developed vegetable cultivars (varieties) with resistance or tolerance to certain pests and diseases. This is a boon for organic gardeners. Study seed catalogues to see what is currently available. Some cultivars only have 'partial' resistance, but this may be sufficient to get a reasonable crop.

## THE SAFER SPRAYS

As already mentioned, sprays should only be used as a last resort, as almost all are liable to damage some beneficial or harmless insects as well as the pest in question. Moreover insects and disease fungi build up resistance to specific chemicals, so the less they are used the longer any one will be effective when urgent measures are required.

Even the less toxic sprays should be handled carefully. Keep them in clearly labelled containers out of the reach of children, in a cool, dry, preferably dark place; follow the manufacturer's instructions meticulously. Always spray in the evening or in dull weather, when pollinating insects are not flying. Never spray near water or rain tubs, or allow spray to drift onto water. Some pesticides can be mixed with others or with liquid fertilizers and/or foliar feeds, and applied together. Consult the manufacturer's instructions.

Sprays based on the following ingredients are approved for use by organic gardeners at the time of writing:

*Derris/Rotenone* – to control aphids (greenfly and blackfly), some beetles, for example flea beetle, small caterpillars, turnip fly, some weevils, thrips, suckers and red spider mite. It has some effect on Colorado beetle if used at double strength.

*Pyrethrum* – to control greenfly, whitefly, many beetles, caterpillars and leaf hoppers.

Note: Derris and pyrethrum are sometimes combined to make a more effective spray.

*Insecticidal Soap* – to control all types of aphids, whitefly, red spider mite and leaf hoppers. It is sometimes used in greenhouses before introducing biological control.

*Bacillus thuringiensis* – a biological spray (based on a bacterium which infects caterpillars) used to control many types of caterpillar.

## MAIN GROUPS OF PESTS

The following is a brief account of the insects and related pests most likely to attack salad crops. As far as possible, use the non-chemical methods of control, outlined on the previous page, to control them.

### Slugs and Snails

In cool, temperate climates slugs are undoubtedly the number one pest on salad plants. They are active almost all year round unless it is freezing, mostly sheltering during the day in the soil or under bricks, pieces of wood or weeds, and coming out at night to feed on roots, stems and leaves – the more succulent and tender the plant the better. Seedlings and young plants are most susceptible. They eat a wide range of plants but have their favourites – lettuce, brassicas (crucifers), French beans, basil to name a few. Snails do similar damage and have similar habits. They are often a serious problem on chalky soil and in gardens with dry stone walls, which are a favourite habitat.

To some extent vulnerable plants can be protected by surrounding them with coarse, scratchy materials such as crushed egg shells, grit, sand, and ashes; the traditional slug repellants of soot and lime also tend to desiccate them. In my experience hunting slugs and snails at night is by far the best method of control. They are most likely to be abroad in large numbers on warm muggy nights or after rainfall. Besides picking off obvious ones look on the underside of leaves and on the ground. I drop the collected slugs into a used drinks can (escape is relatively slow up the smooth sides) and kill them, I hope instantaneously, by pouring in boiling water. This seems 'kinder' than the slow death caused by sprinkling them with salt. I personally never use slug traps, as I find traps catch as many beneficial predatory beetles as slugs. And in any case carpets, black plastic and wooden boards used for mulching act as natural traps. Just pick them up and look beneath.

## Common Soil Pests

Most of these are the caterpillar or grub stages of insects such as moths, beetles and craneflies. See p.58 for identification, typical damage and some control methods. They tend to attack seedlings and young plants at and below ground level. They are worst in freshly cultivated ground and neglected gardens. In some cases the roots are nibbled away; in others the stem is bitten through just above ground, effectively cutting off the growing point. The first indication of trouble is a suddenly wilting plant.

In ground that is being cultivated for the first time it is often advisable to minimize damage by planting a crop of potatoes before growing any salads. The potatoes may be badly holed by the soil pests, but many of the pests will be removed when the potatoes are lifted. At some stage in their life cycle many soil pests use weeds as hosts or hide under debris, so garden hygiene is important in keeping them down. Hunting at night is the main method of control.

## Lettuce Root Aphid

This aphid is unusual in that it spends part of its life cycle in the soil. During this phase the aphids, which are covered in a white waxy powder, feed on lettuce roots, killing the plant which collapses dramatically. (Related species attack other vegetables.) There is no easy control. Prevent a build up by rotation (see Siting and Planning pp.126-7), and if it seems to be a regular problem, try growing some resistant cultivars. Those that are available at the time of writing include 'Avoncrisp', 'Avondefiance', 'Sabine' and 'Musette', but new ones will undoubtedly be introduced before too long.

## Eelworms (Nematodes)

These minute soil creatures cause various devastating plant 'sicknesses', often causing the plants to become bloated, twisted or stunted. Of the salad crops, onion, tomato, potatoes and radish can be affected by different species. Some make cysts which enable them to hibernate in the soil for many years. In practice there are no effective remedies on a garden scale. The best prevention lies in crop rotation, if possible at least on a three-year cycle (see Siting and Planning pp.126-7).

## SOIL PESTS

| PEST | LARVAL FORM | ADULT FORM | TIME AND NATURE OF DAMAGE | SIMPLE CONTROL MEASURES |
|---|---|---|---|---|
| **TURNIP MOTH** / **CUTWORM** | Fat caterpillar Distinct head Sucker Feet Soil coloured Up to 5cm (2in) long | Noctuid moth eg Turnip, heart and dart moth and others | Spring to autumn Larva cuts off stems at soil level Mostly night feeders | Grow under fine nets Search soil by damaged plants and kill larvae Rain/heavy watering in early summer kills larvae |
| **CRANEFLY** / **LEATHERJACKET** | Legless No distinct head Fat and soft Earthy colour Up to 4cm (1½in) long | Cranefly or Daddy-long-legs | Spring to summer Larvae eat roots, bite through stems Ragged feeding on lower leaves | Ensure soil well drained Clear and dig land before autumn especially grassland Control as cutworm |
| **WIREWORM** / **CLICK BEETLE** | 3 prs good legs Tough, wire-like golden yellow, hard shiny body About 2.5cm (1in) long | Click beetle | Spring to autumn; worst first 3 years after digging in grass. Make holes in roots and tubers. Nip off stems at ground level | Hunt around damaged plants and destroy. Plant potato crop initially to reduce numbers of wireworms |
| **CHAFER GRUB** / **COCKCHAFER BEETLE** | 3 prs strong legs Large brown head Tail end body swollen Lies with body bent Whitish; inactive | May-bug (Cockchafer beetle) June-bug (Garden chafer) | Summer to autumn Roots gnawed 5cm (2in) or more below soil surface | Keep garden clean and weed free Search soil near damaged plants and kill grubs |
| **MILLIPEDES** | 2 prs legs on most segments. Up to 2cm (¾in) long. Brown 'flat' type, and shiny, black 'snake' type most harmful | Do not confuse with centipedes which are: fast moving; have one pair legs per segment and are beneficial | Spring to summer Eat pea and bean seeds and seedlings, roots and tubers of many vegetables | Search near damaged plants and remove |

**Aphids**

Aphids, which include greenfly, blackfly and the aptly named cabbage mealy aphid, can be serious on a wide range of salad plants. They pierce the tissue, feed on the sap and weaken the plant, sometimes transmitting virus diseases in the process. They build up rapidly, especially in hot weather, so it is important to spot them early. There are many species of aphid, each usually attacking specific plants or groups of plants.

Their many natural predators such as ladybirds, hoverfly larvae, parasitic wasps and beetles will be encouraged where no chemical sprays are used. Use preventative measures to discourage them; fine nets, sticky traps and reflective mulches to deter them.

**Root Flies**

The adult cabbage and carrot root flies lay their eggs at ground level, and the young grubs tunnel into the stems. This causes young brassica plants to collapse and carrots to become bronzed and feeble. Onions, leeks and shallots may be similarly affected by the onion fly, mainly in dry seasons. Where root flies are a regular problem protect brassicas with discs when planting (see p.54), grow carrots within a 60cm (2ft) high barrier of clear plastic film or fine net, which protects them as the flies only fly low, and grow onions under fine nets.

**Caterpillars**

Caterpillars are most likely to be a problem on salad brassicas (crucifers). Watch out for the eggs and destroy them, or grow plants under fine nets to prevent butterflies and moths from laying eggs in the first place.

**Beetles**

Salad brassicas such as radish, texsel greens and the oriental greens, as well as the closely related salad rocket and land cress, are all prone to flea beetle attacks at the seedling stage. The tiny beetles puncture the leaves with holes. Damage is worse in dry weather. Use grease traps or sow plants under fine nets. They can be removed once the plants are about 10cm (4in) high.

The pollen beetle attacks flowering brassicas like calabrese and flowering oriental greens, radishes grown for seed pods, and a wide range of salad flowers including calendula and nasturtiums. Can control by spraying with derris. In badly affected areas growing under fine nets seems to be the only practical means of protection. Otherwise time sowings to avoid the worst attacks in your area.

**Greenhouse Pests**

In warm weather whitefly and red spider mite are two serious greenhouse pests. In hot climates they may reach serious levels outdoors. Commonly attacked plants include tomato, cucumber, peppers and various types of beans. Both are difficult to control once established, and in greenhouses the appropriate biological control should be introduced at the first sign of trouble. The red spider mite itself is almost invisible to the naked eye, but attacked leaves become bronzed, shrivel up and die. Eventually plants are covered with fine webbing. Whitefly attacks are more obvious as clouds of whiteflies fly up from plants when they are touched. Leaves eventually become sticky and blackened with honeydew and sooty mould.

To lessen the risk of attacks avoid overcrowding, keep greenhouses well ventilated, and damp down frequently to lower the temperature. Scrub greenhouses thoroughly in winter after an infestation. Personally I find that interplanting tomatoes and peppers with French marigolds (*Tagetes*) helps deter whitefly, presumably because of their strong scent. But there is little scientific evidence to support this. Where feasible plants can be protected from whitefly by fine nets but this is impractical with tall and climbing plants.

**DISEASES**

Most plant diseases are caused by fungi, bacteria or viruses. They tend to spread rapidly in favourable conditions. In some cases this is hot weather; others thrive in cold damp conditions. Once established, it is very difficult to eradicate them. There are no suitable sprays for organic growers, so when there is a serious disease attack infected plants must be pulled up and burnt. Sometimes it is sufficient to cut off a few diseased leaves or stems. Practising preventative measures is the key to avoiding disease. If a particular disease is serious in your area, use resistant or disease tolerant cultivars where available. The following are some of the common diseases or groups of diseases on salad crops.

**Fungus Diseases**

Collectively fungi are responsible for a wide range of moulds, mildews, blights, spots, rots and wilts. Some common examples are grey mould (*botrytis*) and downy mildew on lettuce, tomato and cucumber; powdery mildew on cucumber; blight and stem rot on tomato; various onion rots and celery leaf spot. Using resistant cultivars, taking all necessary precautions and acting immediately are the prime preventive measures.

**Damping Off Diseases**
This group of fungus diseases is responsible for seedlings either not germinating at all, or collapsing shortly after they have emerged. It is commonest when seeds are sown indoors, and is usually caused by poor hygiene, overcrowding, or sowing in cold soil. Follow the rules of good husbandry for propagation, and keep seedlings well ventilated once germinated. Chuck out infected batches and start again.

**Clubroot**
This serious disease can attack all brassicas (crucifers), causing the roots to swell and develop gross lumps. Plants eventually become stunted and die. It is a soil borne disease, and soil can remain infected for 20 years, even when no brassicas are grown in it. The long term hope for clubroot lies in the development of resistant cultivars.

Measures which help prevent clubroot from becoming established include improving drainage, rotation, liming to raise the soil pH to 7 (see Soil Fertility pp.18-19), and possibly having high levels of organic matter in the soil. Take care not to introduce clubroot on bought-in plants: examine roots for suspicious lumps. Always burn any infected plants, digging rather than pulling up to avoid spreading infection.

Clubroot can sometimes be cheated by sowing brassicas in modules and potting them on into 10cm (4in) pots before planting out (see Raising Plants 'Indoors' p.83). This may give them a good enough start to gain the upper hand. Keep plants earthed up at the stem to encourage the development of secondary roots which often avoid infection. If you have a clubroot problem in your garden, concentrate on fast growing salad brassicas which can be harvested at the seedling stage before they become infected. Good examples are texsel greens and the many oriental brassicas.

**Soil Sickness**
These are groups of diseases that may build up in soil where the same crop is grown repeatedly over a number of years. The resulting 'soil sickness' makes it impossible to grow a healthy crop. It most commonly occurs with tomatoes, in greenhouses where they are grown year after year. Botanically related crops like peppers and aubergines will also be affected by soil sickness.

Unless the soil is completely replaced future crops have to be grown in containers, either raised off the ground or protected from the contaminated soil by a sheet of polythene film. Another solution is to graft the required variety onto the rootstock of a disease resistant variety. One great advantage of polythene tunnels (see Protected Cropping pp.115–17) is that they are easily dismantled and moved to a fresh site thus avoiding soil sickness. Ideally do so every two or three years, *before* a soil problem develops. In a permanent greenhouse, practise rotation as much as possible (see Siting and Planning pp.126–7).

## Virus Diseases

These serious, incurable diseases are caused by minute sub-microscopic organisms. Common symptoms are badly stunted growth, and mottled, twisted, often yellow leaves. Viruses are spread in various ways, for example by humans using a knife on one plant, and then on the next, by a number of insects, most notably aphids, even by fungi and soil eelworm. They can also be carried in seed.

Of popular salad crops, cucumber is susceptible to cucumber mosaic virus, lettuce to lettuce mosaic virus and beet western yellows, and tomato to tomato mosaic virus. Uproot and burn any suspiciously stunted plants as soon as they are noticed, try to keep aphids under control, and make use of virus–resistant varieties of lettuce, cucumber and tomato where possible.

# Chapter 6
# Seed, Sowing Outdoors and Planting

Most salad plants are raised from seed, so knowing and understanding seed is a vital part of the gardener's armoury.

## SEED STORAGE
Seed naturally deteriorates with age, losing its viability (its ability to germinate) and vigour. This process is accelerated when it is stored in moist warm conditions, but is minimized when it is stored in cool dry conditions. I suspect many gardening failures stem from the practice of keeping seed packets in damp garden sheds or hot kitchens.

Seed should always be stored in as dry and as cool a place as possible. A domestic refrigerator is quite a good place! Ideally keep it in jars or tins, along with a bag or dish of silica gel to absorb any moisture in the air. If cobalt-chloride-treated silica gel is used it will turn pink when moist; it should then be dried in an oven for two to three hours until it turns blue again. If ordinary silica gel is used, dry it periodically as a safeguard. Open packets of seed are particularly liable to deteriorate, so store seed in unopened packets for as long as possible.

Modern seed is often packed in vacuum-sealed foil packs. They are highly recommended, as they slow down deterioration, effectively increasing seed viability by several years. Once opened seed in the foil packs starts to deteriorate normally. They should be stored in dry cool conditions like any other seed.

In reasonable conditions most salad seed can be kept for at least three years. If the viability is in doubt, try germinating a few on moist blotting paper before sowing on a larger scale (see Chitted Seed p.64).

## TYPES AND FORMS OF SEED
### F₁ Hybrid Seed
This is the seed of cultivars that have been bred by crossing two inbred parent lines. Resulting plants are of particularly high quality, exceptional vigour and often very even in their size and development. They are somewhat more expensive than ordinary seed, but in most cases are worth the price. However, be wary of saving the seed for future use (see Saving Seed p.65).

## Pelleted Seed

Here individual 'naked' seeds are coated with a protective substance converting them into tiny round granules. The coating breaks down in the soil. Pelleted seed was originally developed for commercial growers to enable them to sow mechanically, but it is useful for home gardeners, as individual seeds are easy to handle and space accurately by hand. This virtually eliminates the need for thinning. Germination problems sometimes occur if the pellets are sown in dry conditions. Press them into the soil firmly, and if the soil is dry, water gently until the seed germinates.

## Seed Tapes and Sheets

Various systems of incorporating seeds into tapes, or between fine, tissue-like paper sheets have been developed. The seeds are evenly spaced, generally 1.3-2cm (½-¾in) apart. The tapes or sheets, which disintegrate in the soil, are 'sown' by placing them on the soil or in a seedtray, and covering them with soil or compost in the normal way. Because the seeds are well-spaced thinning is very easy. When used indoors there is no need to prick out (see Raising Plants 'Indoors' p.77).

## Primed Seed

Primed seed is seed that has been treated so that it is on the point of germination. It is then re-dried and packeted. When it is finally sown it is 'rarin' to go' and germinates much faster than would otherwise be the case. The technique is used with seed which can be slow to germinate, such as carrot. Primed seed cannot normally be kept for more than a few months after purchase.

## Chitted Seed

Here the germination process has been carried a couple of stages further, to the point where the seed has germinated and the seedling root is showing. Chitted seed is generally sold by mail order seed companies, who despatch it on moist paper in plastic sachets. It must be sown in seedtrays or pots as soon as it is received (see Raising Plants 'Indoors' p.77).

Chitted seed is a great advantage for seeds that are tricky to germinate, for example seeds like cucumber that require a high temperature initially. Not all gardeners have the facilities to meet these early requirements, but can grow the seeds on successfully once germinated.

It is also relatively easy to 'chit your own'. This can be a useful means of overcoming adverse soil conditions. Slow germinating seeds are vulnerable to pest and disease attack in the period between sowing and germination, especially if this coincides with cold or wet weather. If the seeds can be germinated in warm and protected conditions indoors, then sown carefully once germinated, they have a much better chance of survival. In cold climates it is an excellent way of starting tender plants like French beans or sweet corn.

The simplest method is to take a small dish or saucer, cut a piece of foam rubber or sponge to fit it, and cover this with a doubled sheet of paper towelling. Pour in enough water to moisten the paper, then lay the seed on top. Put the dish somewhere warm to allow the seed to germinate. Keep them just moist. Sow the seeds as soon after they have germinated as possible, as the young growing points are easily damaged. This method can be used for testing seed viability.

## SAVING SEED

The practice of saving your own seed is far less common than it used to be, and is not generally recommended for vegetables. For a start, the risk of cross pollination between closely related cultivars is high, so one can rarely be 100 per cent sure of getting pure seed. Another factor is that seed crops require long periods of dry sunny weather when ripening to ensure good quality seed, and most seed ripens naturally in late summer and autumn. Where weather at this time of year is unpredictable, as in the British Isles, getting good seed is a gamble. A third factor is that much seed today is $F_1$ hybrid, and it doesn't come true when saved. The original crosses have to be re-made to reproduce that particular cultivar. Occasionally something useful turns up where $F_1$ seed is saved but that is the exception. Finally, legislation and technology now ensure that the bulk of seed available meets high standards of purity and cleanliness, is disease-free, and has a high level of germination. So there is less incentive to save seed than in the past.

However, where salads are concerned, there are times when it can be useful to save seed. The first is when a species or cultivar is relatively rare. In the interests of economy the mainstream seed-sellers are continually pruning their lists, often cutting out minor salad plants. If you have something that seems unusual (perhaps a wild plant) or has been hard to get hold of, it may well be prudent to save your own. The second case is where you want *lots* of seed, either for making continuous successive sowings, or for cut-and-come-again seedling crops (see Salad Techniques pp.85-95). The meagre quantities of seed in some of today's packets make these basic salad practices something of a luxury. Save seed from just a few plants, and you can indulge in extravagance.

In countries with unreliable weather it is usually easiest, and often very useful, to save seed from the winter hardy salads. They naturally run to seed early in the year, and stand a reasonable chance of encountering good enough weather for the seed to mature and ripen. The following have proved some of the best bets for me: salad rocket, various types of cress, corn salad, cutting celery, winter radish, hardy lettuce, borage, chervil, Japanese mizuna greens and winter purslane (*alias Claytonia* or *Montia*). To maintain the quality of your stock it is probably advisable to start again with commercial seed every two or three years.

### Seed Saving Guidelines
* Always save from the best plants, never from diseased plants, or plants that have bolted prematurely.
* Never try to save seed of more than one cultivar of any crop, or there will be a risk of cross-pollination.
* If necessary transplant a promising or 'special' plant, before it runs to seed, into an out-of-the-way corner, or into a greenhouse or polytunnel. Allow it to seed there.
* Keep plants well watered when they are flowering and when the seed heads are forming, but stop watering when the seed pods are turning from green to yellow.
* Stake or tie tall plants, to prevent them falling on the ground and becoming soiled.
* As far as possible, allow the seed pods to dry naturally on the plant. Cut them down just before the seed pods burst naturally, and hang or lie them flat in a cool dry place, with newspaper beneath to catch seed from any shattering pods.
* If seed pods are in danger of being spoilt by rain or taken by birds or other pests, pull them up before they have dried. Hang them upside down under cover, say in a greenhouse, to dry off completely. Place newspaper beneath to catch any falling seed.
* When the pods are brittle-dry shake out the seed onto newspaper, blowing off as much dust and debris as possible. Put it into paper envelopes, jars, or empty film cassette cans. Store it in cool dry conditions (see Seed Storage p.63).

#### SELF-SOWN SEEDS
It is a characteristic of many salad crops to self-seed, and this can be encouraged if a few plants are left at the end of their season. Provided the soil is reasonably moist, a thick flush of seedlings will appear in due

course. Cut them for use, or transplant individual seedlings into a more convenient spot, where they can be spaced out so they have room to develop into larger plants.

Mother nature can be a perverse customer. Deliberate attempts to sow a seed sometimes fail where self-sown plants succeed. This has often been my experience with both land cress and corn salad. If you leave radishes to run to seed you can, of course, pick the young pods for a delicious salad ingredient.

## SOWING OUTDOORS

Seed is either sown *in situ*, where it will be grown to maturity, or in a 'nursery' seedbed from where it will be transplanted into its permanent position in the garden.

The main methods of sowing outdoors are sowing seeds singly, sowing in narrow drills or flat wide drills, and broadcasting. In all cases the soil, or 'seedbed', has to be prepared first – and preparing a seedbed is probably one of the most skilled gardening techniques. Confusingly, the term 'seedbed' is widely used both to refer to *any* ground where seed is being sown, and to a *specific* area set aside for raising plants that will subsequently be transplanted elsewhere. To avoid confusion, I'll refer to the latter as a 'nursery' seedbed. The preparation of the soil is the same in both cases.

### Preparing a Seedbed

In the perfect seedbed the ground is firm but not solidly compacted. The surface is free of large stones and lumps of soil, and raked to a pleasantly crumbly 'tilth'. The soil should be moist and warm; not wet, cold or dry.

The art of making a seedbed hinges on seizing the right moment to work the soil. If the soil is heavy and would stick to your shoes if you walked on it, it is still too wet. Leave it a little longer to dry out, or give it a helping hand (see Soil Temperature p.68). But don't wait until it has become completely dry and dusty or you may have to water to get the surface into the right state for raking. Clay and chalky soils have a nasty habit of being too wet one moment and drying into intractable solid lumps the next. Light soils can also dry out very rapidly. Sometimes a light shower of rain provides just the right conditions for raking the soil surface to a tilth.

Ideally a seedbed should be prepared several weeks in advance of sowing to allow time for the ground to settle. This will also allow time for weed seeds to germinate; they can then be hoed off before sowing. In practice, however, advance preparation is not always possible or essential.

These are the basic steps in preparing a seedbed.

\* If the soil is rough or fairly compacted, start by lightly forking or hoeing the top 5-7.5cm (2-3in). This makes it easier to work the surface.

\* When the soil surface seems in the right state to work it, possibly the same day, maybe a few days later, use the back of the rake to break down lumps, or crumble them up by hand. Rake off stones and remaining lumps of soil.

\* Then rake the soil gently backwards and forwards until the required tilth is created. Small seeds need a fine tilth, where the soil crumbs are about the size of large breadcrumbs, but large seeds like peas and beans can be sown on a rougher, coarser tilth. It may be necessary to repeat the raking procedure several times, perhaps over several days, to get the soil 'just right' – gradually getting a finer and finer surface. It will probably need one final raking just before sowing.

\* If a prepared seedbed is not going to be sown immediately, cover the surface with a thin mulch of straw, hay, compost, even newspaper, to preserve the tilth and prevent it drying out until you are ready. The strong winds which are so common in spring dry out a surface in no time, and one can be back to square one again. (Cover it with clear film if you want to encourage weed seeds to germinate.)

### Nursery Seedbeds

Plants are raised in a nursery seedbed principally to save space. While a crop is going through its early stages in the seedbed, the space it will eventually occupy in a vegetable bed is used for another maturing vegetable.

Make the seedbed in an open site, resisting the temptation to put it in an out of the way shady corner. This usually leads to drawn, lanky seedlings. However, it doesn't matter if the soil is less fertile than in the permanent bed.

A drawback to raising plants in a nursery seedbed is that seedlings often become overcrowded, and the roots get damaged when torn apart for transplanting. To minimize any potential damage, always sow very thinly in a seedbed, and thin seedlings out before they become overcrowded (see Thinning p.72). For top quality plants, I personally feel that sowing in some kind of module is often preferable (see Raising Plants 'Indoors' p.78).

### Soil Temperature

Seed germinates at different temperatures, but rarely at soil temperatures below 5°C (41°F). Use a soil thermometer to measure the soil temperature. It is *never* worth sowing in cold wet soil where the seed will rot or be attacked by pests or disease before it germinates. It is better to wait until the soil has warmed up, or if necessary, to start seed off indoors (see Raising Plants 'Indoors' p.77). Soil can be warmed up before sowing by covering the seedbed for several days with clear polythene film, cloches, or low polytunnels. Or make the sowing drill first, and then cover it with a cloche to warm the soil before sowing.

## SOWING METHODS

First a word on sowing thinly. SOW THINLY is one of those unwritten rules of gardening that is often ignored. New gardeners are always tempted to sow thickly – just in case! In practice, germination is either so good that masses of seeds germinate (and have to be thinned in time or none will be any use), or some other factor such as cold soil, bad weather, pests, or the age of the seed prevents almost all the seed germinating, so resowing is necessary anyway. Whatever method of sowing is used, err on the side of sowing thinly.

### Broadcasting

Broadcasting, which essentially consists of scattering seed over the surface, is probably the oldest method of sowing. It is used for salad plants that require little or no thinning, such as radish, pickling onions, early carrots, and some of the hardy over-wintering salad plants such as parella lettuce and grumolo chicory which are grown fairly densely. It is also used for seedling and cut-and-come-again crops such as cress, salad rocket, some types of chicory and lettuce, and salad mixtures (see Salad Techniques pp.85-9). It is a quick way of sowing when time is precious, though it is extravagant with seed.

* Make sure the seedbed is free of weeds, as it is difficult to weed in broadcast crops. (If the soil is very weedy prepare the ground, allow a flush of weeds to come up, and hoe them off before sowing.)

* Rake the seedbed to a fine tilth as above.

* Scatter the seed evenly over the surface. The density of sowing will depend on the crop – garden cress, for example, would be sown thicker than radish or lettuce, but whatever the crop aim to sow thinly.

* Cover the seed by raking the soil first in one direction, then at right angles to the first direction.

* If the soil is likely to dry out before the seed has germinated cover it with a light, easily removed mulch such as sheets of newspaper, sacks or straw. Keep inspecting the seedbed. Remove the mulch as soon as any seedlings appear, or they will become pale and drawn.

## Sowing in Narrow Drills

This is the standard method of sowing outdoors in rows. It is often used for fast maturing plants like radishes, or vegetables that are awkward to transplant such as carrots, beet, salsify, parsley, and lettuce in hot weather. It can also be used for seedling crops (see Salad Techniques pp.85-7). Sowings in nursery seedbeds are normally made in narrow drills.

* Prepare a seedbed with a fine tilth as described pp.67-8.

* Mark out the row with a garden line or string attached to a pair of sticks.

* Use the point of a trowel or hoe to make a small furrow in the soil along the length of the line. The drill can be anything from 1.3-5cm (½-2in) deep, depending on the seed. As a general rule seed needs to be covered by about twice its own depth of soil. So tiny seed is barely covered, lettuce is sown about 1.3cm (½in) deep, and so on.

* Put a few seeds in the palm of the hand, take a pinch at a time between the forefinger and thumb, and drop the seeds along the drill. This is better than shaking seed directly out of the packet, which can be wasteful.

* Either space the seed evenly along the drill, or 'station sow', which is sowing in groups of three or four seeds leaving a space between each group. If seeds will ultimately be thinned to say 20cm (8in) apart, station sow 10cm (4in) apart. Station sowing cuts down on the need for thinning. In some cases two different crops, generally one fast and one slow growing, can be intersown in the same row. The classic example of this is fast growing radish sown between slow growing parsnips.

* Press the seed gently into the bottom of the drill.

* Cover it with well-crumbled soil, using the fingers, or hoe or trowel.

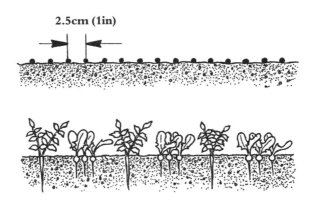

*Evenly spaced seeds (above) and 'station sown' seeds (below)*

## Sowing in Wide Drills

Look on this technique as a halfway house between broadcasting and sowing in narrow drills. It is a quick and practical way of sowing things like radishes and early carrots which are harvested young without thinning, and cut-and-come-again seedling crops (see Salad Techniques pp.85-7). Its advantage over broadcasting seed is that it is possible also to weed between the drills, and if sowing in adverse conditions (see p.72) it is easier to prepare and water or line the drills than it is on a large expanse of ground.

Wide drills are an excellent method of sowing if you want to create patchwork effects with salad plants of different colours and texture. Although sown in separate drills, the seedlings soon spill out over the edges to blanket the ground very attractively.

★ Use the blade of a draw hoe (an onion hoe is ideal) to make a drill about 10cm (4in) wide at whatever depth is required for the seed. If several drills are required, make the second drill parallel to the first and as close as you can without the soil spilling into the first drill.

★ Sow seed evenly across the drill and press it in.

★ Cover it with soil from the edge of the drill.

## Sowing Seeds Singly

This method is used for large seeds such as cucumbers. They can be given an early start in cold weather by covering them with jam jars after sowing. The jars act as a 'mini' cloche.

★ Make a hole with a small dibber at the correct depth for the seed.

★ Drop the seed straight into the hole, making sure that it is at the bottom of the hole and not suspended in a pocket of air.

★ Fill in the soil.

## SOWING IN ADVERSE CONDITIONS

Situations arise where one can no longer afford to wait for perfect sowing conditions. Here are some suggestions for overcoming likely problems.

## Sowing in Very Dry Conditions

★ Make wide or narrow drills as appropriate.

★ Before sowing water the *bottom* of the drill only, very thoroughly.

★ Let the water soak in, sow directly on the moist soil, and press in seeds.

★ Cover the seed with *dry* soil from alongside the drill. This soil acts as a mulch, it breaks the capillary action, and also enables the seed to remain moist until it has germinated.

I have found this method invaluable when sowing in dry spring or summer weather. In dry weather covering seedlings with newspaper or a light mulch also helps to retain soil moisture until they have germinated.

### Sowing in Very Wet Conditions
* Make the drills as above.
* Line the bottom of the drill with sowing or potting compost, leaf mould or a peat substitute.
* Sow the seed on this base, and cover normally.

See also Soil Temperature pp.68-9, for various methods of warming up the soil before making a seedbed.

### THINNING
Seedlings growing rapidly become overcrowded, spindly or drawn, and may never recover. Removing surplus seedlings or thinning so that each plant has enough space to develop is a key operation.

Spare thinnings can often be transplanted or used up in salads. Aim to thin so there is minimum disturbance to the remaining seedlings. Here are a few guidelines.
* Thin when the soil is moist or water it an hour or so beforehand. In hot climates thin in the cool of the evening.
* Start thinning as soon as the seedlings are large enough to handle.
* Thin so that each seedling is just standing clear of its neighbours.
* If possible, nip off surplus seedlings just above ground level. This is much less disruptive than pulling them up by the roots.
* Afterwards firm the soil around seedlings which have been disturbed.
* Remove thinnings, as their smell may attract the plant's pests.
* Thin in stages to offset losses from pests and diseases.

### PLANTING
Unless plants are sown *in situ* they will at some stage need to be planted in their permanent position. The term *transplant* is generally used for young plants that are dug up from the soil from a nursery seedbed for instance, and moved elsewhere. They are often described as 'bare root transplants', as opposed to plants raised in a pot or some kind of module, where the roots take on the compact shape of their container, and suffer very little disturbance when planted.

Most vegetables *can* be transplanted, but root vegetables should be planted before the tap root starts to develop. With bare root transplants, within reason, the younger they are transplanted the better. Young plants make new roots much more easily than old ones, and they recover from transplanting sooner.

**Raising Your Own Plants *Versus* Buying In**
If you want to grow a wide range of salad plants, it is definitely worth raising your own as far as possible, rather than buying plants from either a nursery or a garden centre. Apart from the fact that there are very few suppliers who offer anything other than the most popular (but not necessarily best flavoured) cultivars, there is always the risk of introducing disease into the garden. The other great advantage of raising your own is that the plants are at hand to transplant in their prime, and when soil conditions are most favourable. Where it proves necessary to buy in plants, choose the healthiest looking that you can find. Wherever possible choose plants grown in individual pots or modules as they get established so much faster.

**Planting Guidelines**
The key to successful planting is to minimize the shock to the plant root system that takes place in the process. This is far more important where bare root transplants are involved.
★ Plant in dull, overcast weather, or in the evening.
★ Never plant in waterlogged soil. If the soil is heavy, work a little well-rotted compost or peat substitute into the surface of the planting area beforehand.
★ Unless the soil is already wet, water the seedbed, or pot or module, thoroughly beforehand, preferably overnight or several hours in advance of planting. Compost-raised plants in pots or modules may *never* reabsorb moisture if they are planted out in a dry state. (This is especially true of peat-based composts.)
★ Lift bare root seedlings and young plants carefully with a trowel. Use a miniature trowel or small dibber for very small seedlings. Always hold the plants by the leaves to avoid damaging the delicate root hairs.
★ Use a trowel to make a hole large enough to take the roots without cramping them.
★ Hold the plant in the hole, with the seedleaves (if still evident) just above the soil level
(1). Replace the soil, easing it between the roots of bare root transplants or around the compact shape, or 'plug' of a module raised plant.
★ Firm the soil round the stem with your finger tips (2). Tug a leaf when you have finished: if the plant wobbles, replant it (3).

* Unless the soil is already wet, water lightly around the plant with a rose on the can.

* It is sound practice to mulch after planting. It helps plants to get established quickly and cuts down watering and weeding later on (see Mulching pp.46-50). Don't mulch very small plants or they may be swamped.

* In very hot weather shade the plants until they are well-established. Effective shades can be made with a range of materials including netting, conical 'hats' of newspaper and cardboard.

* If necessary water gently daily until the plants look perky and well-established. This is less likely to be needed with pot-raised plants or where they have been mulched after planting.

* Where necessary, for example with tomatoes, insert stakes after planting. This avoids damaging the roots later.

1

2

3

*Stages in planting*

## Spacing

As already mentioned (see Soil Fertility p.21) it generally makes sense to grow salad crops with equidistant spacing in each direction between plants, rather than in the traditional rows with wide spaces between rows. Research has confirmed that equidistant spacing ensures the optimum use of space, water and nutrients, besides being an effective means of keeping down weeds. Aim to space plants so that when mature, their leaves just touch those of the neighbouring plants.

As many plants grow to fill whatever space is allotted to them, spacing can sometimes be used as a tool to determine the size of a plant. If you want small cabbages and cauliflowers, grow them close together; if you want large ones, space them further apart. Chinese pak choi can be grown 10cm (4in) apart to get a 'baby' pak choi plant, but 30cm (12in) apart for a larger plant that can be cut over a much longer period. Examples will be given where they arise.

To convert recommendations for traditional row spacing into equidistant spacing, add the in-row and between row spacings together and halve them. Plants grown 15cm (6in) apart in rows 30cm (12in) apart can be spaced 23cm (9in) apart each way in an equidistant spacing system.

# Chapter 7
# Raising Plants 'Indoors'

The term 'sowing indoors' is widely used for any situation where plants are raised in protected conditions, rather than being sown directly in the soil outdoors. 'Indoors' can be in a cold or heated greenhouse, in a garden cold frame or under cloches, in a heated propagator (which can be in a greenhouse or in an ordinary house), or on a windowsill or elsewhere inside. In cold climates quite a range of salads are raised indoors, but it can also be a useful practice in hot and extreme climates, if for any reason germination is difficult outdoors.

The main reasons for sowing indoors are:

★ To get an early crop before the normal outdoor season. Spring lettuce and onions can be sown indoors then planted outside in early spring for an early crop.

★ To start the tender half hardy crops, which in cold climates would not have time to mature if sown directly outside. Common examples are tomatoes, peppers, iceplant (*Mesembryanthemum crystallinum*), summer purslane and Mediterranean herbs such as basil.

★ To extend the growing season for slow maturing crops such as celeriac.

★ To control temperature in the early stages. Some oriental greens, for example, will bolt prematurely if there is a sudden drop of temperature while they are in the seedling stage. This can be avoided if they are sown indoors. On the other hand lettuces and onions will not germinate at temperatures above 24°C (75°F), which can easily occur outdoors in hot weather. They can be germinated in cool temperatures indoors and planted out later.

★ To save space. Raising plants indoors shortens the time they occupy the ground, but they are ready to plant as soon as another crop has been harvested. This is an asset where garden space is at a premium.

★ To raise high quality plants. Plants raised indoors are not only protected from the elements and from pests in the vulnerable early stages, but can be given plenty of attention. All this results in top quality plants.

## STAGES IN RAISING PLANTS INDOORS
The following are the main stages involved in raising plants indoors. Not every stage will be necessary for every case. Pricking out, for example,

can be eliminated by sowing in modules (see below). Potting on is only necessary where relatively large plants, such as tomatoes and cucumbers, are required.

1 Sowing
Seed is normally sown in special compost that encourages germination in some kind of container. It is often germinated in warm conditions, for example in a propagator.

2 Pricking out
The small seedlings are transplanted into a larger container to give them more space.

3 Potting on
After a few weeks the small plants are transplanted into larger individual pots which will enable them to grow further.

4 Hardening-off
This is the process of gradually accustoming plants to lower temperatures so they don't suffer 'shock' when finally planted outside.

5 Planting
Plants raised indoors are eventually planted outside or in greenhouses.

**SOWING INDOORS**
Choose one of the following options:
★ Sow in a container such as a seedtray or small pot in a light compost, and 'prick out' into a larger container into richer, coarser compost when large enough to handle.
★ Sow *individually* in 'modules', in which the plants are grown until they are potted on or planted out in the vegetable garden. Modules are filled with, or made of, specially formulated or all-purpose composts. Plants raised in modules – often known as 'plugs' – develop a compact root system which suffers minimum root disturbance when they are planted out. It is, for this reason, a highly recommended method for raising good quality plants.

Modules generally take up more space than a small pot or seedtray, which can be a disadvantage in the early stages if seed is being germinated in a small propagator. A compromise is to sow in a seedtray or pot and prick out seedlings into a module.

## Containers

Seed can be sown in various types of container.

### Standard Containers

The most widely used containers are seedtrays, which need be no more than 3cm (1¼in) deep, or small clay or plastic pots, generally 5-7.5cm (2-3in) deep. Whatever is used must have drainage holes in the base. The small plastic containers in which yogurt and cottage cheese for example are sold can be used if two or three drainage holes are made in the base. Seedtrays are sometimes fitted with plastic domes to retain moisture and encourage germination.

### Modules

A wide range of module is now available for home gardeners, many based on systems originally developed for commercial growers. For example:
*Moulded plastic and polystyrene cellular trays or cell packs* – These are pre-formed trays of round, square or tapered holes or cells, anything from 1.3-5cm (½-2in) in diameter. The young plant or 'plug' is easily pushed or pulled out of the hole when it comes to planting. The larger units require more compost and occupy more space, but allow the plants to grow larger and remain longer in the module before planting.
*Soil blocks* – Discrete 'blocks' are made by compressing soil or potting compost with a blocking tool, which also makes an indentation in the upper block face where seed is sown. Block sizes range from about 1.3cm (½in) square, to 5cm (2in) or more in diameter. It is best to make blocks with proprietary blocking composts which contain an adhesive. Soil or potting compost can work: it is a question of getting the right moisture content.

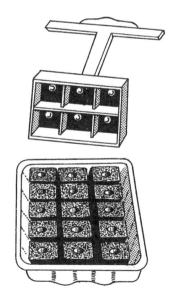

*Soil blocks made with a small hand blocker*

*Compressed netted blocks* – Most of these are flat discs made of compressed peat-based compost encased in netting. They expand into small pot shaped units when soaked in water. The plant roots grow out through the netting and the unit is planted intact. The same system could be used for peat substitutes.

*Divided seedtrays* – Seedtrays are converted into modules by dividing them into sections with interlocking plastic dividers. Makeshift dividers can be made of plastic or cardboard.

Small pots

Any small pot, whether made of clay, plastic, polythene film or any other material, can be used as a module to grow a single plant. Open-ended pots can be made of rolled newspaper, papier-mâché, or the inner spool of a toilet roll. Stand them packed closely in a seedtray, and fill them with compost. The roots will grow through the 'pot' into the soil after planting, the casing eventually disintegrating.

**Sowing and potting composts**

Ordinary garden soil is usually unsuitable for raising plants indoors, as it is generally too coarse and full of weed seed. Various light textured sowing and potting composts have been developed for the purpose. They are sterile, so free of weed seed.

Seed or sowing compost is very fine, and contains little in the way of plant nutrients. It cannot sustain plants beyond the seedling stage. Potting composts are coarser and contain a higher level of plant nutrients, and can sustain plants until they are potted on or planted out. In practice most salad plants (unless the seed is very fine) can be sown direct into a multi-purpose or potting compost with absolutely no adverse effects. Various professional blocking and module composts have been developed for making blocks and for filling modules. Use these where appropriate if you can obtain them.

Types of Compost

*Soil-based composts* – The traditional soil-based composts are made from sieved loam, peat and sand, mixed to a formula devised by the John Innes Institute in the UK. Being soil-based they are quite heavy, but they retain moisture well. Seed can be sown into John Innes Seed Compost or direct into John Innes Potting Compost No.1 (JIP.1), potting on into JIP.2.

*Peat-based composts* – Until recently most of the plant raising composts for home gardeners were peat-based, but in view of the concern about exhausting peat supplies, alternatives are being developed, and should be used where they prove satisfactory. Watch out for developments in the garden press. The advantages of peat-based composts are that they are light to use, sterile, very porous and encourage rapid root growth. Their disadvantage is that they dry out rapidly and can be difficult to re-wet.

*Worm worked composts* – These composts are made by feeding a variety of waste materials to earthworms. Although not yet widely available, in my experience they are excellent for plant raising.

*Comfrey compost* – The recipe for this compost has been developed by a committed organic gardener Terry Marshall, and has produced excellent results. The main ingredients are leaf mould and Russian comfrey *Symphytum* x *uplandicum*, preferably the highly productive cultivar 'Bocking 14'. This is easily grown from root cuttings or plants obtained from organic suppliers. Plant them in good soil any time from spring to autumn, spacing plants 75cm (30in) apart. (For making leaf mould see Manures and Fertilizers pp.28–32.)

★ Cut the leaves of well-established comfrey plants in early autumn.

★ Take a strong plastic sack and line the bottom with a roughly 7.5cm (3in) deep layer of well-rotted leaf mould, ideally 12–18 months old.

★ Cover the leaf mould with a layer of comfrey leaves of a similar depth, pressed down lightly.

★ Alternate comfrey and leaf mould layers until the sack is full.

★ Tie the sack at the neck, make a few ventilation holes with a garden fork, and leave it in a sheltered place until spring, when it is ready for use.

*Homemade sowing compost* – For a sowing compost mix two parts of peat, leaf mould, or peat substitute, with one part of coarse builder's or silver sand. The peat, leaf mould or peat substitute can be soaked beforehand in a weak solution of liquid seaweed to encourage healthy seedling growth. Sowing compost can also be made by sieving the topsoil from a hardwood forest through a 3mm (⅛in) sieve.

For potting add an equal weight of good sieved loam, plus some well-crumbled compost-heap compost and seaweed based liquid fertilizer.

### Source of Heat

Most seeds germinate better in warm soil, with a heat source coming from below. A soil temperature of 13–16°C (55–61°F) is suitable for most salad plants. Where necessary this can be obtained by germinating seeds in a propagator. Domestic propagators range from units in which the heat is supplied by a light bulb beneath the seedtray, to electrically heated plates and coils placed beneath a seedtray. Propagators can be built on greenhouse staging using insulated electric cables buried in sand. Whatever system is used, cover the seedtray or container with a sheet or dome of plastic or glass to retain moisture and prevent the soil from drying out. Lift the cover daily and wipe off condensation.

Alternatively seeds can be started in a warm cupboard, or above, but not directly on, a radiator.

## Sowing Procedure
In Standard Containers
★ Fill the container with moist compost. With peat-based and similar composts it may be easier to fill the container with *dry compost*, then to stand it in a tray of water so the compost can soak it up.
★ With a small board or the bottom of a flower pot press the compost to make it reasonably firm, then level it. Leave a 1.3cm (½in) space below the rim of the container.
★ Sprinkle the seeds evenly over the surface, or space them carefully 1.3-2.5cm (½-1in) apart, depending on the seed.
★ Cover seeds by sieving a little dry compost or sharp sand over them. Sand seems to reduce the risk of seedlings being attacked by fungal diseases. As a rule, seeds need to be covered by about twice their depth. Very small seeds can be left uncovered. Firm the soil after sowing.
★ If necessary, water the surface lightly, or stand the container in water until the top surface is moist.
★ Cover the tray with a sheet of glass or plastic dome, or slip it into a plastic bag to prevent it drying out. Remove the covering once the seedlings have germinated.

In Modules
Essentially the same procedure is followed, but the aim is to have only one germinated seedling in each cell. To achieve this, either sow one seed per cell, or sow several seeds, and nip out all but the strongest once they have germinated. (Resist the temptation to leave several seedlings rather than 'waste' seedlings by uprooting them: an exception is 'multi-sowing', see p.82.) If doubtful about the seed, do a germination test before sowing (see Seed, Sowing Outdoors and Planting pp.64-5).

Large seeds are easily sown individually, but this is more awkward a method to use with small seeds. One method is to push them carefully off a piece of paper. An alternative method is to pick them up carefully from a saucer on the moistened tip of a piece of broken glass. A single seed will

*One method of sowing seeds singly*

adhere to the glass, but drop off when the glass is touched on the compost. When sowing in blocks gently push the compost over the seed to cover it.

There are a few cases where several seeds can be sown together in a cell, left unthinned, and eventually planted out 'as one' at wider spacing than normal. This 'multi-sowing' is only suitable for plants which are not affected by competition from close neighbours, such as onions and round beetroot. Examples will be mentioned in the text as they arise. This sowing technique saves on space and time.

## Post Germination

A word of warning about the 'post-germination' problem. As soon as there is a sniff of spring in the air, gardeners get itchy fingers and start sowing indoors. Many of those fingers get burnt! While it is relatively easy to *germinate* seeds in late winter to early spring, especially with a propagator, it is much more difficult to provide suitable growing conditions in the weeks after germination. This is most crucial with tender plants which cannot be planted until all risk of frost is past.

Seedlings soon outgrow the limited space in a propagator, and to continue growing steadily they must have good light (or they become lanky and drawn), reasonably warm day temperatures and at least frost-free night temperatures. These requirements may be hard to meet in certain domestic conditions. The moral is not to raise too many seedlings too early, *unless* you will definitely have somewhere light and warm to house them all.

Once seeds have germinated they need to be watched carefully as they are delicate at this stage.

★ Keep tiny seedlings away from bright sunlight; shade them if they are on exposed sunny windowsills.

★ Turn them 90 degrees every day so that they do not become drawn towards the light.

★ Keep them moist but not overwatered, watering either with a rose on the can, or by using the soaking-up method.

★ Keep them out of draughts.
★ Prick them out before they become overcrowded.

## PRICKING OUT

On the whole the earlier seedlings are pricked out the better, provided they are large enough to handle or have developed their first true leaves. Discard unhealthy seedlings – the 'duds' rarely recover.

★ Prepare a tray or pot with potting compost as for sowing.

★ Water the seedlings first, then lever them out gently with a miniature dibber or blade, disturbing the roots as little as possible. Handle them by the leaves.

★ Use a miniature dibber or even a large nail to make a tiny hole in the compost just large enough for the roots.

★ Hold the seedling in the hole and press compost gently around it, making sure the roots are in contact with the soil and not hanging in an air pocket. The seed leaves should be just above soil level. Space the seedlings 2–5cm (¾–2in) apart, depending on the plant. If transplanting into modules put them in the centre of the cell or pot.

★ Water if necessary water, using a fine rose on the can, or the soak–up method to ensure that you don't overwater the compost.

★ Shade seedlings from direct sun for the first two or three days.

★ Put them in an airy, well lit place.

## POTTING ON

Most salad plants can be grown in the container that they were pricked out into. Plants which need to be held longer before planting out, or will eventually be grown in large pots or containers, may need to be replanted into larger pots to give them more room to develop. To supply the necessary plant nutrients, add some well-rotted compost-heap compost to the potting mixture, or feed them with dilute seaweed fertilizer.

It is never advisable to move a plant from a small pot into a *much* larger one at one go; move to an intermediate size first. Where a soil-based compost is used, put a drainage layer in the bottom of the pot, such as broken crocks covered by old leaves. (This is unnecessary with peat-based and similar composts, which are naturally very well-drained.) Always water a plant before knocking it out of a pot for potting on or planting. Pot it up in the same way as planting (see pp.73-4).

Plants that are growing rapidly should be constantly moved further apart so they are not crowded, otherwise they will compete for soil nutrients and are unlikely to thrive.

## HARDENING-OFF

Plants raised indoors tend to be very soft-leaved, particularly if raised in peat-based or equivalent composts. They need to be 'hardened-off' by being acclimatized gradually to colder, more exposed conditions before being planted outside, to avoid a setback when planted. Harden-off over a two to three week period, first by increasing the ventilation, then by putting the plants in a cold frame or sheltered place outdoors for longer periods each day. Either cover the plants at night (this is easy in a garden frame), or bring them back indoors. Eventually they will only need protecting on exceptionally cold nights.

The Japanese have developed an alternative method of hardening-off, which saves moving the plants outdoors. Seedlings are brushed or stroked to produce the toughening effects of exposure to lower temperatures and wind. Using a piece of paper or cardboard, brush them backwards and forwards for up to a minute a day. It can be done twice daily.

*Hardening-off seedlings by stroking, to avoid moving them outside*

# Chapter 8
# Salad Techniques

## CUT-AND-COME-AGAIN

It is a happy accident that many salad crops will resprout after the first cut, giving one, two, sometimes as many as four more cuts – hence the name 'cut-and-come-again' or 'CCA'. It can be done with seedlings, with semi-mature plants and with mature plants. For cut-and-come-again to succeed the soil must be fertile, the crop healthy and well watered, and the timing right. Seedlings can be cut with scissors, but for semi-mature and mature plants use a sharp knife.

### Cut-And-Come-Again Seedlings

The list of salads that can be grown as CCA seedlings is very long, ranging from certain types of cresses, lettuce, endive and chicory to salad rocket, salad rape, summer and winter purslane, spinach, fenugreek, and many of the various oriental greens. In the seventeenth century even orange and lemon seedlings were grown for salads! (For further information, see Chapter 12.)

The seedlings are grown fairly thickly, and generally cut from 2.5-7.5cm (1-3in) high. At this stage they are exceptionally tasty and very nutritious, in some cases even having twice the vitamin content of their mature leaves.

As CCA seedlings are highly productive, this is an excellent method of growing 'salading' (a nice old fashioned word for salad plants) if you only have a small garden or are restricted to a balcony or window box. It is amazing how much can be obtained from even a tiny patch of ground sown to CCA seedlings. They can be sown in the ground in the open or with protection (see Chapter 10), in a 'growing bag' after the main crop has been harvested, in a window box or even in a seedtray filled with good potting compost. Being fast growing, they also make excellent catch crops and are ideal for intercropping (see Siting and Planning p.128). Patches of CCA seedlings can look very pretty and are ideal in the potager.

On the whole CCA seedlings grow best in the cooler seasons – in spring, early summer, and autumn outdoors, and in winter and early spring under cover. In the heat of summer many run to seed rapidly so

SALADS FOR SMALL GARDENS

fewer cuts can be made, or they become coarse and bitter. In cold climates autumn sowings under cover are especially useful: seedlings can be sown after say tomatoes are lifted, and a cut or two may be made before winter sets in. They will stop growing during the worst of winter, but as soon as there is any warmth, burst into growth providing welcome salading when it is most scarce.

For a summary of when and where to sow, the advice given by Richard Bradley in 1720 still holds good in temperate climates: early spring under glass or frames; late spring in the open; while hot, in shady places; autumn as in early spring; frosty weather on hot beds. And he also suggested that if seedlings were frosted, they should be steeped in hot water for two hours to revive them.

How to Sow
Unless sowing in a seedtray or 'growing bag' the best way to sow most CCA seedlings is in wide drills (see Seed, Sowing Outdoors and Planting p.71). They can also be sown broadcast or in single drills. Aim to space the seeds no closer than 1.3cm (½in) apart. As far as possible, ensure the ground is weed free before sowing, as weeding between seedlings is a tedious business (see p.67). If you know or suspect the soil is weedy, lay a piece of black plastic film on the soil, anchor it at the edges, cut out strips the width of your drill, and sow in these cut-out strips. I have found this a most useful way of keeping down the weeds between drills.

If sowing in seedtrays or other containers simply scatter seed over the surface, covering it lightly with soil.

Harvesting Seedlings
While fast growing seedlings such as salad rocket, salad mustard and garden cress may be ready within a few days of sowing, others may take several weeks. A lot depends on the season. Make the first cut just above the tiny cotyledons or seed leaves; if they can't be distinguished cut no lower than 1.3-1.5cm (½-⅝in) above ground level. Clear away loose leaves, as they may cause the leaves around or beneath to rot. Depending on the crop and season, the second cut may be made within days. As soon as the seedlings become coarse or show signs of running to seed, they should be pulled out. Again, this could be within a few weeks, or under some circumstances, not for several months. In some cases it is possible to thin out the seedlings and allow a few plants to grow to maturity. This works well with 'Sugar Loaf' chicory. If a seedling patch is flagging, revive it with a seaweed-based foliar feed.

*Patch of CCA seedlings, some already sprouting, some not yet cut*

Seedling Mixtures
In western Europe there is a tradition of sowing a mixture of different salads together, resulting in a range of plants which can be cut over a long period. Fast germinating species such as salad rocket would come through early and be cut first, but slower crops such as the chicories might be ready several months later. In the early stages the mixture would be cut as seedlings, but later a few plants could be left to develop to a mature state. Traditional salad mixtures were known as 'Mesclun' in France, 'Misticanza' in Italy, 'Salatsamenmischung' in Germany, and have been dubbed 'Saladini' in the English speaking world. Other salad mixtures include 'Misuglio', a colourful mixture of various types of chicory, and 'Oriental Saladini', a mixture of six oriental brassicas, which I developed with the seed company Suffolk Herbs. All these mixtures are suitable for use as CCA seedlings.

(For seedling sprouts, which would normally only be cut once, see Seed Sprouting and Seedling Sprouts pp.96-104.)

**Mature and Semi-Mature Cut-And-Come-Again**
With a number of salad vegetables the mature head can be cut, rather than pulling up the whole plant, and the stump will in due course produce a further crop of useable leaves. It is usually best to cut the head so that a few basal leaves remain on the main stem or stump.

In most cases this secondary growth is loose-leaved, but occasionally a compact secondary head, or heads, is produced. Spring and early summer cabbages are an example. After cutting the head make a shallow cross in the top of the stump. Provided the soil is fertile and the plants well watered, a second crop of four or five heads will develop, at the corners of the cross, by the late summer or autumn.

Another case where a second head may develop is with over-wintered lettuces. Cut the head in spring, leaving the stump in the ground. I have done this with the cold greenhouse cultivar 'Kwiek'. Within five weeks a secondary head had developed, admittedly not as perfectly formed as the first, but quite edible. This is a great time saving, compared with sowing and waiting for three months for a reasonable head. In my experience heading lettuce (as opposed to 'Salad Bowl' types) cut later in the year tend to produce rather bitter secondary growth. This may be a question of cultivar and climate, and it is worth experimenting in your own vegetable garden.

Other salads that make compact heads, such as standard Chinese cabbage and red and 'Sugar Loaf' chicories, will only produce loose leaves after cutting the first head.

Many salad plants that naturally form an open- or loose-head, rather than a compact head, can also be cut and left to resprout in this way. This can be done either when the plants are fully grown, or at earlier, semimature stages of growth. Corn salad, mizuna and mibuna greens, looseheaded Chinese cabbages, 'Salad Bowl' types of lettuce, broad- and curly-leaved endives are typical of those that respond well to this cut-and-come-again treatment.

Besides cutting right across the head, it is often practical to take a few leaves at a time from a plant. It is usually best to take them from around the outer edge.

Hidden Benefits
Apart from increasing the useful life of a plant and its total yield, cut-and-come-again has other benefits.

Increased Frost Resistance
The larger and denser the head on a plant, the more vulnerable it will be to frost damage. In my experience, a relatively bare stump, kept trimmed back by cut-and-come-again treatment so that there is a collection of loose leaves, can usually survive temperatures several degrees lower than one would normally expect it to withstand. This can be a great asset with plants such as Chinese cabbage and 'Sugar Loaf' chicory which are normally killed by frost. While these plants may not be productive at very low temperatures, they will *survive*, ready to start into growth again early in spring. Where these plants are grown under cover in winter, the cropping period can be extended dramatically by this treatment.

Enhanced Colour
For some reason secondary growth is often a deeper colour than the original leaves. This is very marked with some of the red 'Salad Bowl' lettuces – a useful factor if you want dramatically coloured leaves in a salad, or a brilliant effect in a potager.

Forestalling Bolting
Vegetables that show signs of bolting and are becoming tough and coarse can sometimes be cut back, and will continue to produce useful leaf. This is the case with texsel greens and some forms of Chinese cabbages.

## BLANCHING
Many salad plants are naturally bitter, or at least too bitter for the average palate. To make them sweeter and more palatable they can be blanched, literally 'whitened', by being kept in the dark, usually for a period of a week to ten days. Salad plants are sometimes blanched for aesthetic reasons. The gracefully curved white and yellow tipped blanched dandelion leaf is beautiful, as is the pink and white chicon of 'Treviso' chicory, or a frizzy, pale, curly endive leaf.

Various parts of a plant are blanched: mature leaves in endives and dandelion, young shoots of seakale, scorzonera, and Chinese chives, stems of celery and the Japanese herb mitsuba, secondary growths or 'chicons' in 'Witloof' chicory. Most plants are blanched *in situ*, but there are instances where they are transplanted for blanching, usually when there is an element of forcing in the procedure (see Forcing Plants in Darkness p.91).

Whether to blanch or not is sometimes a matter of taste. In the past a wider range of salad plants were blanched, but cultivars that are sweeter have been developed and blanching has become less necessary. It is not very common, for example, to blanch Chinese cabbage or cos lettuce today. The natural bitterness in leaves can also be alleviated simply by shredding them fairly finely before use.

### Blanching Guidelines
A few general rules apply to most blanching operations.
★ Never blanch wet plants, as they will soon rot. Dry them under cloches for a few days beforehand if necessary.
★ Only blanch healthy plants, for the same reason.
★ Remove any dead, decayed or diseased leaves before blanching.
★ Once blanched the plant tends to deteriorate rapidly, so only blanch a few at a time – enough to keep up a regular supply.

\* Use plants as soon as they are ready. If necessary cut them and keep them in the dark in a refrigerator. They soon become bitter again on exposure to light.

### Blanching Methods

#### Tying

Tie leaves towards the top of the plant using either raffia or elastic bands. This very simple method only blanches the central leaves, but is quick and easy (see diagram right).

*The tying method of blanching*

#### Covering Individual Plants

Cover the plant completely with for example a lightproof bucket, or a large flowerpot with the drainage hole blocked to exclude light, or a 'cloche' made from a heavy black polythene bag slipped over a wire frame. If the leaves are sprawly it is a good idea to tie them loosely first.

#### Blackout Frame for a Row of Plants

A row of plants can be covered with a homemade wooden frame, either box-like or an inverted 'V' in shape. Similarly black polythene could be anchored over a row of low wire hoops to make a darkened tunnel over a row of plants.

#### The Plate Method for Low Plants

Cover any low growing endives with a large dinner plate, simply placed on the mature plant. Some sprawling outer leaves may not be blanched, but the central leaves will be well blanched (see diagram right).

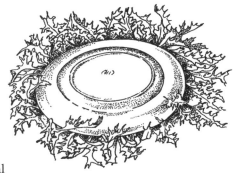

*Blanching using a large plate*

Bracken or Straw Cover
Cover plants with a loose
layer of straw or bracken,
kept in place if neces-
sary with wire hoops.
This works partic-
ularly well with
red chicory and
also gives some pro-
tection against frost. Cover
the plants in autumn before
cold weather sets in (see diagram right).

*Blanching using straw
or bracken*

Earthing Up
Celery stems can be blanched by gradually earthing up soil around them.
Alternatively polythene or paper collars can be wrapped around the
stems. (For details see Salad Plants pp.139–141.)

Transplanting into a Garden Frame
This method is generally used in the autumn, in fairly cold climates. It is
popular for salad plants like endive and dandelion. Dig up the plants and
replant them, packed closely together, in a garden frame. Traditionally
light was excluded by covering the frame with straw mats, but black polythene film is one modern alternative. Plants can also be transplanted into
boxes of soil and then housed in a dark cellar, or into the ground beneath
greenhouse staging. Exclude light with any of the methods that have
been suggested. Transplanting methods are frequently combined with
forcing (see below).

**Forcing Plants in Darkness**
Forcing is done at the point where a root is starting into growth, either
from a natural state of dormancy (as with seakale or rhubarb in spring), or
because the top has been cut back artificially (as with 'Witloof' chicory).
It is done in darkness so the plant is also blanched, making the new leaves
exceptionally tender and good in salads. Plants are sometimes forced at
higher temperatures to bring them on earlier, but it is widely felt that
flavour is better if they develop naturally at lower temperatures. Forcing
is either done *in situ* or by lifting plants. The general rules for blanching
apply equally to forcing. The most commonly forced salad plant is
'Witloof' chicory.

Forcing 'Witloof' Chicory
in Pots or Boxes

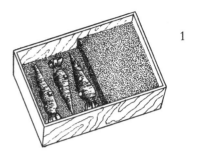

This is the most popular method of forcing 'Witloof' chicory. It can be adapted to other salads, such as Treviso chicory and dandelions.

★ Dig up the plants in late autumn to early winter. Leave them somewhere sheltered outdoors, for example in a barrow in a lean-to shed, for about a week or so. This allows the moisture to pass back into the roots.

★ Trim off the leaves about 2.5cm (1in) above the neck.

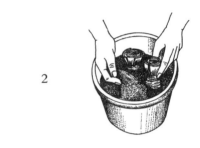

★ Trim off any side roots, and discard roots that are less than 4cm (1½in) diameter across the top.

★ Store roots in boxes until required for forcing. Lie them horizontally in layers of sand in a box in an outdoor shed (1). Alternatively lay them in a 30cm (12in) deep trench in the garden, covered with soil.

★ Force a few at a time in a 23-30cm (9-12in) flower pot. Select three to five roots of roughly the same size, and pack them fairly close together in any soil or old potting compost (2). (Soil quality is immaterial, as all nourishment comes from the root.) If necessary cut off the tips of the roots so they fit into the pots. After planting the necks should be about 2.5cm (1in) above the soil.

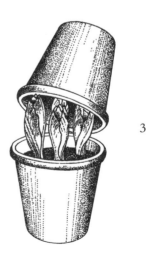

★ Water lightly, and then cover the pot containing the chicory with another upturned pot of the

*Stages in forcing 'Witloof' chicory*

same size, with the drainage hole blocked to exclude all light (3).

★ Put the pot indoors, ideally at a temperature of 10-18°C (50-64°F).

★ Inspect it from time to time. Remove any rotted leaves and water lightly if dry. Firm chicons normally develop within about three weeks.

★ Cut them about 2cm (¾in) above the root. If not eaten immediately wrap them in brown paper and keep them in the fridge. If the roots are left they resprout to produce a smaller second crop of loose, but tender, blanched leaves.

Forcing can be done in boxes or any other container if preferred, instead of flower pots. Just allow at least 20cm (8in) headroom for the chicon to develop.

Forcing 'Witloof' Chicory in a Greenhouse

The same procedure is followed, but instead of planting in a pot, transplant the chicory root into the soil in a greenhouse. It is easiest to plant under the greenhouse bench or staging. Make the area dark by boarding it in, or covering it with black polythene film anchored over wire hoops (see diagram below). When temperatures rise in spring aphids may build up rapidly, and the chicons may start to rot in the close, warm conditions. The only remedy is to use the plants up quickly.

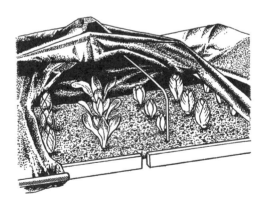

*Forcing chicory beneath black polythene film*

Forcing 'Witloof' Chicory *In Situ*

This is a slower method of forcing as the chicons will not normally be ready until spring. This makes a nice succession to a crop forced indoors. Leave the roots in the soil, but in late autumn cut back the leaves as for lifted chicory. Cover the stumps with a 15-20cm (6-8in) layer of sand, light soil, or sieved cinders to make a ridge over them. In due course the chicons will push through. Scrape away the covering to cut them. If the ridges are covered with cloches or low polythene film tunnels they will be ready a little sooner.

Essentially the same method can be used for blanching the chards (young growths) of plants that naturally die back in winter such as scorzonera, salsify and dandelions. In these cases a tight chicon would not develop, so a looser covering can be used, such as straw, hay or bracken. Keep it in place with wire hoops if necessary. If covered in autumn, blanched shoots will be ready in spring.

Forcing in Cellars: the Traditional Method

Cellars are still used in parts of Europe for storing and forcing winter vegetables. The following method of forcing dandelion, wild chicory, and small 'Witloof' chicory roots (or large ones which have already been forced once) is used in Belgium. Make a heap of soil 10cm (4in) deep against a cellar wall. Lay trimmed roots on this layer, with their necks protruding over the edge. Cover them with another 10cm (4in) layer of soil, then another layer of roots and so on. Water the heap gently with a rose on the can. If the final layer of soil is made about 20cm (8in) deep, the final layer of roots can be planted upright. The blanched leaves are cut as they are ready, just above the neck. Some will resprout several times.

## STORING VEGETABLES

The quality and flavour of almost all vegetables starts to deteriorate once they are picked, and continues to decline in storage. So salad vegetables should only be stored when it is essential to do so, for winter reserves or when weather conditions threaten the crop. Appropriate storage methods will be given in Chapter 12, but there are a few general, common sense, guidelines:

★ Only store vegetables that are in prime condition. Reject any which are diseased, damaged by pests, or showing signs of bruising or rotting.

★ Handle them very gently. Bruises are often the starting point for rots, particularly with onion bulbs and garlic.

★ Examine them regularly in storage, and remove any that are rotting.

## KEEPING LEAFY SALADS FRESH

Ideally leafy salads should be picked at the last possible moment, but this is not always practicable. One thing we have learnt from marketing bags of fresh salad is that they keep much better *without* being washed. So where salads have to be picked several hours, or even days in advance, pick them first thing in the morning when they are at their most fresh, remove any soiled outer leaves, then put the salads in paper bags in a fridge until required. Wash them in cool water just before use. (Paper bags are considered less likely to encourage infections such as listeria than polythene bags.) We have found, as have other professional organic growers, that organically grown vegetables keep fresh noticeably longer than vegetables grown with chemicals.

# Chapter 9

# Seed Sprouting and Seedling Sprouts

The idea of germinating seeds, and eating the tiny nutritious young sprouts and/or seedlings is not a new one; it is probably at least five thousand years old. The Chinese and other races such as the Aztecs and Navajo Indians practised it centuries ago, but it has only become popular in Europe and North America relatively recently. For salad lovers, this opens up a whole new range of 'crops' available at any time of year.

Sprouting is a useful technique for several reasons. Above all, it requires little space or time. Several days' supplies can be grown in a jam jar or sprouter on a windowsill, and most seeds, under normal conditions, will grow to an edible stage within four to five days. It is simple, requiring only rudimentary and inexpensive equipment, and it is economical. Many seeds yield up to ten times their weight when sprouted. In some ways it is the perfect packaged food: nutritious, lightweight and easily stored until required.

There are two distinct types of sprout, depending on the particular stage they are eaten.

*Seed sprouts* – These are used at any point from immediately after germination until just before the development of the first tiny leaves. The sprout length could be anything from 6mm (¼in) to about 4cm (1½in). Most beans are used at the 'seed sprout' stage.

*Seedling sprouts* – These are allowed to grow into seedlings 5-7.5cm (2-3in) long, with the first small leaves developed. Traditional 'mustard and cress' is harvested at this stage, as are radishes.

## WHAT CAN BE SPROUTED?

Very many seeds can be sprouted and eaten, but only the tastiest and easiest to sprout have become widely used for the purpose. Watch out for interesting new developments. Popular sprouting seeds include many beans, ranging from the well-known mung and soya beans of Chinese bean sprout fame, to the round red azuki, now commonplace in health food shops, to the familiar large white Lima bean. Of the cereals, rye, wheat, barley, rice and maize can all be sprouted. So can numerous legumes, including alfalfa (lucerne), some types of clover, fenugreek, lentils and peas. Many members of the brassica (crucifer) tribe, including mustard, salad rape, various oriental greens and closely related radish are sprouted, as are some common garden plants like pumpkin, sunflower, onions and leeks. Bamboo, buckwheat, burdock, chickpea, Mexican chia, Japanese mitsuba, chrysanthemum greens and mint are among more unusual sprouted seeds.

Seeds for sprouting can usually be bought in health food stores or from mail order seed firms. In some cases it is quite easy to grow your own, examples being radish, cress, sunflower, alfalfa and pumpkin. With pumpkin and sunflower it is necessary to grow a cultivar with hull-less seeds, which are the only ones suitable for sprouting.

Always buy seed which is *intended* for sprouting or human consumption, or is guaranteed untreated. Seed which is sold for sowing is often treated with chemical dressings, generally insecticides or fungicides, and it goes without saying that such seed would be dangerous to use for sprouting. Remember, also, that seed for sprouting is living; it should be stored in cool dry conditions, preferably in airtight jars, to retain its viability (see Seed, Sowing Outdoors and Planting p.63).

**Nutritional Factors**
Sprouts are a highly nutritious form of food, particularly rich in vitamins, high quality protein, enzymes and minerals such as iron, calcium, potassium and iodine. However, they grow very rapidly and soon pass their peak, from the nutritional and flavour point of view. They should always be used in their prime. Harvest them as soon as they are ready: don't let them go on growing. If necessary keep them in a fridge for a couple of days, in a jar, or a bowl of cold water, or wrapped in film to preserve them. Bean sprouts are easily infected by bacteria, and to be on the safe side, should be kept for no more than 24 hours before consumption, at a fridge temperature of 4°C (39°F).

If a constant supply of sprouts is needed, sprout small quantities at regular intervals.

Apart from being used fresh in salads, sprouts can be used in many other ways – in soups, in baking, for stuffing and as an accompaniment to meat dishes. Many wholefood recipes make use of ground dried sprouts. For this purpose they can be dried gently in an oven, stored in jars, and ground just before use.

Sprouts can be deep frozen, though much of the fresh flavour will be lost. Blanch them by steaming for a minute then cool rapidly before freezing. They can be frozen without blanching, but should then be used within four to six weeks.

Toxicity in Legume Sprouts
A word of warning on eating raw legume sprouts – that is members of the
pea and bean family, including lentils, alfalfa, fenugreek and clover. In
varying degrees raw legumes contain toxins. Among the most toxic raw
are French haricot and broad beans; azuki beans, lentils, alfalfa, fenugreek
and buckwheat are relatively toxic, while mung and soya beans are
among the least toxic. To some extent toxicity is reduced by soaking the
seed, by sprouting and by cooking – frying, boiling or steaming – but it is
a complex situation. The point is that one shouldn't eat large quantities of
*raw* legume sprouts on a regular basis, no more than about 550g (20oz)
daily; eating small quantities would be unlikely to have harmful effects. A
nutritionist advises me that quick frying sprouted beans for a few minutes
in oil, followed by ten minutes' steaming as part of a mixed vegetable
dish, would render them safe.

Seed Sprout Mixtures
Mixtures of seeds are sometimes sold for sprouting. Some consist of various beans, some are based on alfalfa, and some are blends of different
seeds. They are worth trying, but a likely snag is that they germinate at
different rates.

**SEED SPROUTING**
Although seed sprouting is easy, it is by no means foolproof, and begin-
ners sometimes have failures. If you are new to sprouting, I would suggest starting with one type of seed, and growing it by several methods
until you find the best for your conditions. Having acquired a feel for it,
you will soon be able to produce a successful crop and it will be easy to
move onto others.

Sprouting seeds must have warmth, moisture and air, but the combination of warmth and moisture encourages the growth of moulds.
Moreover, germinating seeds generate considerable heat, and unless they
are cooled (for example by rinsing with cold water), they soon go
mouldy. Preventing this is the challenge of seed sprouting. Cracked, dead
or diseased seeds are especially liable to rot during the sprouting process.

The commonest causes of failure are:
★ Seeds drying out or being swamped with water.
★ Temperature too high or too low.
★ Insufficient rinsing.
★ Dirty equipment.
Successful sprouting seems to depend on developing an unshakeable

routine. In hot weather neglecting even one rinse can result in seeds going 'sour'. Once this has happened there is no remedy other than throwing them out and starting again. Here are a few guidelines.

**Sprouting Guidelines**
★ Wash all equipment thoroughly between batches.
★ Before you start, remove any obviously cracked, unhealthy or off-colour seed. Remove any other poor seeds you notice once sprouting has started too.
★ Keep the seeds fresh by rinsing them night and morning. In a few cases they will need rinsing three times a day.
★ Grow the seeds as fast as possible without actually forcing them. 'Lingering' seeds never grow well. For each kind there is an optimum temperature range, and finding it is largely a matter of trial and error. For the majority, temperatures between 13 and 21°C (55 and 70°F) are suitable. A few require higher temperatures.

**Darkness or Light?**
Seeds can be sprouted in the dark or light; it is a question of whether you prefer the flavour of the crisp-textured, whitened (and less nutritious) sprouts obtained by growing in the dark, or the usually softer-textured, yellow and greenish sprouts when grown in the light. Chinese bean sprouts are traditionally grown in the dark. I usually grow mung and similar beans in the dark, and most other sprouting seeds in the light. Seedling sprouts are grown in the light, though they are sometimes started in the dark to encourage germination.

For growing in the dark a cupboard is usually quite suitable provided it is not too close an atmosphere. An airing cupboard is handy in winter when windowsills may be cold. Otherwise, jars can be darkened by wrapping with black polythene or aluminium foil or by putting them into some kind of lightproof container. Dishes can be darkened with lightproof lids or foil covers.

If grown in the light the best place is a windowsill, but avoid a very sunny window.

**SEED SPROUTING METHODS**
Seeds can either be sprouted 'loose' in a container, or on a 'base'. When sprouted loose there is no wastage as the entire sprout can be used. When sprouted on a base there may be some wastage, as the sprouts may have to be cut off from the base. Growth is generally a little slower in the base

method, but the sprouts remain in good condition longer by rooting into the base. They can be allowed to develop into seedling sprouts where required, so this method is useful for sprouts which can be eaten either as seed or seedling sprouts. They can be grown in attractive dishes, and served in them at table.

**Loose Container Methods**
Choose a container which is deep enough to allow for the expansion of the seeds: most increase their volume seven- to ten-fold while sprouting.

Sprouting is simplest if the container has a perforated base, and is therefore self-draining. This is the principle on which most patented seed sprouters work. Some are single units, others have several perforated tiers stacked on top of each other to allow different kinds of seed to be sprouted simultaneously. Water is poured in at the top, filters through, and drains away or is poured away at the lowest level, cooling the sprouts.

For a cheap, homemade sprouter, take any plastic carton or container and poke small holes in the base, effectively converting it into a sieve.

Jam jars can be used for sprouting if the lid is replaced with a nylon mesh top, or with muslin held in place with a rubber band. (Mesh tops which fit standard size jars can sometimes be bought.) Sprouts are rinsed by pouring water in and out of the mesh or muslin. Personally I have always found this awkward, and prefer to use one of the perforated sprouters above. Muslin has the added disadvantage that it quickly becomes stained. Where a jar is used sprouting is more even and seems to be faster if the jar is laid on its side.

General Sprouting Procedure
* Remove poor seeds (see p.99).
* Rinse the seeds in fresh water and drain them so they are just moist. To do this either tip them into a sieve and run water through, or use your sprouter if it is self-draining. Some seeds, for example beans, sprout faster if soaked overnight first. Rinse and drain before starting to sprout.
* Put a layer of seeds in the bottom of the container, generally no more than 6mm-1.3cm (¼-½in) deep, though this will vary with the seed: the larger the seed, the deeper the layer.
* Cover if necessary; put them somewhere warm if temperatures get too low in winter. Otherwise germinate them at room temperature.
* Rinse the seeds night and morning with cold water. Drain thoroughly after each rinsing, so the seeds are moist, but not submerged in water. In very hot weather rinsing may have to be more frequent.

★ Sprouts will be ready for use within a few days, depending on the temperature. Give them a rinse before use to remove ungerminated seeds.

Sprouting Mung Beans

In the past my mung bean sprouting was a dismal failure. Although small, skimpy sprouts would develop, I could never replicate the fat, crunchy sprouts of a Chinese restaurant. It wasn't until I went to China and Taiwan that I discovered the secret is to subject the sprouting seeds to some kind of pressure. Traditionally this was simply the pressure exerted by the sprouting seeds pushing against the sides of a curved clay sprouting pot. I have found that putting a weight on top of the sprouting seeds seems to have the same effect. I use a homemade container as described on the previous page.

★ Soak the beans overnight and then put them to sprout in a perforated container.

★ Cover them with a moist cloth.

★ Lay a weight on the cloth. I have used old fashioned weights or stones. How heavy the weight is a matter of trial and error under your conditions. I use approximately 900g (2lb) in a 13cm (5in) diameter container with 1.3cm (½in) of sprouts in the bottom. Less weight can be effective. Unless the weight fits snugly on the container, put it on a saucer to distribute the weight more evenly.

★ Rinse regularly, removing the weight (and saucer) when rinsing the seeds.

*Sprouting mung beans:
perforated container (top);
seeds covered with moist cloth
and weight (centre);
rinsing (bottom)*

## Sprouting on a Base

The sprouts are grown on a dish or in a container, lined with a moisture-retentive base. If they are left beyond the seed sprout stage they will root into the base and stand upright, becoming seedling sprouts (see below).

A wide range of containers can be used, from shallow dishes and plastic cartons to seedtrays. For the base use several layers of paper

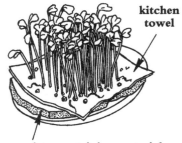

*Sprouts growing on a base*

**kitchen towel**

**moisture retaining material**

towel or blotting paper, absorbent cloth or flannel, thin foam rubber or sponge. I often use a piece of thin sponge or foam rubber, cut to fit the dish, covered with a couple of layers of paper towel. This allows the foam to be re-used several times (see diagram above).

★ Clean and rinse the seeds and spread them in a single or very shallow layer over the base. Cover the container or put it in the dark if you want blanched sprouts.

★ Rinse the seeds by pouring water gently into the container, and swilling it around before tipping it out. The seeds may need to be held in place with the back of the spoon in the early stages. On the whole less rinsing is necessary when grown on a base.

★ If the medium is very clean the sprouts may be used whole. Otherwise cut them just above base level.

For details of the best stage to eat the most common sprouted seeds, and the average time taken for sprouting, see the entries in Chapter 12.

## SEEDLING SPROUTS

Seedling sprouts are my favourite fast food. They have two advantages over seed sprouts:

★ The stage of eating is much less critical, as they keep in good condition for that much longer.

★ They provide 'greenery', and all can be eaten raw in crunchy salads and are good in sandwiches.

## What to Grow as Seedling Sprouts

The ideal seedling sprout has an interesting flavour and germinates and grows very quickly. Almost any salad crop can be used, as most are tender and succulent even when very young. In the seventeenth and eighteenth centuries cresses, spinach, radish, turnip, mustard, rape, lettuce, orange and lemon seedlings were all grown for use in salads. There are many salad crops to choose from today, with new ones continually being introduced: therefore keep an eye out for them. It can be a good way of using up any old packets of salad seed where germination is in doubt. Little is lost if they fail.

The following are all good value. For a spicy or piquant flavour try mustard, cress, radish, and salad rocket; for a milder flavour there is alfalfa and salad rape (often substituted for mustard in commercial packs of so called 'mustard and cress'), besides many members of the brassica (crucifer) family such as cabbage, kales, turnip, komatsuna and the hybrid 'senposai'. Fenugreek tastes very like peas in the seedling sprout stage, as do peas themselves! More curious flavours can be found in chrysanthemum greens and the Japanese herb mitsuba – though neither germinate very fast. The Japanese bunching onions are among the best bets for an onion-flavoured seedling sprout.

Mixtures
It is quite feasible to grow different seedling sprouts together. Mustard and cress is the classic example; alfalfa and radish another possibility. The slower germinating seeds (in these cases cress and alfalfa) need to be sown first so the two are ready at the same time. It is fun to experiment with your own mixtures. To plan the sowing, sow small trials of each variety first, noting how long they take to germinate.

**Growing Methods**
Seedling sprouts are normally grown in the light, although direct sun should be avoided. They are sometimes started in the dark, so that elongated seedlings will develop, then a couple of days after germination are moved into the light to 'green up'.

They can be sprouted on a base, if preferred, or by the 'raft' method (see diagram p.104).

Sprouting on a Base
The types of containers and the method used are essentially the same as those for seed sprouts. However, besides being sown on an inert base such as paper towelling or foam for instance, seedling sprouts can be grown on a thin layer of sowing or potting compost, one of the peat substitutes, fine leaf mould, or light sandy soil. These will supply a few nutrients so enabling the seedlings to grow to a more advanced stage or to

stand longer without deteriorating. Cover them lightly with soil or what-ever medium is used.

Most seedlings can be eaten when 4–5cm (1½–2in) high. If the base is very clean they can be pulled up by the roots and the entire seedling eaten; otherwise cut them off at base level with scissors. Sometimes a second crop will grow up, generally from seeds which did not germinate the first time. If kept moist, mature seedlings will stand up to ten days or so in good condition. Where a soil or similar base is used they may resprout after the first cutting to give a second cut. For this to happen, they should be cut above the first pair of seed leaves.

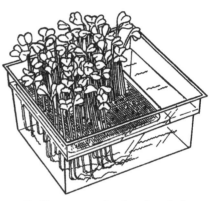

### The Raft Method

In this excellent method of growing seedling sprouts the seed is sown on a small screen. This screen is usually made of rigid nylon, which floats on water, like a raft. When the seedlings germi-nate their roots go through the screen and dangle in the

*Seedling sprouts using the raft method*

water. They develop into a dense mat of upright seedlings, and keep in good condition for as long as two weeks, depending on the temperature. Change the water at least every two days to keep it fresh.

Various types of sprouter are marketed, but they tend to come and go. A favourite of mine is a Japanese rectangular plastic container about 5cm (2in) deep and roughly 13cm (5in) wide, in which a nylon screen fits onto a ridge 2cm (¾in) below the top. Seeds are sown in a single layer on the screen, and the container is then filled with water up to the level of the screen (see diagram above).

Cheap sprouting rafts can be made from any rigid screening material which is fine enough to prevent seeds falling through. Attach it to a frame to make it buoyant, then float it in a bowl or dish of water. It is easiest to put the seeds onto the dry raft, then to float it into the water, rather than putting them straight onto the floating raft.

The perforated dishes or trays in seed sprouting kits can be converted into seedling sprouters by placing them over a dish of water. The seedling roots grow through and dangle in the water.

# Chapter 10
# Protected Cropping

For salad lovers in cold and temperate climates protected cropping is the key to having fresh, varied, good quality salads all year round, especially very early and very late in the year when salad is most scarce. It also enables warmth loving, tender crops such as tomato, cucumber and pepper to be grown where an outdoor crop would otherwise be a gamble.

Cloches, frames, low plastic film tunnels, walk-in polytunnels, greenhouses and the various films known as 'crop covers' are all forms of 'protection'. In *very* severe climates some kind of heated greenhouse or structure would be necessary for year round supplies, but that is outside the scope of this book. In the British Isles and areas with a roughly similar or warmer climate it is unnecessary and expensive to grow salads with artificial heat. Besides, salads pampered in artificial heat seem to be insipid in flavour.

Protection benefits salad crops in a number of different ways.

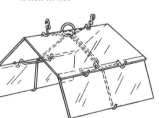

*Glass barn cloche (below). Ends should be closed as in glass tent cloche when in use*

*Rumsey clip to join loose panes*

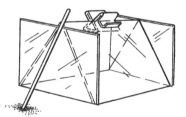

*Glass cloche (above), end panels held in place with angled canes*

Increasing the 'Growing Days'
Most salad plants only grow when the mean daily temperature rises above 6°C (43°F), a temperature reached some time in spring; they cease growing when it falls below that temperature. The days between these two points are termed 'growing days'. In the British Isles, to take one example, the number of growing days varies from about 300 a year in the south

west to 250 in the north of England, eastern Scotland and other cold areas – an appreciable difference.

All forms of protection warm up the soil and air around plants and, to a greater or lesser degree, slow down the rate at which heat is radiated from the soil at night. This effectively increases the number of growing days for any protected crop. So protection is most valuable in cold, high and exposed areas where the growing season is shortest. A gain of as much as three weeks at the beginning and end of the season can be made by protecting crops. Moreover, provided the plants have sufficient moisture, the higher the temperature rises the faster they grow; so protection increases the rate of growth.

### Minimizing Frost Damage

Salad crops vary in the amount of frost they can stand without being killed or damaged. Cloches and greenhouses give some protection against frost, though on cold clear nights, due to soil radiation, the air temperature under cloches and plastic tunnels can be as low, and in freak cases, even lower, than the temperature outside. (The only complete guarantee against frost is a heated structure.)

However, it is the *combination* of low temperatures and strong wind that is most lethal to plants: if protected from wind the frost damage is far less severe. Protection keeps plants dry, so disease is less likely to set in when they thaw out. It also keeps the soil around plants in better condition than if exposed to the elements.

Further protection against frost damage can be given by spraying cloches with water immediately before a heavy frost is expected. The ice layer formed gives extra insulation. Spraying plants the morning after a frost, before the sun reaches them, enables them to thaw out gently, and often prevents fatalities.

### Improving the Quality of Plants

A surprising number of salad plants *survive* remarkably low winter temperatures, but when exposed to the full brunt of winter weather the leaves become battered, tough and coarse. This may not matter if they are to be cooked, but they make for a miserable salad. Protection preserves their quality and flavour.

### Protection from Pests

All forms of protection are to some extent a physical barrier, so can be very useful in preventing attacks from pests such as birds and rabbits.

They also give protection, in varying degrees, against flying insect pests such as butterflies, moths, and flies and pests like flea beetle. (See also Pests and Diseases p.53.) The reverse side of the coin is that some pests and diseases – notably pests like red spider mite and whitefly – will build up much faster in protected situations.

## Materials used for Protected Cropping

In the past glass was almost exclusively used for greenhouses, garden frames and cloches, but today it has to compete with a wide range of synthetic plastics and other materials, most of which are cheaper. Their differing qualities have to be weighed up when choosing or making forms of protection.

### Glass

Glass, provided it is kept clean, transmits light very well, which is particularly important in winter when lack of light limits plant growth. It also traps heat well. During the day the earth absorbs the sun's energy in the form of short waves, but at night some of this heat is lost from the soil by long wave radiation. Glass transmits the incoming short waves, but unlike most plastic materials, to some extent holds back the outgoing long waves, so retaining heat that would otherwise be lost. Glass lasts for many years without deteriorating, and always looks good.

Its disadvantages are that it is expensive, heavy, breakable and somewhat awkward to erect.

### Rigid plastics and synthetics

Some of the modern transparent plastics can transmit light almost as well as glass, although moisture tends to condense on them, cutting out some light. The opaque plastics *appear* to cut out light, but it has been shown that plants grow well in their even, diffuse light. The corrugated forms lose more heat than flat sheets, but have more rigidity and are usually easier to erect. A few rigid plastics such as polyvinyl chloride (PVC) are like glass in being impermeable to long wave transmission, so retain some heat at night. All these materials are lighter than glass, so can be erected on less substantial structures. They are also more flexible, but, if used for cloches or frames, will require more anchorage.

Their main disadvantage is that they are relatively short lived, easily become scratched (which cuts out light), and become brittle with age, due to ultra-violet (UV) radiation. Buy the longer lasting UV treated plastics if possible, and store them out of sunlight when not in use.

Among the most useful materials currently available are PVC sheeting and acrylic sheeting (originally known as 'perspex') both of which transmit light and retain heat well and normally last about five years. Glass fibre is opaque, but very strong and will last many years, though it is fairly unsightly in the garden. Watch out for any useful new materials that may be developed in future.

Semi-rigid plastics

These are generally used for making frames or cloches. Polypropylene 'board' is a double layered, corrugated plastic, with fluted channels between the two layers. The double layers have good insulation properties, and this is another case where plants seem to grow well in the diffuse light. Its average life expectancy is three to five years, provided it has been UV treated. It can be attached to metal or wooden frames. Use it with the flutes running horizontal at ground level, otherwise moisture and dirt are sucked into the flutes, causing discoloration.

Wire-reinforced plastics are cheap materials which can easily be bent into any required shape, so are useful for making cloches, frames and other forms of protection. They last between three and five years.

Polythene films

These cheap, lightweight films are used for making cloches, frames, low tunnels and walk-in polytunnels. They range from very thin 150 gauge films (used for low tunnels), to the much more substantial 500–700 gauge used for polytunnels. With UV treatment the lightest films last a year or so, and heavy films up to three years. During the day temperatures rise rapidly under the films but fall rapidly at night. They are excellent for providing protection against the elements. The film of moisture which condenses on the underside of clear polythene films apparently helps prevent heat radiation from the soil. (For perforated polythene films and fleecy films, both used for 'crop covers', see pp.123–5.)

## CLOCHES

A cloche is any small unit used for protected cropping, which is easily moved from one part of the garden to another. Cloches are normally designed so that they can be placed end to end to cover a row of plants.

The traditional cloches were made of glass, and were tent-shaped (made from two pieces), barn-shaped (made from four pieces) or flat-topped (from three pieces). They were fastened together with a series of special wire clips. For low growing salads, tents and low barn cloches made from panes 45 x 30cm (18 x 12in) are quite adequate, though taller crops such as tomatoes will require larger cloches. Various devices are sold for joining loose panes of glass together to make cloches, the best known being the Rumsey clip (see diagram p.105). Simple tent cloches can be made from two panes, kept in place with pairs of canes pushed into the ground on opposite sides at each end. By the way, glass is less likely to break if the edges are rubbed with a carborundum stone before the pieces are put together. Broken glass usually can be mended with an appropriate glue.

With some of the more flexible modern materials that have been developed cloches can be made in a variety of shapes – semi-circular, tunnel-shaped, or bell-shaped for example.

### DIY Cloches

Cloches can be made from a range of modern materials, by tacking, nailing or screwing them to a wooden frame. Polythene film is best battened to a frame to hold it firm. Very primitive cloches can be made from large plastic bags, slipping bent pieces of wire (such as coat-hangers) down each side of the bag, and piercing the plastic with the wire for anchorage (see diagram right).

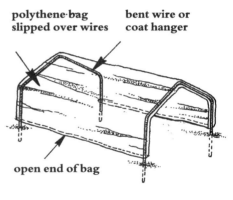

*Simple homemade cloche*

### What to Look for in Cloches

The following are some of the practical factors, other than cost and appearance, to consider when choosing or making cloches.

Light transmission
Choose materials with good light transmission, bearing in mind that an evenly diffused light is acceptable. The light factor is most important in the short days of autumn and winter, in industrial areas where atmospheric pollution reduces the light, and when cloches are being used to grow, rather than merely protect plants.

Insulation
Where possible choose materials which limit heat loss from the soil. In practice it is not always easy to get the technical information to evaluate prospective materials.

Stability and anchorage
Cloches are most useful in exposed areas and in autumn, winter and spring when cold winds and gales are most frequent. So avoid flimsy cloches. You will find yourself constantly retrieving them, whole or in pieces, from your own or neighbours' gardens. Avoid sharp angles which catch the wind.

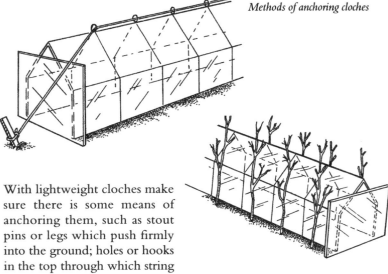

*Methods of anchoring cloches*

With lightweight cloches make sure there is some means of anchoring them, such as stout pins or legs which push firmly into the ground; holes or hooks in the top through which string or wire is threaded along the length for extra anchorage (see diagram above left); or flanges at the base which can be weighted down. In very exposed situations push pea sticks or short canes into the ground on either side of the cloches to keep them in place (see diagram above right); or weight them down with a pair of bottles, attached together with heavy string tied around the necks and strung over the ridge of the cloche.

Handling and storage
One of the great advantages of cloches is their versatility, so make sure they are easily moved. Anyone short on muscle power may find the larger

sized glass cloches awkward and heavy to handle. Cloches which are difficult to erect and dismantle tend to spend much of their life idle. Look for cloches which stack or fold on top of each other when not in use.

## Ventilation

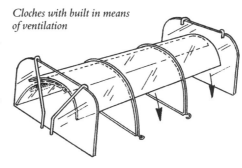

*Cloches with built in means of ventilation*

Temperatures can build up rapidly under cloches, and ventilation is often necessary, especially in summer. Glass cloches have gaps in the tops which can be adjusted for ventilation. In some cloches roofs can be raised for ventilation. Other ventilation systems include sides or panels that can be removed, raised or rolled back (see diagram above), or replaced with nets to maintain protection against birds. Where there is no built-in means of ventilation, move cloches apart on hot days, leaving small gaps between them.

## Preventing draughts

If cloches are left open-ended they become wind tunnels, (see Shelter, Water and Weeds pp.39-40), so completely offsetting the benefits. There must be a means of closing off the ends. This can be closely fitting pieces which hook on to the main body, anchoring rods inserted down the vertical flutes of double-layered polypropylene; or simply by using panels of glass or plastic, held in place with canes or sticks. Put the canes into the ground at an angle rather than upright, or they work themselves loose (see diagram p.105).

## Size

Cloches must be large enough to cover crops with a little room to spare, so that air keeps circulating and disease is prevented. In summer foliage should not be too near glass or it will scorch; in winter, plants touching glass may be affected by frost. In some models cloche height can be increased with side or roof extensions, otherwise stand cloches on bricks or boards to raise them. With some of the flexible materials the width/height ratio can be adjusted to cover a wider or narrower area of ground. On very light, well-drained soil only (or there will be a water-logging problem) crops such as tomatoes can be planted in a shallow trench. Straddle the top of the trench with cloches to gain some more height.

When plants have outgrown the cloches some types can be put on their sides and 'wrapped' around the plants to continue to give some form of protection. Anchor them with a cane through the handle, or canes pushed into the ground on each side (see diagram right).

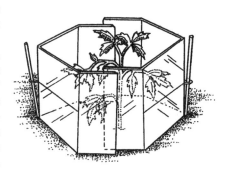

*Cloches used as windbreak*

## Making the Most of Cloches

Cloches are a valuable resource, and to get the most benefit from them, should be used for a variety of tasks throughout the year, moving them around the garden accordingly. They also deserve the best soil.

### Soil and Moisture

Work plenty of organic matter into the soil where cloches are going to be used (see Manures and Fertilizers pp.27-38). This not only encourages plant growth but helps to retain the moisture in the soil, which can dry out rapidly under cloches. Where feasible, keep plants well mulched for the same reason.

There is generally no need to remove small cloches for watering, as rain water runs down the sides of cloches, percolating down to the roots. If necessary they can be watered from above with a can or hose. It may be necessary, however, to remove them to water small seedlings, or to remove large cloches to make sure that water is reaching plants in the centre. Poke a finger about 2.5cm (1in) deep into the soil to check if it is moist. Cloches can, of course, be lifted off when it rains to give the soil a thorough drenching.

### Year Round Use of Cloches

Here are some of the ways cloches can be used to grow salads.

### *Early spring*

★ To prepare the soil for sowing. Put cloches on the soil to dry it out or warm it up before making a seedbed.

★ For early sowings, either in boxes or pots, or *in situ*. Virtually all salad crops can be started off ten days or so earlier in spring by sowing under cloches. To make maximum use of precious space under cloches, inter-crop as much as possible. For example radish, corn salad, spring onion, carrot, beetroot, and seedling crops can all be carefully sown towards the outside of the cloches, with lettuce, peas and dwarf beans down the middle of the planting area.

★ For hardening-off. Tender seedlings and young plants raised in propagators indoors can be hardened-off by putting pots or boxes under cloches. Move the cloches a little further apart each day, then leave them off during the day but cover the plants at night. Finally expose the plants continually before planting out in permanent positions.

★ For early plantings. Any salad plants which have been sown indoors can be planted out earlier under cloches than into open ground.

★ In greenhouses or polytunnels cloches may be used as an extra layer of protection inside unheated greenhouses and tunnels in winter and early in the year. Soil and air temperatures under the cloches will be a few degrees higher than in the rest of the greenhouse. In winter this may prevent frost damage; in spring it can enable tender crops such as tomatoes to be planted out earlier, and other salad crops to be brought on faster. In early spring these extra days of growth are invaluable.

*Late spring/early summer*
★ For sowing or planting hardy crops. Tender crops such as cucumber, peppers, summer purslane, iceplant and basil can be started under cloches. Cloches can be removed when they are outgrown or needed elsewhere.

*Summer*
★ Growing tender crops to maturity. Provided the cloches are large enough, they can be used to crop peppers, cucumbers (trained horizontally), tomatoes (grown as bushes or trained horizontally).

*Autumn*
★ To ripen fruits at the end of the season. Peppers, and dwarf and bush tomatoes can be covered completely. Loosen cordon tomatoes from their supports and bend them down to fit under cloches.

★ To dry bulbs. Put harvested onions and garlic under cloches to dry out.

★ To dry seed crops. Gently bend down the stems and support them to keep the seed heads off the ground.

★ To protect late summer sowings and plantings. Use cloches for seedling crops, and salads such as endive, lettuce and radish for use in autumn, winter or early spring *or* for transplanting the following spring.

*Winter*

★ To protect some of the winter salad crops from the elements. These include hardy types such as winter lettuce, spinach, hardy oriental greens like mizuna and komatsuna, as well as less hardy types that stand some cold but not very severe weather, for example sugar loaf and red chicories, endives, various types of Chinese cabbage and oriental greens.

★ For protecting over-wintering seedlings while they develop sufficiently for planting out in spring.

★ Inside greenhouses and tunnels. In cold climates use them to give extra protection to winter salads which are on the borderline of hardiness.

## Strip Cropping

Probably the most efficient way of using cloches is what is known as strip cropping, whereby vegetable sowing and planting is planned so that cloches can be moved to and fro between adjacent strips of ground. Strip cropping is a subject on its own, but one simple example based primarily on salad crops is given below.

| Strip 1 | Strip 2 |
|---|---|
| **EARLY AUTUMN** | |
| *Winter hardy lettuce or mizuna greens planted under cloches; inter-sown with radish for late autumn use* | |
| **SPRING** | |
| Cloches removed for lettuce to mature unprotected | *Spring salads (lettuce, corn salad, CCA seedlings) sown under cloches* |
| **EARLY SUMMER** | |
| *Tomatoes (or cucumbers or peppers) planted under cloches. If large enough, crops can mature under them* | Spring salads followed by short term summer crops eg dwarf French beans grown in the open |
| **EARLY AUTUMN** | |
| | *Winter hardy lettuce or mizuna greens planted under cloches; inter-sown with radish for late autumn use* |

*Italic type* shows crops covered by cloches in any one season.

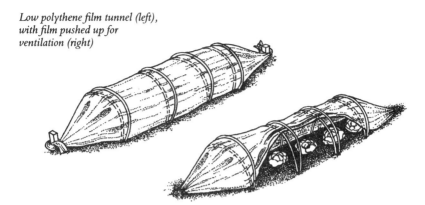

*Low polythene film tunnel (left), with film pushed up for ventilation (right)*

## LOW FILM TUNNELS

A low film tunnel is made of polythene film laid over a series of hoops, to form a tunnel over a row of plants. A basic low film tunnel is one of the cheapest forms of protection, although sophisticated systems with high quality hoops work out more expensive.

Hoops can be made of flexible galvanized steel rods or piping, flexible polythene piping, steel wire or similar materials – as long as the surface is smooth so the film does not get snagged. The height and span of the tunnel depends entirely on the length of the hoops, and can usually be adjusted according to the crop being grown. Take a piece of wire and bend it into a hoop to work out the size of hoop which will suit you best. Hoops are usually spaced about 90cm (36in) apart, and should be pushed at least 10cm (4in) deep into the ground.

The film is normally lightweight 150 gauge, though slightly heavier film can be used. It must be light enough to pull taut over the hoops, and wide enough to cover the hoops generously on either side. The tunnel shape stands up to strong winds surprisingly well but the film sometimes rips. It can be mended with special tapes sold for the purpose. Use UV treated film wherever possible, and always store it out of the sun.

### Anchoring the Films

Polythene films are very light and easily blown about, so must be laid tightly over the hoops. It is something of an art to get a low tunnel nicely taut. The film must be anchored at both ends of the tunnel, and kept in place along the length of the tunnel. Secure the ends by one of the following methods:

* Bunch the ends of the film together and knot them around a stake, put into the soil at a 45° angle about 60cm (24in) beyond the last hoop. (See Pests and Diseases, diagram p.53.)

* Bury the ends into the soil.

* Weight the ends with stones or heavy pieces of wood. (See Pests and Diseases, p.53.)

Several methods are used for keeping the film in place along its length, the method depending on the type of hoop.

* Earth one side in the soil. (Don't use this method if you are likely to want access from both sides.)

* Tie strings to each side of the hoop over the top of the tunnel. (To do this hoops must have an eye at ground level.) Tie the string on one side with a permanent knot, throw it over the tunnel, and attach it to the far side with a knot that can be undone easily. This will make moving the tunnel a quicker and easier operation, which is especially valuable in cold, finger-numbing weather. The strings can be left permanently attached to the hoops. (Fine wire can be used instead of string if preferred.)

* Roll edges of film around pipes laid on the ground beside tunnel. Some patented systems use a neat clip to hold the film tight around the pipes.

* Anchor the film with some kind of weight, such as wooden boards, piping, or small polythene bags filled with sand or soil.

Spare hoops can be put over the top when extra security is needed.

**Ventilation and Operations**

One of the advantages of low tunnels over cloches is that the film is easily pushed up on one or both sides for watering, cultivation, picking and ventilation. Ventilation is often necessary in late spring and summer when a humid, close atmosphere, which would encourage disease, builds up under the films. Keep the film in place with clothes pegs clipped to the hoops, or, where extra strings or fine wire is used to secure the film, bunch it up between them and the hoop (see diagram p.115).

**Use of Low Tunnels**

Low tunnels are used for the same purposes as cloches, although they are probably most useful in winter and spring. In Spain and Italy low tunnels are widely used in spring for early plantings of melons and tomatoes. 'Portholes' are cut at regular intervals along their length for ventilation. Like cloches, tunnels are useful inside greenhouses and walk-in polytunnels for bringing on salad crops, and for early plantings of indoor tomatoes.

Where tunnels are used outdoors in winter, snow should be brushed

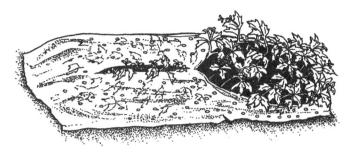

*Growing tomatoes under perforated film (see Tomatoes p.212)*

off to prevent the film sagging onto crops as this could damage them. Where the plants are robust, leave some snow on to act as insulation.

## GARDEN FRAMES

The garden frame is virtually a bottomless box with a sloping lid or roof – a halfway house between a cloche and a greenhouse. More substantial than a cloche, it is more permanent and offers more protection from frost, but is less mobile and flexible in use. Frames were once built over hotbeds of fermenting manure and were extensively used for forcing early salads. Today they are sometimes heated with electric cables in the soil.

### Types of Frame

Frames can be portable or permanent, lean-to or free-standing, single or double span. The sides of permanent frames were traditionally made of brick, concrete or wood. Portable frames which are more common today have timber, galvanized steel or aluminium frames, the sides often constructed with transparent materials such as glass, any rigid or semi–rigid material (see Materials p.107) or of film. (Use heavy film, as recommended for polytunnels.) Frames made with glass or transparent sides let in maximum light, an important factor late and early in the year. An opaque-sided frame will generally have better insulation, but it should not be too deep, or seedlings and young plants will be drawn towards the light.

*Aluminium and glass frame*

The roof or lid, traditionally a glass 'light' in a wooden frame, can also be made of a range of modern materials. Some frames are hinged to open

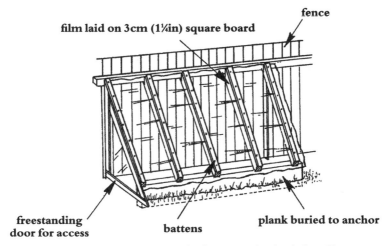

*Simple homemade lean-to garden frame covered with polythene film*

upwards, while others slide on or off sideways or forwards. These are all factors to consider when erecting a frame in a confined area. Where lids are made of lightweight material there should be some extra means of securing them in windy weather.

Frames are normally made lower at the front and higher at the back, to catch the maximum light, being sited, wherever possible, in a sunny position. For low-growing salads a height of 18cm (7in) in front and 23cm (9in) at the back is adequate. Taller crops such as cucumbers, self-blanching celery and melons would require deeper frames, say 45cm (18in) at the back and 30cm (12in) in front. A simple lean-to frame built against a wall to grow tomatoes would need to be at least 1.2m (4ft) high at the back, reaching down to ground level at the front (see diagram above).

Many people construct their own frames, usually made of wood coupled with glass or one of the other materials mentioned on the previous page. Most rigid and semi-rigid materials can be drilled and screwed to the frame bars; polythene film should be battened down, while glass is best fitted into 5cm sq (2in sq) glazing bars, dry glazed with sprigs to hold it in place.

### Siting and Managing Frames

Frames should generally be positioned in the open, never under trees or in the shade. As with cloches, work in plenty of well-rotted compost to make sure that the soil is fertile. Ventilation is an important factor: frames are relatively airtight and a muggy atmosphere encourages disease. Most frames are ventilated by propping the roof lights open (see diagram right) or sliding them back; in summer the lights can be removed completely. When watering, try to water the soil rather than the leaves of the plant, to minimize the risk of fungus diseases. Seed boxes in deep frames may have to be raised on upturned boxes or pots to prevent seedlings becoming too drawn.

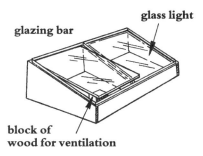

*Homemade garden frame with glass lights fitted into glazing bars*

### Use of Frames

In many ways frames are used like cloches, though they cannot be moved from one crop to another so readily. Being in the main more substantial than cloches, they are more suitable for providing frost-free protection in winter. Common uses include:

★ Raising plants in early spring in boxes, or *in situ* for transplanting.
★ Growing early salads.
★ Hardening-off.
★ Growing tender crops in summer.
★ Over-wintering mature lettuce and other hardy salads.
★ Over-wintering seedlings for spring planting.
★ Forcing and blanching chicories and endives during the winter, and forcing early roots of mint and seakale in spring.
★ Storing winter vegetables.
★ Maintaining a winter supply of parsley, mint and other herbs, by lifting mature roots in the autumn, and planting them in the frame.

### PERMANENT GREENHOUSES

A permanent, glazed greenhouse is a luxury, although in cold climates they are widely used in summer for growing tender vegetables such as tomatoes, cucumbers, peppers and aubergines. Cost aside, the major drawback to permanent structures is that where crops such as tomatoes are grown for several years consecutively in the same soil, the soil becomes 'sick' through a build up of pests and diseases. As a result crop failure becomes increasingly likely. The measures that can be taken to solve the problem are all tedious (see Pests and Diseases p.61).

One of the merits of walk-in polytunnels (see p.120), is that they can be moved to a fresh site every two or three years, to avoid soil sickness.

## Winter Use of Greenhouses

To me it is heartbreaking to see how many greenhouses, cleared of their summer crops, lie idle in winter when they could so easily be carpeted with winter salading. In all but very severe climates late-planted oriental greens, cut-and-come-again seedlings, and any of the winter salad vegetables suggested for cloches or frames, can be grown successfully in greenhouses during the winter months. (For detailed suggestions, see Use of Polytunnels p.122.) Sowing or planting can take place as soon as the summer crops are cleared – starting plants off earlier in boxes or pots if necessary. Anything remaining in spring can be sacrificed with very little loss when the time comes to plant the tender summer salad vegetables once again.

## WALK-IN POLYTUNNELS

Small 'walk-in' polytunnels, on the lines of those used by commercial growers, offer salad growers a viable and cheap alternative to a permanent greenhouse. Shaped like a giant, semi-circular cloche, they are essentially a frame of galvanized tubular hoops over which heavy polythene film is stretched. The hoops are sunk into foundation tubes knocked into the ground, and the film is anchored by laying the edges in a shallow trench, which is then filled in with soil.

The film lasts roughly three years, depending on the severity of climate and the quality of the film, and is cheaply and easily replaced when it becomes necessary. (For choice of film see Polythene Films p.108.) It is a relatively minor operation to put up a walk-in tunnel, or to dismantle it and move it to a new site, for example, if the soil develops soil sickness, or when the tunnel needs to be re-covered, or for any other reason that may arise.

The polytunnels available for amateurs at the time of writing are on average 2.4-3m (8-10ft) wide, nearly 2m (6½ft) high, and up to 10.5m (35ft) long. If longer than this they would require additional ventilation in the centre.

The main drawback with polytunnels is poor ventilation, as the basic models rarely have built-in windows, as would be the case with a greenhouse of a similar size. High temperatures and high humidity can easily build up under the film, encouraging pests and diseases. So in choosing a tunnel opt for maximum ventilation, if possible having a door at each end, with ventilation panels in the doors.

To make the most of a polytunnel, site it on good, well-drained soil, on as level a piece of ground as possible.

## Hints on Putting Up a Polytunnel

★ Put it up on a calm, warm day. Warmth makes the film supple, so enabling it to be pulled tighter. This helps to eliminate the slack points which flap in the wind, so leading to tears in the film.

★ Erect the hoops first. Before putting on the film, cover those sections of the hoops which will be in direct contact with the film with insulated anti-hot spot foam tape. This insulates the film at the most vulnerable points, and can prolong its life by at least a year. Alternatively paint the hoops with white reflecting paint.

★ Dig a 23-30cm (9-12in) deep trench around the outside, except where there will be doors.

★ Lay the edges of the film in the trench. It is easiest to tighten the film when it is weighted down, so cover the film by half filling the trench with soil. Then line helpers along the tunnel, each holding the outer edge of the film. Get everyone to heave together to remove any wrinkles in the film. Then fill in the rest of the trench.

★ Put in the doors according to the manufacturers' instructions. Insulate any rough corners, at the top of doors for example, by binding them with rags or tape.

## Managing a Polytunnel

★ Build up the soil fertility with plenty of organic matter. This will help to make the soil more moisture-retentive, an important point as soil dries out rapidly with the high temperatures reached under films. In my experience it is inadvisable to use farmyard manure, as it introduces pests which are normally destroyed when manure is used in the open.

★ Keep the plants mulched as much as possible, both to keep down weeds and to conserve moisture. I find straw mulches excellent under cover, as they encourage a good earthworm population. Various plastic film mulches, such as the black permeable mulches, are very effective in polytunnels (see Mulching p.47).

★ Repair tears in the film as soon as they develop, using the strong purpose-made tapes. Polythene film is much more rugged than it might seem, and can stand a surprising amount of patching.

★ Discolouring green algae may develop on the surface of the film, initially on the shadiest side. Sponge them off carefully; this is easiest to do when the film is wet.

★ In very hot conditions increase ventilation by cutting semi-circular dinner plate size 'portholes' along the side, 30-45cm (12-18in) or so above ground level. Leave the lower edge uncut, and tape it down securely on the inside to prevent flapping. They can be taped up again in winter if necessary.

* Crops in polytunnels (and greenhouses) obviously need far more watering than outdoor crops. Trickle hose and semi-automatic systems can be installed to lighten the load.

* Grow annual plants along the outer edge to soften the appearance. They need to be fairly robust, as the soil will sometimes be very dry, sometimes very wet. I have found pot marigolds, *Bellis perennis* and parsley among those which do well.

## Use of Polytunnels

*Spring*

* Early sowings in boxes or pots, both of salads for planting outside, and tender crops to be grown under cover.

* Catch crops of cut-and-come-again seedlings such as cutting lettuce, salad rocket, salad mustard, cress, salad rape, purslane, texsel greens, slow bolting cultivars of pak choi, oriental saladini, radish, sugar loaf chicory and curly endive.

* Late harvest of autumn planted salads, for example corn salad, land cress, sugar loaf and red chicories, oriental greens, winter lettuce and salad rocket.

*Summer*

* Grow tender summer salads to maturity. In temperate climates this would be an early crop, followed by an outdoor crop. In more severe climates it will be the only crop. Typical subjects: tomatoes, cucumbers, peppers, melons, basil, iceplant and summer purslane.

*Early autumn/winter*

* Dry bulbs and seed crops.

* Late plantings of oriental greens, winter lettuce, sugar loaf and red chicory, curly and broad-leaved endive, chrysanthemum greens and texsel greens. These will be cropped during winter and into spring.

* Late sowings of spinach, fenugreek, alfalfa, oriental saladini, and other cut-and-come-again salad crops which can also be sown in spring (see above).

* Protection of over-wintering seedlings that are intended for planting out in spring, for example early lettuce, red cabbage and biennial herbs such as clary sage.

## Miscellaneous Polythene Structures

Apart from purpose-made polytunnels, handy amateurs can easily build themselves 'mini' tunnels, or simple structures of a traditional greenhouse design, using polythene film and a timber or galvanized pipe framework. There are various easily assembled polythene structures on the market, falling into a category somewhere between a giant frame and a small greenhouse. All are useful for extending the salad season, and improving salad quality all the year round.

## CROP COVERS

The term 'crop covers' embraces various very light films which can be laid directly on a crop to give it protection. They are also known as floating mulches or floating films.

They have a certain 'elasticity' so within limits they expand over the crops as they grow, supported by them. They provide useful protection from wind and other elements, giving earlier, heavier and better quality crops, early and late in the year. They are invaluable where no other form of protected cropping is available. Buy UV treated films wherever possible to extend their useful life.

The introduction of these films is still relatively new, so salad growers should be prepared to experiment with them under their own conditions, trying them out on different salad crops. It is a rapidly developing field, so watch out for potentially useful new products.

## Types of Film Cover

The main types available at the time of writing are clear perforated polythene films, and the much softer fleecy films made from polypropylene combined with other compounds.

Characteristics of Clear Perforated Films

★ These very light films are either perforated with numerous small holes of 1.3cm (½in) diameter, or with myriads of tiny slits. The latter type is much more expensive, but more 'elastic'. Perforated films will last for two seasons if handled with care.

★ They offer very little protection against frost but the ground warms up rapidly beneath them. In sudden spells of hot weather temperatures can rise very high and be damaging.

★ They are relatively impervious to rain and irrigation, so if left on for too long the plants grown in them can become short of water, and may also be chafed and damaged.

* For every crop there is a critical point at which the film must be removed, either because of chafing or temperature rises. For this reason they are generally used in the first few weeks or months of growth.
* They are normally laid directly on the crop, but they can also be laid over low tunnel hoops, to cover taller crops such as tomatoes or peppers in their early stages.

Characteristics of Fleecy Films
* These spun fibre, 'non woven' films have a soft, cheese-cloth texture and drape easily over plants. 'Agryl P17' and 'P34', 'BASE UV17' and 'UV40', 'Agrifleece' and 'Reemay' are products available at the time of writing. They are made in various thicknesses, the higher the number (the weight in gms per sq m) the heavier and thicker the film. Those made with reinforced edges are longer lasting and more easily anchored.
* Fleecy films are more expensive than perforated clear films, but gentler in action, so there is less chafing of plants. Depending on the film, they can last several seasons if handled carefully.
* They are more permeable to air and water, so less subject to temperature fluctuations. The ground is less liable to dry out, and they can be watered from above.
* They give protection against several degrees of frost: the heavier the film, the greater the protection.
* They can be left on plants much longer than perforated films, sometimes until harvesting. They are especially recommended for early and late sown crops and over-wintering leafy crops. They improve growth and quality of the plants.
* They give protection against birds and flying insect pests such as aphids, cabbage root fly, carrot fly, flea beetle, butterflies and moths provided they are securely anchored at soil level with no gaps, and there are no holes in the fabric. Japanese radishes, for example, can be protected against cabbage root fly by covering them with fleecy films until shortly before lifting. Unless very hot weather is experienced, carrots can be grown under fleece until near maturity to protect them against carrot root fly.

**Managing Crop Covers**
* Prepare the soil very well. Film covers will not improve poor soil, though they help conserve the structure of the soil, especially during the winter months.
* Covers are most easily managed on gently mounded raised beds, where

they fit snugly over the surface.

★ Anchor the edges with any of the methods suggested for low tunnels (see pp.115-16), or with purpose-made pegs.

★ Make sure the ground is weed free before being covered, as weeds will flourish under covers and weeding is awkward once they are in place.

★ Lay the films over plants after planting. With perforated films allow a little slackness so the films can stretch. Fleecy films should be laid so they are fairly taut, but fold the edges of the film at the sides, so it can be released in stages as the crops grow.

★ Consider covers primarily as a means of *shortening the growing season* and improving quality. Except where heavy fleece films are being used, don't plant out much earlier than would otherwise be the case. Once planted, however, the crops will grow much faster than they would normally do in the open. Covers are an effective method of capitalizing on the advantages of early sites.

★ Watch plants carefully, and remove covers as soon as plant growth seems to be slowing down or the plants look stressed.

★ Growth under covers is rather soft, so plants must be 'weaned' carefully when the covers are removed, particularly with perforated films. Ideally remove covers towards the evening on still, overcast or damp days. Weaning can start by slitting the covers several days beforehand. First make intermittent slits along the cover, subsequently slitting along the entire length.

★ Water gently shortly after the covers are removed if the ground is dry, as will often be the case.

★ When the flowers appear, remove covers from insect pollinated crops such as tomatoes and courgettes.

## Main uses of Crop Covers
*Spring and early summer*
★ For the early stages of many vegetables, including salad potatoes, lettuce, tomatoes, beetroot, celery, spinach, cabbage, endive and other leafy salad crops. Fleecy films will give some protection against frost.
★ To grow radishes and carrots to maturity (under fleecy films only).

*Autumn and winter*
★ As extra protection for over-wintering lettuce, spring cabbage, late sowings of beetroot, spinach, radish, and cut-and-come-again seedlings
★ Emergency frost cover. If heavy frost is forecast drape fleecy films over outdoor crops or crops under cover as extra protection against frost.

# Chapter 11
# Siting and Planning

There are many approaches to planning a salad garden. Salads can be an integral part of the overall vegetable garden plan, which is usually based on a standard rotation system. Alternatively they can be fitted into a decorative vegetable garden scheme or 'potager'. For people with very small gardens intensively grown salads may be the only vegetables that are practical to grow. Space can be saved by intercropping, undercropping and growing in containers. Most gardens have difficult areas: among the many diverse salad plants, there is usually one to suit that awkward spot.

Planning a garden is a very personal business, based on the site and your needs. Here are some of the factors to consider when drawing up plans.

## ROTATION
Rotation is a traditional gardening practice, where closely related vegetables are grouped together, and grown in a different bed, or different part of the garden each year, generally over a three or four year cycle.

The reason for rotation is that some pests and diseases in the soil attack a range of plants within the same botanical group or family but no others. If the plants they attack are continually grown in the same place, the pests and diseases are likely to build up seriously. If, however, there is a break of several years when other crops are grown, they will decline and may disappear altogether.

In practice some of the more serious pests and diseases, clubroot and some nematodes (eelworm) for example, require a break of at least six or seven years to have any effect, and rotating over a six or seven year cycle is impractical in most small gardens. Even so, rotation is sound preventive medicine, helping to prevent pests and diseases reaching serious levels. Arranging the vegetable garden on the bed system rather than in large plots (see Soil Fertility pp.15-26), gives far more scope for working out a rotation system.

Rotation Guidelines
* As far as possible, rotate crops over at least a three or four year cycle; a five, six or seven year system would be even better.
* Never follow a crop with the same crop, or another from the same

group. Leave as long a gap as possible to minimize the possibility of that area of your garden developing pest or disease problems.

* Watch for any signs of pest or disease build up in the soil so that you can take action immediately.

The following are the most important plant groups from the rotation point of view:

*Brassica (crucifer) family* – Cabbage, cauliflower, kales, turnip, swede, radish, salad rape, mustard, texsel greens; all oriental brassicas; green manures such as mustard, salad rape, fodder radish.

*Legume family* – All peas and beans, including green manures such as alfalfa (lucerne), fenugreek, clovers.

*Onion family* – Onions, leeks, garlic, Chinese chives, shallots.

*Solanaceous family* – Potatoes, tomatoes, peppers, aubergines.

*Umbelliferous family* – Carrots, celery, parsley, parsnip.

Fewer problems arise with salad plants like lettuce or chicory, but where lettuces have been attacked by lettuce root aphids, avoid planting in the ground for at least a year.

### SALAD PLANTS USED DECORATIVELY

Very many salad plants are colourful, decorative, or have beautiful texture, and can be happily worked into a 'potager' or grown in flower beds and borders where they will blend in with purely decorative plants (see Introduction, pp.6-14). Make the most of these qualities when drawing up plans.

They can be used as edgings, or planted in small groups in the centre of a bed, or, where appropriate, grown as tall architectural plants at the back of a border. Remember that they generally need more fertile conditions and more moisture than flowers, so cater for this when growing them in flower beds.

In the summer months use red-leaved lettuces, iceplant, golden-leaved purslane, endives, fennel and the many pretty herbs. In the cooler months the best candidates for adding colour and attractive texture to the garden are ornamental cabbages and kales, hardy oriental greens, hardy chicories, and hardy herbs like salad burnet and chervil. Flowers such as borage, nasturtium, calendula (pot marigold), bergamot, pansies, violets, geraniums, chrysanthemums, roses, anchusa, and the flowers of herbs like rosemary, sage, lavender, ordinary and Chinese chives can all be used in salads and look beautiful growing. Salad plants with decorative features will be indicated in the chapters which follow.

127

## SALADS FOR PROBLEM SPOTS
If parts of the garden are too wet, too dry, or too shady for most vegetables, try the following salad plants in these places.

Light shade
Angelica, chickweed, chrysanthemum greens, chervil, cress, mitsuba, Hamburg and ordinary parsley, sorrel, and in summer lettuce, radish, and mangetout peas. Red lettuce tends to develop a deeper colour when grown in light shade.

Damp, heavy soil
Chickweed, chicories, hairy bitter cress, land cress, and celery and celeriac if the soil is reasonably fertile.

Dry soil
Nasturtiums, pickling onions, winter purslane, thyme and other Mediterranean herbs.

## ACCESSIBILITY
In winter especially, picking salads is much easier if they are near paths — one of many arguments in favour of narrow beds (see Soil Fertility, pp.21-5). Dwarf-growing winter salads, for example lamb's lettuce, salad burnet and land cress, can be used as edgings to paths or beds. It makes sense to grow the most commonly used herbs as near the kitchen as possible. In areas where snow is likely mark the ends of winter salad rows with a cane, so that they can be found if covered with snow!

## HARVESTING TIMES
Within the broad outline of the rotation system, try to grow fairly close together crops that will be sown or harvested at roughly the same time. This enables a piece of ground to be cleared at one go to make room for something else. Think in terms of spring-sown salads, summer crops, autumn crops, and hardy over-wintering crops. Setting aside small areas for a range of cut-and-come-again seedlings also seems to work well.

## INTERCROPPING AND CATCH CROPPING
As salad crops are among the fastest growing vegetables, they are particularly suited to intensive, space-saving techniques such as intercropping and catch cropping. *Intercropping* is when two (occasionally more) crops are grown together in the same piece of ground. Either one is fast and the

other slow maturing, or one is tall and the other dwarf or spreading; in this case the dwarf, spreading one *undercrops* the other.

*Catch cropping* is when a crop is sown in the gap between one long-term crop (such as winter brassicas) being cleared and another (such as peas or sweet corn) being sown or planted. No ground need ever be idle provided the 'window' is sufficient for a quick salad crop. Almost all the plants suggested below for intercropping are also suitable for catch cropping. For both intercropping and catch cropping raising plants in modules, so they are ready to plant as soon as required, is recommended (see Raising Plants 'Indoors' p.78).

## Suggestions for Intercropping

John Evelyn had a few suggestions for his gardener in the seventeenth-century: 'One may sow Reddish & Carrots together on the same bed: so as the first may be drawn, whilst the other is ready: or sow Lettuce, purselan, parsneps, carrots, Reddish on the same beds, & gather each kind in their season, leaving the parsneps to Winter . . .'

Here are a few twentieth-century ideas:

★ Between rows of slow-growing crops such as shallots, leeks, maincrop onions or maincrop carrots, sow radish, spring onions, cress, mustard, or any other cut-and-come-again seedlings; or plant small lettuces (such as 'Tom Thumb') or corn salad.

★ Between slow-growing widely-spaced crops such as brassicas, marrow, pumpkin, or between blocks of peas, dwarf beans or broad beans, sow and plant those plants mentioned above. If there is sufficient space plant larger plants, for example salad rocket, medium-sized lettuce, pak choi, mizuna and chrysanthemum greens. Remove the salad crop as soon as the ground is needed by the slower growing plant. It may only be possible to get one cut from CCA seedlings.

★ When climbing marrows, cucumbers or beans are grown on tripods or trained up tall canes cut-and-come-again seedlings and radish can be sown, and lettuce, corn salad, chrysanthemum greens planted, on the ground between them in the early stages. The latter will have matured, or can be cleared, before the ground is shaded by the climbing plant.

★ Under sweet corn sow or plant any of the salad plants suggested above. Mature sweet corn only shades the ground lightly, so the salad plants may be left for their full term if kept well watered. Trailing plants such as gherkins and marrows can be grown among sweet corn, as can courgettes and dwarf beans. Mizuna greens grow very well beneath sweet corn.

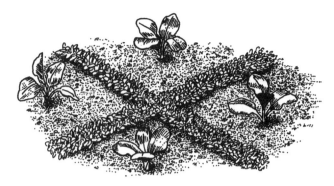

*Intercropping: bands of CCA seedlings sown between young brassicas*

* Mix carrot and pak choi seed in a ratio of 2:1 and sow them together in a patch. Cut the pak choi young; the carrots will continue developing among them and can be pulled in due course.
* Mix carrot seed with the seed of flowering annuals such as love-in-a-mist, cornflower, larkspur and flax and sow them as above in a flower border or decorative vegetable bed. While the annuals are flowering the carrots will develop, and can be pulled as ready. This method seems to ward off carrot fly.
* Station-sow between the slow growing crops (see Seed, Sowing Outdoors, and Planting p.70). Radish, small lettuce, spring onions, salad rocket, small pak choi are all suitable salad plants for sowing between the

*Interplanting sweet corn with lettuce: the two crops are planted together*

*Mature crops of sweet corn interplanted with lettuce*

'stations' of slow-maturing crops like parsnip, salsify, scorzonera. The secondary crop must mature and be cleared before the main crop has grown to occupy the space.

## GROWING IN CONTAINERS

Where gardening is restricted to balconies, patios, roofs and window ledges people display enormous ingenuity in growing vegetables in a variety of containers, ranging from pots and barrels to window boxes and the patented 'growing-bags'. Many of the fast growing and less demanding salad plants, of which cut-and-come-again seedlings and edible flowers are prime examples, are ideal for containers.

Below are a few general guidelines to choosing and using containers (see Further Reading p.251).

★ As containers dry out rapidly and the soil soon becomes exhausted, the larger the container the better. For vegetables such as ornamental cabbage they should be about 20cm (8in) wide and deep. Small herbs could be grown in 10cm (4in) pots.

★ Make sure there are good drainage holes in the bottom of the container you are using.

★ Most ordinary garden soil becomes very compacted in containers, so fill them with good potting compost, mixing in plenty of organic matter (see Raising Plants 'Indoors' pp.79-80).

★ Always keep plants well watered and apply liquid feed regularly.

★ Keep the plants well mulched.

★ Place the containers out of wind and draughts.

### Follow-on Crops in 'Growing-Bags'

The various 'growing-bags' on the market are generally used for large plants such as tomatoes, peppers, cucumbers or courgettes. At the end of the season there is usually enough fertilizer residue in the bag for a late crop of a quick growing or undemanding salad crop, such as cut-and-come-again seedlings, salad rocket, corn salad, summer or winter purslane. If necessary add a liquid feed to grow a slightly hungrier crop such as winter lettuce, sugar loaf chicory, pak choi or mizuna greens for use during the winter and spring months. Put the bags in a sheltered position, preferably in a greenhouse or frame. Used bags are also handy for raising seedlings in spring.

# Chapter 12
# Salad Vegetables

Now for the many plants which can be used in salads, starting with what are recognizably salad vegetables – some well-known, like lettuce and radish, and some less well-known, like the chicories and oriental greens.

In practice it is hard to draw the line between vegetables that are mainly eaten raw in salads and the many dual-purpose vegetables, beans, potatoes, asparagus to name a few, which although primarily grown for cooking and eating hot, are also excellent as cooked, cold salads. It's curious how the distinctive flavour of root vegetables like parsnips, and the delicate flavours of sprouting broccoli and Chinese broccoli, are brought out when they are cooked and then eaten cold. As these vegetables are widely grown, they will only be covered briefly in Secondary Salad Vegetables pp.216-21. For further reading on their cultivation, see p.251.

Space will be given instead to the many unusual and less known plants that can find their way into salads – the weeds and wild plants our ancestors gathered, the edible flowers which add such colour and drama, and the many herbs which, deftly used, make each salad unique.

As I mentioned in the introduction, seed supplies of the more unusual salad plants have improved enormously in the English speaking world in the last 15-20 years, largely through a handful of very enterprizing and dedicated seed growers and suppliers. Unfortunately for those of us within the European Union, bureaucratic seed legislation is leading to the loss of some old, and often excellent varieties of established vegetables. If they are not in demand by *commercial* growers, and no-one is prepared to bear the costs of having them 'listed', they can no longer be sold. It is more than likely that varieties I would recommend will be withdrawn from the 'Common Catalogue' – the list of varieties that can be offered for sale in the EU. Partly for this reason, I will only recommend a few varieties with exceptional qualities.

I must point out that 'varieties' should now be called 'cultivars' (abbreviated to cvs) – the correct term for 'varieties raised in cultivation'. Old habits die hard, but I'll try to adopt this practice from now on! Another recent innovation from the nomenclature experts is to subdivide the very large groups, such as the 'Brassica' tribe, into several smaller, closely related 'Groups' – hence the word 'Group' after some Latin names.

So far the EU list only applies to cultivars of the main vegetables. The threat to more unusual items lies mainly in economic pressures. If demand is insufficient to justify their production, they too may become hard to obtain. It is up to us salad lovers to exert as much pressure as we can on the powers that be, to halt and reverse this trend. The bodies fighting to conserve our seed heritage deserve all the support we can give them.

My personal observations on sowing, planting and harvesting the salad plants covered in this book are based on my experience in East Anglia – an area with fairly cold winters and relatively warm and dry summers (rainfall roughly 500mm (20in) a year). In the *average* winter minimum temperatures go down to about -7°C (20°F), but this is rarely maintained for more than about a week. Vegetables like chards, spinach and spring cabbage normally survive winter in the open. The average mean temperature in the hottest month of the year (generally mid-summer) is roughly 15°C (59°F). I rarely risk planting tender vegetables like French beans, peppers or courgettes outside until early summer. In what follows *temperate* indicates a climate much like the one described above, *warm* would indicate an area with longer, hotter summers and milder winters, while *severe* would indicate a climate with much cooler winters where few or no vegetables survive in the open. I hope these generalizations will enable gardeners in different climates to adapt the information in the book.

I have concentrated on growing plants outdoors in the vegetable garden or in cold greenhouses, as few of us can afford the luxury of heated greenhouses for salads. Wherever cold greenhouses are mentioned, frames or cloches could also be used, but are, of course, less efficient. I have also assumed that salad plants are being grown at equidistant spacing. So unless stated to the contrary, where the advice is to thin or plant say 10cm (4in) apart, the rows would also be 10cm (4in) apart.

The chapters that follow are written almost in note form, to save space and to make reference easier. When I started growing vegetables I was always rushing indoors to look things up, fingers dirty, guiltily tiptoeing over carpets in muddy boots . . . and I remember being very irritated if I had to wade through long paragraphs to extract the information I needed. So this is an attempt to overcome the 'information retrieval' problem!

Lastly, a reminder of the value of keeping your own records. I find that hardly a day goes by without my looking up previous records to see what I sowed, when and where, and what the results were.

In the following pages CCA = cut-and-come-again; see pp.85-9.
For seed sprouting techniques see pp. 96-104.

| | |
|---|---|
| JANUARY    *MID-WINTER* | JULY    *MID SUMMER* |
| FEBRUARY    *LATE WINTER* | AUGUST    *LATE SUMMER* |
| MARCH    *EARLY SPRING* | SEPTEMBER    *EARLY AUTUMN* |
| APRIL    *MID-SPRING* | OCTOBER    *MID-AUTUMN* |
| MAY    *LATE SPRING* | NOVEMBER    *LATE AUTUMN* |
| JUNE    *EARLY SUMMER* | DECEMBER    *EARLY WINTER* |

## ABYSSINIAN MUSTARD (*see* Texsel Greens)

## ALFALFA Lucerne or Purple Medick *Medicago sativa*

Fast-growing, evergreen, hardy perennial legume with decorative spikes of blue and violet flowers. Deep-rooted plants, growing over 1m (3½ft) high. Traditionally used as green manure and animal fodder plant, but highly nutritious for humans. Can grow as a perennial, as CCA seedlings, as sprouted seeds or seed sprouts.

### Soil and Situation

Grows in any soil; tolerates extremely dry conditions. Can grow as low hedge dividing garden into sections.

### Cultivation

As a perennial: best sown *in situ* in spring and late summer to autumn; thin to 25cm (10in) apart. Cut young shoots for salads. Cut back hard annually after flowering (unless seed required). Renew every three or four years or becomes straggly. For CCA seedlings: sow wide drills spring or late summer. Make final sowing autumn, under cover, for winter use. Sprouted seed: ready within two days. Seedling sprouts: can grow in dark or light, or start in dark, move to light after two days. Ready in four to six days. Eat from about 1.3–4cm (½–1½in) long, when green seed leaves appear.

### Use in Salads and Cooking

Tips of young shoots used raw in salads almost all year. (Older leaves may be coarse.) In China young shoots cooked lightly and mixed into dishes.

## AMARANTHUS (*see* Secondary Salad Vegetables)

## AMERICAN CRESS (*see* Cress, Land)

**ARTICHOKE, CHINESE** *Stachys affinis*
Perennial plant in mint family, about 45cm (18in) high, producing ridged, white, shiny tubers up to 5cm (2in) long. Roots fairly hardy; but tops frost sensitive.

**Soil and Situation**
Does best in open site on rich light soil; must not be allowed to dry out in summer. Useful ground-cover plant.

**Cultivation**
Plant tubers in spring, upright, covered by at least 2.5cm (1in) of soil, or deeper on very light soils. (Can start indoors in seedtrays of moist peat, and plant out when sprouted.) Space tubers about 30cm (12in) apart. Earth up around stems when plants about 30cm (12in) high; keep mulched; liquid feed if growth poor. Cut back flowers in summer. Tubers ready five to seven months after planting. Best to lift as required as they dry out rapidly.

**Use in Salads and Cooking**
Delicious nutty flavour, crunchy texture. Scrub and use raw in salads; or scrub, steam, slip off skin and eat cooked and cold in salads.

**ARTICHOKE, GLOBE (***see*** Secondary Salad Vegetables)**

**ARTICHOKE, JERUSALEM (***see*** Secondary Salad Vegetables)**

**ASPARAGUS (***see*** Secondary Salad Vegetables)**

**AUBERGINE (***see*** Secondary Salad Vegetables)**

**BARLEY** *Hordeum vulgare*
Can be sprouted, but may be difficult to obtain untreated seed. Sprouts easily in jar. Normally ready within three to five days. Wispy roots appear first. Eat shoots when very tiny or they may become bitter.

**BASELLA (***see*** Secondary Salad Vegetables)**

**BEANS, general use in salads (***see*** Secondary Salad Vegetables)**

**BEANS, for sprouting**
Azuki *Phaseolus angularis* Best sprouted at 30°C (86°F). Takes four to

eight days. Rinse frequently. Eat when 1.3-2.5cm (½-1in) long.

Mung *Phaseolus aureus* Best sprouted in dark; ideal temperature 20°C (68°F). Ready in three to six days. Eat when 5-7.5cm (2-3in) long.

Soya *Glycine max* Best sprouted in dark at temperature of 21-25°C (70-77°F). Takes four to eight days to sprout. Eat from just over 1.3-7.5cm (½-3in) long (see also Seed Sprouting and Seedling Sprouts pp.101-5).

**BEETROOT (*see* Secondary Salad Vegetables)**

**BRASSICAS, Crucifers *Brassica* sp.**
*(see under individual crops)*
**Seedling Sprouts**
Any of the brassicas – cabbage, cauliflower, kales, oriental greens – can be sprouted. Seed sprouts generally ready within three days. Use when 1.3-2.5cm (½-1in) high. Seedling sprouts excellent value; ready within a week. Use up to 5cm (2in) high. Flavour ranges from mild (Chinese cabbage, turnip) to spicy (mustards).

**BROCCOLI, Purple Sprouting (*see* Secondary Salad Vegetables)**

**BROCCOLI, CHINESE (*see* Secondary Salad Vegetables)**

**BUCKWHEAT *Fagopyrum esculentum***
Useful fast growing green manure, but the seeds can be sprouted. Ready for use in two to four days; eat when 2-2.5cm (¾-1in) long.

**CABBAGE (*see* Secondary Salad Vegetables)**

**CABBAGE, CHINESE Chinese leaves, Napa cabbage *Brassica rapa* var. *pekinensis***
One of the most attractive brassicas for salads: mild flavoured, crisp texture, pretty leaves. Can grow up to 4.5kg (10lb) in weight. Some forms hearted, some loose-headed with lovely creamy centres. Colour ranges from delicate light green to deep green. Leaves often have broad white midribs, prominent white veins giving a marbled look, and frilled, wavy leaf margins. Extremely fast-maturing crop; ready six to twelve weeks from sowing. Main types: headed – compact hearts, either round barrel-shaped or long, narrow, and cylindrical very much like a large cos lettuce.

Loose-headed – much less compact; often pretty creamy centres.

## Soil and Situation

Likes rich, moisture-retentive soil, limed if acid. Work in plenty of organic matter. Has poor root system so dries out easily. Good 'follow on' crop after potatoes and early peas. Needs open situation. Don't over-crowd or may get rotting, especially in humid weather. In temperate and cold climates grows well under cover in autumn/early winter.

## Cultivation

Grows best in coolish weather: ideal temperature 12-20°C (54-68°F). Most useful as late summer/autumn crop. Mature plants tolerate light frost. Susceptible to same pests and diseases as western brassicas, especially slugs, flea beetle, caterpillars, cabbage root fly, clubroot. Take appropriate measures. Growing under fine nets recommended. Can be grown as headed crop, as semi-mature CCA, or as CCA seedlings.

Bolting: runs to seed rapidly if sown in 'long days' in spring/early summer in northern hemisphere, so transplanting best avoided unless raised in modules. When sown in spring/early summer tendency to bolt if weather unduly cold. Also prone to bolting in dry conditions.

Watering, feeding: Chinese cabbage needs plenty of water and also nourishment to sustain its high growth rate. Water little and often to compensate for poor root system. Can give liquid feeds during growth: key times a month after planting and as head starts to develop. Plants respond well to being kept mulched.

Sowings

Headed crop: sow late spring/early summer until late summer. For first sowings use bolt-resistant cultivars; try to keep temperature above 10°C (50°F) during period between germination and planting out (generally between two to four weeks). Cover with fleecy films if necessary (see Protected Cropping pp.123-5). Sow *in situ* or in modules, finally spacing plants 30cm (12in) apart. Very upright cultivars can be planted closer. Late sowings can be planted under cover for early winter crop.

Semi-mature CCA crop: sow as above. Can also make an early autumn sowing for planting under cover for a winter crop. Plants can be treated as CCA both *after* cutting first head (see Harvesting and Storage p.138) and where they fail to develop a full head. Can also space late sown plants under cover about 13cm (5in) apart, for regular cutting when leaves no more than 8-10cm (3½-4in) high, keeping plants small. These cropped plants withstand far lower temperatures than mature plants. Very useful source of tender winter salading.

Seedling CCA crop: being cut young these succeed where a headed crop may bolt. Loose-headed cultivars most suitable. Sow *in situ* from spring (under cover in cool areas) to early autumn, making last sowings under cover.

### Harvesting and Storage

Headed types: harvest when they feel firm. Cut 2.5–5cm (1–2in) above ground level, leaving the stump to resprout. Heads can be stored for about two months in cold cellars; several weeks in fridge. Plants generally only withstand a light frost, but some cultivars are more frost-resistant than others. It can be protected with cloches or low film tunnels in late autumn to prolong the growing season and also to improve quality. May last well into mid-winter if the weather is mild. At end of season flowering shoots develop. Generally it is very sweet and mild flavoured. Use in salads at bud stage.

### Cultivars

Cultivars continually being improved. Watch catalogues for new introductions. Headed types: $F_1$ cultivars generally most productive. Use bolt-resistant barrel-shaped cultivars for earliest sowings; use cold resistant cylindrical types for latest sowings. Loose-headed type: 'Santo' cultivars well-known; 'Ruffles' typical of fluffy top types.

### Use in Salads and Cooking

Unique delicate fresh flavour and crisp texture, quite unlike western cabbage. Use leaves and leaf stalks finely shredded in salads; alternatively cook very lightly – steamed, stir-fried, or in soups. Makes some excellent quick pickles.

**CALABRESE (*see* Secondary Salad Vegetables)**

**CARDOON (*see* Secondary Salad Vegetables)**

**CARROTS (*see* Secondary Salad Vegetables)**

**CAULIFLOWER (*see* Secondary Salad Vegetables)**

**CELERIAC (*see* Secondary Salad Vegetables)**

**CELERY** *Apium graveolens* var. *dulce*

Biennial, traditional salad crop grown primarily for long leaf stalks, eaten raw or cooked. Foliage of some types used sparingly as salad herb. Essentially cool weather plants of variable hardiness. Types: trench celery – moderately hardy, white or pink/reddish stems, stems blanched artificially when growing. Characteristic flavour and crunchy texture. Self-blanching – more recently introduced, frost tender, yellow/off-white stems; grown closely spaced to induce some blanching but essentially eaten as they are. Considered less flavoured than trench celery, but easier to grow; good alternative for summer use. American green – green-stemmed, self-blanching type; good flavour, no blanching necessary. Cutting (wild, leaf, green, branched) celery – exceptionally hardy, bushy varieties from Europe for use in soup, for garnishing and for salads. (French: *céleri à couper, céleri vert*; Italian: *sedano da taglio*.)

### Soil and Situation
Marshy plants in origin; require very fertile, moisture-retentive soil, rich in organic matter, neutral or slightly alkaline. Peaty soils ideal.

### Cultivation
Seed sowing: celery germinates best in the light; sow shallowly or on soil surface covering lightly with sand.

Bolting: celery has tendency to bolt if seedlings subjected to temperatures below 10°C (50°F) for more than twelve hours. Don't sow early unless this minimum temperature can be maintained. Good hardening-off over about two weeks and a steady supply of moisture are important factors in preventing bolting.

Pests and diseases: celery fly/leaf miner – common pest. Tiny maggots tunnel into leaves leaving pencil-thin white trails and causing blisters. Can be serious. Never plant blistered seedlings; remove blisters on growing plants by hand; burn diseased foliage. Avoid planting near infected parsnips, or where infected parsnips/celery grown previous year. Can spray with pyrethrum or derris, or grow under fine nets. Leaf spot – often serious seed-borne disease. Chemically-treated seed available (but not recommended to organic gardeners). Don't save your own seed; clear up and burn all diseased foliage in autumn. Can spray several times with Bordeaux Mixture when spotted leaves first noticed. Slugs – very partial to celery; take precautions.

Water/feeding: all celery benefits from copious watering and regular liquid feeding during growing season.

Trench Celery
Sow on the surface in seedtrays or modules in early spring and keep at a gentle heat. Prick out if necessary, harden-off carefully, plant late spring/early summer. Easiest to blanch if planted in single rows spacing plants 30-45cm (12-18in) apart. On heavy soils plant on the flat and blanch with collars or by tying stems with brown paper or black film. On medium and light soils can plant in trench and blanch by earthing up. Ideally prepare trench previous autumn; make it at least 38cm (15in) wide by 30cm (12in) deep; work plenty of well-rotted manure or compost into bottom layer. Replace soil to within 8cm (3½in) of soil level, leaving surplus soil alongside for earthing up.

Blanching: start when stems about 30cm (12in) high, generally mid-summer. Where grown flat – tie purpose made collars, or 23cm (9in) strips of heavy lightproof paper or black polythene film around stems. Do in stages, leaving about one third of plant exposed. Tie fairly loosely so stems can enlarge. Earthing up in trenches – tie plants loosely with raffia to keep upright. Then draw up soil around stems about 8cm (3½in) at a time; repeat at least twice at two-week intervals until only tops exposed. Try to avoid soil falling into heart of celery plant.

Self-blanching and American Green Celery
Sow, prick out, harden-off, as for trench celery. Plant evenly spaced in block formation, plants 15-27cm (6-11in) apart. (Closer spacing gives slender hearts; wider spacing gives higher yields, good blanching.) With self-blanching celery put straw around outer plants for extra blanching.

Cutting Celery
Sow spring to late summer, in seedtrays or modules, in a seedbed or *in situ*. Thin or plant 23-30cm (9-12in) apart. Can plant closer initially, removing alternate plants progressively. Use throughout summer, winter and early spring. Can pot up single plants in large pot to bring indoors for convenience in winter; otherwise leave outside. Many cultivars survive -12°C (10°F). Self-seeds with abandon: just allow a few plants to run to seed in spring for next year's crop. The cultivar known as 'Parcel' has very beautiful, deeply curled, glossy leaves. It is decorative and well-flavoured for winter salads.

**Harvesting and Storage**
Discard outer stalks if coarse. Trench celery ready late autumn until heavy frost. Lift plant as required. Pink/red cultivars stand more frost than white

ones. Self-blanching celery ready mid–summer until first frost. Cut stems as required. Cut slender, leafy green celery stems all year round.

## Use in Salads and Cooking
Generally used as appetizer, dipping stalks into salt or olive oil. Chop stalks and tender leaves into mixed salads.

## CHARD, SWISS (*see* Spinach)

## THE CHICORY FAMILY *Cichorium intybus*
Large and variable family of perennial plants, generally cultivated as annuals. Grown since ancient times for roots, leaves, flowering shoots and flowers, for culinary and medicinal use. Unusual salad plants with unique qualities; especially useful in period from late summer to spring. Characteristic, somewhat bitter flavour: in salads often used blanched, or shredded very finely, to modify flavour. Red-leaved chicories wonderful source of winter colour.

Generally remarkably robust, disease-free and easy to grow. Strikingly decorative plants when flowering. Flowers can be used raw in salads or pickled (see Flowers in Salad p.233). Some forms almost unknown outside Italy; all deserve to be far better known; has been increased interest of late. Wild chicory native in Europe and Asia, now naturalized in North America. (See also Wild Chicory p.147.)

Chicories can be grouped arbitrarily according to the part eaten. In practice groups overlap and within each group there are many cultivars, with varying degrees of hardiness. For characteristics/cultivation of new cultivars be guided as far as possible by information on packets.

Main types: green leafy chicories including 'Grumolo', 'Spadona', 'Sugar Loaf' and various 'cutting' and wild chicories. Red-leafed chicories, outside Italy, are now widely known as 'radicchio'. Root chicories including types that are grown for edible root and 'Witloof' chicory grown for forced chicons. 'Catalogna' chicories grown for young shoots or *puntarelle* (see Secondary Salad Vegetables pp.218-19). Italian general names for chicory family: *cicoria, radicchio.*

Seed availability: the less common chicories are still very hard to obtain outside Italy. Travellers in Italy should buy seed whenever the opportunity presents itself. 'Misuglio' is an extremely colourful, attractive mixture of green, red and wild leaf chicories. Highly recommended. It produces very colourful patches in winter in temperate climates (see Salad Techniques p.87).

CATALOGNA CHICORY (*see* **Secondary Salad Vegetables**)

GRUMOLO CHICORY
Exceptionally hardy plant. Survives abominable winter weather to produce beautiful, ground-hugging rosette of smooth, rounded, jade-like leaves in spring. It is like a green rosebud at ground level. In spring and summer plants looser and taller; rosettes form in autumn and winter. Widely grown in Northern Italy. Flowers edible (see Flowers in Salad p.233).

**Soil and Situation**
Said to do best on light, well-worked, well-manured soils; but I have grown it successfully on very heavy, weed-infested, waterlogged clay! A patch sown in a derelict corner of the garden could well be left to perpetuate itself. Also lends itself to intercropping, for example sown between sweet corn or winter brassicas.

**Cultivation**
Traditionally sown broadcast as thinly as possible; alternatively sow the seeds thinly in wide drills (see Seed, Sowing Outdoors and Planting p.71), or rows 15cm (6in) apart. Summer sowings are traditionally covered lightly with straw or sacking until the seedlings have germinated; fleecy films are an excellent modern substitute. Mid-summer crop should be lightly shaded in hot areas. Protect the seedlings, young plants and winter crops from birds. Thin to 10-13cm (4-5in) apart in autumn if the plants seem to be on top of one another.

Main Sowings
Spring outdoors: once or twice during summer cut off young leaves when about 5cm (2in) high for use in salads or for chickens or rabbits. This encourages the formation of the rosette. Leave plants from autumn onwards. Use late winter, early spring. Mid- to late summer outdoors: for use mainly in following spring. Late summer outdoors: cover with low tunnels or cloches in late autumn for tender, very early crop. Early autumn under cover: for very tender, early crop. Although 'Grumolo' chicory very hardy and plants can be picked from under snow, protection encourages earlier, faster, renewed growth in spring.

**Harvesting**
Cut rosettes just above ground level; plants regrow several times, but leaf

formation never again quite as perfect as original rosette. Later leaves tend to be larger and coarser, but still useable. Plants finally throw up flowering stems over 2m (6½ft) high covered with spikes of pale blue flowers. Either uproot at this stage if ground required, or leave a few for decorative value or to seed themselves. The leaves on the flowering stems are bitter, but can be fed to hens and rabbits.

## Cultivars
Dark and light green forms. Known under many local names in Italy, for example *cicoria grumolo verde, ceriolo, sciroeu, cicorietta*. 'Dark forms' – *scuro*, light forms – *bionda*.

## Use in Salads
Flavour bitter to many palates, but compensated by freshness of appearance. Blends well with milder plants. Very useful late autumn, winter and early in the year. Use small rosette leaves whole; larger leaves shredded.

### RED CHICORY
Large group of low growing relatively hardy plants grown widely in Italy, mainly for use in late summer and winter. Have become known outside Italy as *radicchio*. Characterized by colourful pink, red, and bronze leaves often with creamy, white and yellow variegation. With old cultivars leaves green in early stages, only becoming coloured with onset of low night temperatures in early autumn. Modern cultivars selected for ability to develop colour much earlier in season. Onset of colour associated with leaves turning in to form dense tightly packed nugget-like heart with paler, crisper, sweeter, very attractive leaves. (Heart formation said to be protective mechanism against cold weather.) With good modern cultivars heart develops earlier and more consistently than in the past, when hearting was a lottery – many plants remaining loose-leaved. The very hardy, loose-leafed 'Treviso' type doesn't form a heart, but the upright, pointed leaves develop brilliant colour in winter.

Red chicory cultivars vary in hardiness, from those tolerating only mild frost to the very hardy 'Treviso'. Judging from the seed samples I sent to Taiwan, red chicories can be grown in warm climates in the cool season. Chicory has intriguing bitterness, mollified by shredding the leaves, by blanching, and probably on exposure to cooler temperatures. Inner leaves sweeter than outer ones and therefore preferable in salads. Some 'Verona' and 'Treviso' cultivars can be forced and blanched like 'Witloof'. Resulting chicons beautiful – mainly white tinged with red or pink.

'Treviso' chicons particularly elegant. All cultivars can also be grown as CCA seedling crops.

## Soil and Situation
Does best in fertile, moisture-retentive soil, but adaptable to different climates, tolerating wet and dry conditions. Grows well partially shaded by other crops. Can be grown under cover from autumn to spring.

## Cultivation
Traditionally broadcast, eventually thinning plants to 23-30cm (9-12in) apart if necessary. In practice patches often seem to thin themselves out! Can also sow in seed boxes or modules and transplant. When transplanting, leaves may be trimmed back to within 8-10cm (3½-4in) of base to encourage rapid regrowth. (Another traditional practice.) Average spacing for modern cultivars 25-35cm (10-14in) apart. Relatively pest and disease free, but may need to protect against slugs and birds. Aphid attacks may occur under cover in warm weather. Plants sometimes rot: remove affected leaves and they may recover.

Main Sowings
Headed chicory. Summer crop: sow mid- to late spring, using suitable early cultivars or plants may bolt prematurely. Can protect with perforated films or fleece in early stages to encourage growth. Main autumn/early winter crop: sow early/mid-summer. Some of these plants will survive outside until following spring. Winter crop under cover: sow mid-/late summer, transplant under cover or cover *in situ* late summer/early autumn. Should provide pickings all winter.

CCA seedlings: sow *in situ* late spring to late summer. Leave hardy cultivars for cutting in winter when leaves most coloured. Patches can be thinned allowing a few plants to heart up (see Sugar Loaf Chicory).

Winter Treatment
In late autumn protect remaining outdoor plants, either by covering with cloches or low tunnels, or with light cover of straw, bracken, or even dried leaves. This sometimes entices vermin, but seems to preserve quality of plants. Plants often withstand snow well, but rotting more likely if exposed to heavy winter rain. Plants under cover should be kept well watered in dry weather or may suffer from tipburn at leaf edges.

Both 'Verona' and 'Treviso' cultivars can be lifted in succession for forcing and blanching in same way as 'Witloof' chicory (see Salad

Techniques pp.89-94). This produces attractive, sweeter leaves, but plants useable without forcing.

**Harvesting**
Cut heads leaving 2.5cm (1in) or so above ground level. Stumps resprout to give succession of small red leaves for use in salads – often until late spring/early summer following season. Can leave a few plants to run to seed in late spring/early summer for use of flowers (see p.233).

**Cultivars**
Many new cultivars and improved strains of old cultivars are frequently being introduced. Watch out for them in the gardening press. $F_1$ hybrids particularly productive. Recommended – 'Cesare', 'Medusa $F_1$' (cropping early to mid-season); 'Rubello $F_1$' (mid- to late season). Hearting variable with traditional cultivars, for example 'Rossa Verona', 'Castelfranco' (highly variegated).

**Use in Salads and Cooking**
Leaves used whole or shredded in salad, in Italy, often with oil, vinegar and salt. Popular garnish; adds striking colour to salads. Flavour changes subtly and delicately when cooked, for example grilled, in soups, in rice dishes. Small pieces of root sometimes eaten with heads of the plants.

ROOT CHICORY
Hardy chicories with very large roots, some of which are ground, dried and roasted as coffee additive or substitute. Roots well-flavoured, used in winter grated raw, sliced or finely chopped in salads. Sow *in situ* late spring/early summer. Thin to 15-20cm (6-8in) apart. Lift as required during winter. Best known traditional cultivars: 'Magdeburg', 'Soncino'.

SPADONA CHICORY **Sword, Dog's Tongue**
An extremely hardy, robust chicory, comparable to grumolo chicory, but producing narrow bladed leaves rather than a rosette. Grow as grumolo; it will stand frequent cutting. In Italy widely used for hens and rabbits during the summer, then for human consumption in colder months when leaves more tender.

SUGAR LOAF CHICORY
Pale green chicories, eventually forming tightly folded conical heads, in which inner leaves become naturally blanched. This makes them sweeter

than most chicories, although still sharper than lettuce. Underrated salad plant, with attractive, refreshing crispness, flavour and appearance. Recent experience indicates it has better drought tolerance than most leafy salads, possibly because of deep root typical of chicories. In past considered only slightly frost hardy; newer cultivars seem to have greatly improved frost resistance. Versatile plant, can be cut at any stage. Grown for heads, for CCA at semi-mature stage, and CCA seedlings. Various 'cutting' chicories probably types of sugar loaf and/or closely related; grown mainly as CCA seedlings.

**Soil and Situation**
Does best on fertile, moisture-retentive soil. CCA seedling crops require high fertility if being cut frequently.

**Cultivation**
Headed crop originally grown mainly for autumn/early winter supply; lifted and stored before severe weather. Improved modern cultivars survive much lower temperatures, can be used fresh over longer period. Sow *in situ*, or in seedtrays or modules, thinning or planting 25-30cm (10-12in) apart. For CCA seedlings see below.

Main Sowings
Headed crop: spring/early summer for early crop maturing summer (only some cultivars suitable); early/mid-summer so heads can form by autumn; late summer – in which case heads may form in autumn, but will otherwise form following spring if protected. Can transplant under cover in early autumn; or cover *in situ* with cloches, film, or straw in late autumn. Can also be treated as semi-mature CCA (see Salad Techniques p.87). Note: Immature and 'cut back' plants withstand temperatures several degrees lower than mature, headed plants. For best value recommend sowing as CCA seedling crop, then thinning to allow some plants to develop heads (see below).

CCA seedlings: sow late winter/early spring to late autumn/early winter, making first and last sowings under cover using hardiest cultivars. Sow in succession if continuous supply of fresh young leaves required. Cut seedlings and young leaves at ground level, generally at about 15-day intervals. Regrowth is very rapid. Continue cutting as CCA seedlings over several months as long as leaves tender; then thin remaining plants to 25cm (10in) apart, leaving to heart up. In summer keep well watered, and unless soil very rich in organic matter, give occasional liquid feeds.

(Nitrogen requirements very high.) Early protected spring crop can be excellent source of rapidly-growing, fresh salad when salad usually scarce.

### Harvesting and Storage
Headed: always cut heads across neck about 4cm (1½in) above ground level and leave to resprout. If kept cropped some new leaves will be produced over several months; sometimes productive almost all the year round. Late autumn/winter crop may begin to rot, especially when subjected to prolonged cold and wet weather; remove rotting leaves but leave stump, as regeneration likely in spring.

Traditionally headed sugar loaf chicory was lifted before frost and stored outdoors in circular heaps about 1m (3½ft) high, with heads facing towards the centre. Heap was covered with straw. Also stored indoors in cellars and sheds. Less necessary with modern cultivars.

CCA seedlings: see Cultivation opposite and Salad Techniques p.85. Once beyond small leaf stage plant can be uprooted, or if ground not required for the season left in ground. Some sugar loaf types naturally form small heads in summer or autumn; in Italy such plants uprooted and eaten with small portion of the root. Coarser 'cutting' chicories can be fed to hens or rabbits.

### Cultivars
Typical traditional headed cultivars: 'Groenlof', 'Sugar Loaf'. New cultivar with good frost resistance: 'Jupiter'; reasonable frost tolerance: 'Poncho', 'Snowflake' ('Winter Fare'). Some round headed cultivars being developed. For CCA seedlings use above and traditional 'Trieste' (quite tender, fairly hardy) or 'Milan' (coarser, summer only). The various Italian 'cutting chicories' *cicoria/radicchio da taglio* are probably forms of sugar loaf chicory or closely related; can be grown as CCA seedlings.

### Use in Salads and Cooking
Use hearts cut into small pieces, shredded or as single leaves. Large leaves can be shredded or cooked like spinach. Use seedling leaves whole for salad. In Italy young spring leaves served with chopped hard boiled egg.

WILD CHICORY **Capucin's beard** *Barbe de Capucin*
Jagged leaved chicory with strong resemblance to dandelion. Grows wild but can be cultivated. Naturally bitter. Young leaves used raw in salads, often shredded to make less bitter. Mature plant can be blanched and used like dandelion. Top of root considered specially well flavoured.

147

Sow late spring/early summer *in situ*, thinning to about 15cm (6in) apart. In late summer can blanch by covering completely to exclude light or by any methods used for 'Witloof' chicory, for example earthing up *in situ*, by lifting and repotting or replanting under cover, or by the Belgian cellar method (see Salad Techniques p.94).

## WITLOOF **Belgian Chicory**

Root chicory originally grown as coffee substitute; roots now forced during the winter months to develop the white, pointed, leafbuds or 'chicons'. According to one account technique 'discovered' by a Belgian farmer throwing old chicory roots into a dark shed and finding the resulting growths tender. Surprisingly easy to grow. Hybrid cultivars developed for forcing commercially in plastic trays without a soil covering, are excellent for domestic use.

### Soil and Situation

Any reasonably fertile, but not freshly-manured soil; open site.

### Cultivation

Sow thinly *in situ* late spring/early summer. Germinates very easily. Thin to 23cm (9in) apart. Keep weeded and watered during summer so roots develop well.

Forcing

Lift plants for forcing from mid-autumn to early winter. Various methods of forcing can be used. For treatment prior to forcing, and for forcing *in situ*, in pots, in greenhouses and by the Belgian cellar method see Salad Techniques pp.92–4. For a method of forcing in pits or frames see below.

Forcing in pits or frames: plant trimmed roots side by side in frame or shallow pit. Cover with 2.5cm (1in) sifted soil; water gently so soil works between roots. Two days later cover with 20cm (8in) of light soil or sifted ashes. Cover this with layer of straw, and finally cover whole with black plastic or sheet of corrugated iron to ensure darkness and keep out rain.

### Cultivars

The $F_1$ hybrid cultivars are much more productive than traditional 'Witloof' cultivars.

### Use in Salads and Cooking

Chicons make excellent crunchy, delicately flavoured, very mildly bitter salad. In Holland sliced very finely and served with mayonnaise. Good eaten plain with cheese, or in mixed salad. Flavour subtly changed by cooking for example braised, in casseroles. When lifted for forcing paler inner leaves, which are trimmed off, can be used raw in salads, though fairly bitter.

**CHOY SUM (*see* Secondary Salad Vegetables)**

**CHRYSANTHEMUM GREENS (*see* Secondary Salad Vegetables)**

**CLOVER *Trifolium* spp.**
Seeds can be sprouted. Sprouting takes one to two days. Eat sprouts when very tiny, or when 2.5–5cm (1–2in) long. Seedling leaves edible. Many species can be used as excellent green manures (see Manure and Fertilizers p.33).

**CORN SALAD Lamb's lettuce, mâche, feldsalat *Valerianella locusta***
Low–growing, hardy annual, rarely more than 10cm (4in) high with small leaves. Fragile-looking, but extraordinarily robust. Found wild all over southern Europe; closely related species occur in North America. Cultivars more substantial than wild forms. Widely grown in western Europe; one of the most useful winter salad plants.

**Soil and Situation**
Undemanding crop; grows well on a wide range of soils, tolerating both fairly dry and fairly wet situations. Likes full sun, but can be grown in light shade in summer. It is an ideal plant for summer intersowing and intercropping. In Europe often broadcast on onion bed prior to onions being lifted. Shallow soil cultivation sufficient, but needs to be sown in firm soil.

**Cultivation**
Can be sown *in situ* or transplanted. Thin or plant to about 10cm (4in) apart. (Use thinnings in salad.) Can also be broadcast and treated as CCA seedling crop; Italians use tiny young leaves in salad. I personally find corn salad more productive when grown as single plants.

Germination can be slow in hot weather. After sowing cover beds with wet sacking, newspaper or fleecy films until seedlings are through. Can sow throughout the growing season. Sow early/mid-spring outdoors for late spring/early summer crop. This comes in at a very useful time; can sow or plant between early brassica plantings. Sow late spring to mid-summer outdoors for late summer/early autumn crop, though in hot weather summer sowings may run to seed rapidly. Sow late summer/early autumn outdoors for main autumn, winter and spring crop. Sow mid-autumn/early winter under cover in unheated greenhouses or other forms of protection for additional, good quality spring crop. This can be sown after summer greenhouse crops are cleared.

Quality and growth rate of early autumn outdoor sowings onwards improved by using crop covers (see Protected Cropping pp.123-5). Remove covers about ten days before harvesting. Although corn salad is very hardy, over-wintered outdoor plants are more tender and grow faster in spring if protected with cloches, low film tunnels, bracken in severe weather. Plants left in spring/early summer will seed themselves naturally.

**Harvesting**
Can start picking as soon as three to four leaves per plant. With more substantial plants, cut just above neck and leave to resprout. Leaves tend to become tougher once flowering starts; if flower spikes cut off plant may get a new lease of life. The young flowers are edible.

**Cultivars**
Two main types: large seeded – generally larger, floppier, narrow leaves, paler in colour; considered less hardy, more adapted to warm weather, more productive. Most suitable for summer sowings but can be sown throughout the growing season. Cultivars include 'Broad leaved English', 'Dutch large seeded', 'Italian large leaved', 'Valgros'. Small seeded/'green' – more compact, crisper, perkier, rosette-shaped, generally rounder, darker leaves; said to be hardier, better flavoured, more suited to late sowings. Cultivars include 'Coquille de Louviers', 'Verte D'Étampes', 'Verte de Cambrai', 'Vit'. In practice difference in hardiness and flavour between the two types may be exaggerated!

Variegated forms: occasionally found in European catalogues, and mentioned in old gardening books. One with mottled, white-marbled leaves; one with bright yellow central leaves – colour intensified in cold weather giving 'rather pretty effect'. (Have no personal first-hand experience.) French names: *mâche, doucette, boursette, salade de blé*. Italian: *dolcetta, valeriana, lattughella di campagna, songin, galinella*.

**Use in Salads and Cooking**
With several sowings can be available all the year, but most appreciated in

winter months when fresh lettuce scarce. Very mild flavour; some people adore, some find insipid. Soft, faintly buttery texture; blends well with other salad plants. Best when freshly picked.

**COURGETTE (*see* Secondary Salad Vegetables)**

**CRESS, GARDEN Peppercress *Lepidium sativum***
Hot-flavoured, delicate-leaved plant, of very ancient usage in salads. Early this century grown in huge quantities by London market gardeners in late winter and early spring under vines, and also in hotbeds and temporary frames.

Best known as a CCA seedling crop, and extremely useful very early and very late in the year, often grown on windowsills and in seedtrays. When sown in garden grows rapidly to height of 30–60cm (1–2ft) and useful over longer period.

**Soil and Situation**
Grows on any soil. Although high fertility unnecessary, needs reasonable fertility if many successive cuts being made. Does best on light, well-drained soil; lighten very heavy soil by working sand or potting compost into surface. Patches of cress very even in height and decorative when growing; look good in flower beds/decorative potagers, especially when intercropped. Good subject for sowing on spent growing bags.

**Cultivation**
For cultivation as seedling sprouts, see Seed Sprouting and Seedling Sprouts pp.96–104 and Mustard, black p.179. For CCA seedlings, sow outdoors from early spring to mid-autumn, sowing at fortnightly intervals for continuous supply of leaves. Can run to seed very rapidly in hot summer weather unless sown in light shade and kept watered. Sow under cover mid-autumn to late winter, providing temperature of 10°C (50°F) can be maintained. Secret of tender cress is fast growth, light soil and adequate moisture. Becomes too hot flavoured if grown in dry conditions, especially as it becomes older.

Sow in wide drills (see Sowing Outdoors p.71) or broadcast on surface fairly thickly, but seeds not touching. Cover by raking; water with rose on can. Cover with newspaper or plastic or fleecy film until germinated. Germinates normally in three to four days, but slower in winter.

In my experience, following sowings best 'value for money' with cress in temperate climate: 1. Late autumn sowing under cover. May get one or two cuts before winter sets in. Will remain dormant in mid-winter, but starts regrowing rapidly very early in the year. 2. Late winter/early spring sowing under cover. Provided soil reasonably fertile and kept watered will resprout at least five times before losing vigour. Can cut at almost any height from 4–15cm (1½–6in). (Patch sown in my cold greenhouse in early spring was cut five times in two and a half months – with one seaweed foliar feed to boost growth.)

Can also grow in boxes and seed pans in soil or spent compost. Quick method of resowing in boxes is to scrape off stalks after cutting, sprinkle with fresh soil, and resow on top of old crop. Same technique can be applied to cress sown outdoors in spring. (For 'mustard and cress' see Mustard, black p.179.)

**Harvesting**
Start cutting for use when seed leaves open and have turned green; this usually occurs within ten days of sowing. Cut with scissors just above ground level, and above lowest seed leaves. Then leave to resprout. Keep cutting at intervals until the stems have become hard or the plants have started to run to seed. It can be relatively easy to save seed (see Seed, Sowing Outdoors and Planting pp.65–6).

**Cultivars**
Standard cultivars: common, fine leaved/fine curled cress; various improved faster-germinating cultivars are now available. 'Broad-leaved' and 'Greek' cress: fairly distinct, very productive forms. Australian cress: maybe a lost cress; gold-leaved form sounds most distinctive and valuable if it could be found. Apparently it is rather like land cress in appearance but with more pointed leaves. French: *cresson alénois commun* (common cress), *à large feuille* (broad-leaved), *frisé* (curled) and *doré* (Australian gold-leaved form).

**Use in Salads**
Surprisingly sharp flavour adds spiciness to salads all year round.

CRESS, LAND **American land cress, Belle Isle Cress, Early winter cress, Upland cress (occasionally)** *Barbarea verna/B. praecox*
Very hardy, biennial plant, remaining green all through the winter months. Low growing until running to seed, when it can reach up to up to 60cm (2ft) high. Leaves deep green, shiny. Excellent substitute for watercress.

**Soil and Situation**
Tolerates wide range of soil and situation, including fairly wet soil, shady borders, but grows best in moisture-retentive soil rich in organic matter. Light shade an asset for summer crop. Easily grown as intercrop, or undercropping brassicas, sweet corn. Makes good winter edge for vegetable beds.

**Cultivation**
Sow *in situ*, or in seedtrays or modules for transplanting. Sow early spring to early summer for summer crop; sow mid- to late summer for autumn and over-wintering spring crop. Plant or thin to about 15cm (6in) apart. Can also sow in wide drills or broadcast on fertile soil for CCA seedling crop. Young plants may be attacked by flea beetle; control with derris or pyrethrum. Keep well watered, as plants may bolt prematurely in dry conditions. Land cress is best when grown fast. Naturally grows most vigorously in spring and autumn.

In early summer of second season plants run to seed. Leave a few and save the seed or allow them to seed themselves. Somewhat perversely, land cress may fail to germinate when you sow it, but will successfully 'self sow' itself – especially in summer months when germination often erratic. Seedlings easily transplanted if ground well watered. A few seedlings transplanted into greenhouse late autumn or early spring provide very useful early crops. If some left to seed under cover may produce lovely 'broadcast' crop of seedlings following spring. Cloches improve quality of outdoor winter crop and encourage early growth in spring.

**Harvesting**
Generally ready eight weeks after sowing, though seedlings ready sooner. Seedlings, leaves from the basal rosette, and leaves from stems of flowering plants can all be used; select the most tender. Can be available all the year round if sown twice a year.

**Cultivars**
I know of no named cultivars at present. French: *cresson de terre*.

**Use in Salads and Cooking**
Undoubtedly most useful in winter. Leaves can have slightly hard texture unless used young or grown under cover. Piquant flavour very similar to watercress; use in small quantities in salad or in mixtures calling for watercress. Can be cooked like watercress.

## CUCUMBER AND GHERKIN *Cucumis sativus*

Tender, normally climbing plants, grown for the crispy long fruits. Require warm conditions; minimum 10°C (50°F); ideal growing temperature 18-30°C (64-86°F). Will not tolerate frost. Types: greenhouse/frame/indoor – traditional long smooth European 'slicing' cucumber, grown in greenhouses or frames. Very vigorous climbers. Some shorter fruited 'mini' cultivars have been developed. Ridge/outdoor – far more rugged, disease resistant types, with cultivars that sprawl rather than climb. A few, non-climbing bush types introduced recently. Fruits short, prickly-skinned, 10-15cm (4-6in) long. Originally grown on ridges to give good drainage – hence the name. Group includes the short thin or stubby gherkins/pickling cucumbers, and the round 'apple', for example 'Crystal Apple', and 'lemon' cucumbers. Japanese hybrids – outstanding, relatively new type of ridge cucumber with excellent disease resistance and cultivars tolerant of cold and hot weather; fruits much smoother than traditional ridge cucumber, often over 30cm (12in) long. Developed for outdoor use but grow well under cover. All types of ridge cucumber are insect pollinated, so no need to remove male flowers, as was the case with traditional greenhouse cultivars to prevent pollination which makes the cucumbers bitter.

### Soil and Situation

Outdoor cucumbers must have warm site sheltered from wind; tolerate light shade in summer. In cool climates must grow in greenhouse or frames, but may require shading on sun facing side in summer. Diffused light, for example light that comes through opaque films, is excellent for indoor cucumbers. Roots need to ramble freely through highly organic, moisture-retentive, fairly fertile soil. Good drainage essential. Can be grown in large pots, boxes, or growing bags, indoors or outdoors, if root medium good. Very acid soils should be limed. Basically prepare ground by digging holes (or trenches) about 30cm (12in) deep, 45cm (18in) wide, filled with very well-rotted manure, compost or rotted straw. Cover with about 15-20cm (6-8in) good soil, to make slight mound.

### Cultivation

Traditional greenhouse cucumbers: require heated greenhouses in early stages at least to maintain minimum night temperature of 20°C (68°F). Also require high humidity. Careful pruning required as fruits mainly borne on secondary laterals. With older cultivars must remove the male flowers to prevent cross pollination which results in bitter, swollen fruit.

Suggest instead using modern all-female F$_1$ hybrid cultivars which bear fruit on main stem, and don't require flower removal. Careful ventilation and watering necessary to prevent diseases which are encouraged by the warm, humid conditions. Plants must be trained up supports. For detailed cultivation see general vegetable books in Further Reading p.251.

Traditional ridge and Japanese hybrid cucumbers: use methods below for growing indoors or for growing outside.

Plant Raising

Cucumbers need soil temperature of 20°C (68°F) to germinate. They don't transplant well unless raised in modules. Only sow *in situ* in warm soil. Only plant outside after all risk of frost is past.

In temperate climates sow indoors four to six weeks before planting out. Sow mid-spring, in gentle heat, in modules (see Raising Plants 'Indoors' pp.76-84). Sow seeds on their side about 2-2.5cm (¾-1in) deep. Sow seeds singly, or two to three seeds per module, removing weakest seedlings after germination. Seedlings generally grow fast once germinated. Transplant at three- to four-leaf stage. Generally plant indoors late spring/early summer. Plant outdoors early summer after hardening-off well. Advisable to protect with cloches, low covers or some shelter in early stages outdoors. Can sow outdoors *in situ* early summer. If necessary sow under cloches or individual jam jars for extra protection (see Seed, Sowing Outdoors and Planting pp.63-75).

Space plants 45cm (18in) apart if climbing; 90cm (3ft) apart if grown flat. Don't bury crown of plant. Planting on mound (see Soil and Situation opposite) ensures good drainage and also lessens risk of plants rotting off at neck just above the ground level. Mulch plants with thick layer of straw or well-rotted manure.

Supports

Gherkin plants normally not vigorous so can trail on ground; other types can be left to trail, but growth better and fruits cleaner if trained up supports. (The exception is naturally compact bush cultivars.) In greenhouse make simple framework by stretching wires across the greenhouse, spacing them about 30cm (1ft) apart, about 15cm (6in) from edge of greenhouse. (Follow contours of greenhouse from floor to roof ridge.) Train each plant up cane, string, or wire, attached at right angles to wire framework. Outdoors, erect any kind of strong frame, trellis or tepees from wire, bamboo or rigid net. Cucumbers largely self-clinging, but may need some tying, especially in early stages.

Training

Allow main stem to grow as high as space allows; nip out growing point when no more room to train main shoot upwards or horizontally. Train laterals along wire framework; stop them when becoming entangled with neighbouring plants, or if showing no signs of fruiting. Stop laterals on which fruits are borne two leaves beyond any fruits. New Japanese hybrids bear fruit prolifically on main stem; older types bear more on the secondary laterals.

Watering/feeding

Cucumbers need regular watering and feeding. Once fruits start to form can feed with weak liquid feed every watering; foliar feeding seems to be beneficial. When grown in greenhouses damp down plants and greenhouse with water, once or twice daily in hot weather. This creates a moist atmosphere which suits cucumbers and discourages red spider mite.

Production of cucumbers may decline in late summer after initial spurt. Remove all dead leaves and any surplus shoots which bear no signs of fruit; give foliar feed; top dress roots by covering with 5-8cm (2-3½in) of soil mixed with well-rotted compost. This treatment is often effective in stimulating further production which will usually continue until the onset of frost or low temperatures.

Pests and diseases

Cucumber family unfortunately prone to a fairly large number of pests and diseases. Good husbandry essential. Avoid planting in cold soil and cold weather; keep greenhouses/frames well ventilated, damp down as above when hot; shut up greenhouses/frames early in evening when nights cold. Many modern cultivars have good resistance to one or more diseases; use them where available. Slugs often serious in early stages.

Red spider mite – frequently a serious pest under glass in hot weather; leaves become speckled white on back, then 'rusty'. Remove and burn leaves. (For control see Pests and Diseases p.60.)

Cucumber mosaic virus – virus disease spread mainly by aphids; worst on outdoor crop. Leaves become mottled, yellow-green, growth stunted. Young plants often die but established plants may outgrow it though yields are lower. Only remedy is to uproot and burn plants. Try to control aphids earlier in season.

Mildew – powdery spots appear on leaves and eventually weaken plant seriously. Avoid by keeping plants well ventilated, well watered and by growing resistant cultivars.

**Harvesting and Storage**
Unheated indoor crop normally starts fruiting early summer; outdoor crop mid–summer. Ends rounded in mature cucumber, pointed in immature cucumber. Keep picking to encourage formation of further fruit; do not allow fruits to yellow on plant. If a whole cucumber is too much to use, slice in half on plant: end will callous over and keep well. Or grow half–sized 'mini–cucumber'. Pick gherkins at size required while still firm.

**Cultivars**
New cultivars being introduced constantly. For greenhouse types use all female hybrids with good disease resistance. Established Japanese F$_1$ hybrids include 'Burpless', 'Kyoto', 'Tokyo Slicer'. Mini–cucumber – 'F$_1$ Petita' (all-female greenhouse cucumber; can be grown successfully in cool greenhouse).

**Use in Salads and Cooking**
Use raw, sliced, peeled or unpeeled in salads. Can use to make soups. Gherkins mainly used for pickling but can be eaten raw. We have pickled ordinary small cucumbers, whole and sliced. Flowers can be used raw, fried in batter, or in soups (see Flowers in Salad p.231 and p.235).

**DANDELION** *Taraxacum officinale*
Perennial wild plant; selected, greatly improved forms of common dandelion have for centuries been widely cultivated in western Europe, especially France, for use primarily in autumn to early spring salads. Purists debate whether improved forms as well–flavoured as wild! Leaves either eaten green (most nutritious) or blanched (sweeter but less nutritious) or forced and blanched (generally to bring on earlier where winters severe). Roots and flowers also eaten. (For wild plant/flowers see Wild Plants and Weeds p.245.) In temperate climates leaves often remain green all winter, unless damaged by heavy frost.

**Soil and Situation**
Thrives on almost any soil and in any situation, other than waterlogged soil conditions.

**Cultivation**
Can be raised from root cuttings, but normally raised from seed. Sow early spring to early summer *in situ* or in seedbed. Thin or plant 35cm (14in) apart; dandelions best not overcrowded. Alternatively, can thin to

5cm (2in) between seedlings, so that a group of small plants can be blanched under one pot. Keep weed free – though there is a theory that dandelions left among weeds become naturally blanched. Can leave a permanent patch, but if so advisable to remove flowers before they seed to prevent seeding all over garden. Normally very healthy, but occasionally attacked by mildew.

Blanching and Forcing
If preferred blanched, use one of the following methods, ideally blanching a few plants in succession for a continuous supply. Blanching takes seven to fifteen days to complete. (For blanching guidelines see Salad Techniques p.89.)

Covering *in situ*: cover single plants or groups with pot or box, or row of plants with blackout frame. Do in autumn or winter (if plants still green), or in spring when fresh leaves appear. Growth can be accelerated by covering plants or pots with straw or dead leaves. After leaves cut, let them grow naturally for use the following autumn.

Earthing up *in situ*: (see Forcing 'Witloof' Chicory *In Situ* pp.93-4). Earth up plants in late autumn with spade. (Ample space must be left between rows where this method is used.) Cut plants across neck when ready, earth up again for second picking in spring. This method is believed by many to produce the best flavour.

Lifting methods: in cold climates dandelion plants are lifted mid-autumn onwards, and forced like 'Witloof' chicory (see pp.92-3). Can also be forced by the cellar method (see p.94). If cut carefully when ready, about 1.3cm (½in) above root, will resprout a second crop.

**Harvesting**
Green leaves generally used autumn onwards. Gather inner leaves as outer leaves are tough.

**Cultivars**
Most improved cultivars French in origin, for example 'Amélioré Géant' – large-leaved, succulent, productive, upright form, good for forcing. 'Vert de Montmagny Amélioré' – withstands damp well; good for use all winter. 'A Coeur Plein Amélioré' – neat compact almost self-blanching cultivar for winter use. French name: *pissenlit*.

**Use in Salads and Cooking**
All parts have culinary use, from flowers to roots. Most valuable from late

autumn to late spring. Raw leaves, especially lower parts, make very tasty, succulent salad. Leaves also cooked like spinach and used in many recipes. Roots can be trimmed, scrubbed and used raw.

### ENDIVE *Cichorium endivia*

Attractive, vigorous, crisp leaved salad plants closely related to chicory. Outer leaves distinct sharp flavour; inner leaves whiter and milder. Can blanch to render paler and sweeter, but blanching not essential, especially with modern cultivars. Different cultivars tolerant of hot and cold conditions: often grown as summer lettuce substitute in hot climates, winter lettuce substitute in temperate climates. Can be grown outside and under cover in winter months, for heads, as CCA semi-mature crops, and also as CCA seedlings.

Types: Broad-leaved/escarole/Batavian – robust, productive plants with broad leaves, often fairly upright in stature. Most cultivars resist and survive light frost. Many traditional and new cultivars grown in western Europe; considerable variation between cultivars in leaf colour from bronzy to green, some with fairly crisp, yellow-white hearts. New cultivars like 'Golda' relatively sweet and do not require any blanching. Broad-leaved endive can be grown for much of the year. In the winter months in temperate climate grows much more happily than the standard winter lettuce – far less adversely affected by low light levels and cold damp weather; far better disease resistance. Curled/frisée – very pretty plants with finely-divided crisp leaves. Flatter habit, anything from 12-35cm (4½-14in) in diameter. Generally less hardy than broad-leaved type, and more liable to deteriorate in prolonged cold, damp weather. More widely grown for spring and summer crops; most suitable type for CCA seedlings. In practice intermediate cultivars now being developed, and old distinctions between types being eroded. Watch out for new introductions which you can find out about in the gardening press.

### Soil and Situation

Normally grown in an open situation, but summer crops can tolerate light shade. Summer crops require reasonably fertile, moisture-retentive soil to thrive. Autumn/winter crop needs good drainage but otherwise less demanding; too much nitrogen results in lush growth which is then prone to rot.

### Cultivation

Can be available all the year round with successive sowings. Use the appropriate cultivars for the season (see Cultivars opposite). Germinates best at a reasonably high temperature of 20-22°C (68-72°F). For headed crop sow either *in situ* or in a seedbed, or in seedtrays or modules. Plant 30-35cm (12-14in) apart depending on cultivar. Thinnings can be transplanted to give succession. Summer sowings require rapid germination or they may bolt; shade, or protect with fleecy film, until germinated (see also Seed, Sowing Outdoors and Planting, Sowing in very dry conditions, p.72). Normally takes three months to mature.

Main Sowings
Headed crop: for summer use – sow late winter/early spring to mid-spring. Make the first sowings indoors in gentle heat. Early crops may bolt prematurely after planting if temperatures fall below about 4°C (39°F) for 20 days. For autumn/winter use outdoors – sow early to mid-summer. For late autumn/early winter use under cover in temperate areas sow late summer; transplant under cover early autumn. Outdoor crop benefits from extra protection, for example cloches, low polytunnels or fleece, in late autumn.

CCA seedlings: sow from late winter to early autumn. Make the earliest and latest sowings under cover; inadvisable to sow unless soil temperature above about 15°C (59°F.) Seedlings of curly type more attractive than broad types, but both acceptable. Recommended for intersowing and intercropping. Patches and strips very decorative.

Blanching
See Salad Techniques, pp.89-91. Whether to blanch or not is largely a matter of personal taste. In most situations *in situ* blanching sufficient. Blanch upright types by tying or by using any method for covering whole plant; blanch flatter types by covering: plate method very successful with curly endive. Plants normally ready ten to fifteen days after blanching. Blanching process can be accelerated by covering whatever used for blanching with straw or litter.

In cold areas plants traditionally lifted before heavy frost, and blanched whole, without cutting back leaves, by planting in pots or boxes in dark cellar, or in darkened area under staging in greenhouse or in frame.

**Harvesting**
Cut headed plants about 2cm (¾in) above ground and leave to resprout. Respond well to CCA treatment, especially later in season. May be productive over many weeks. 'Cut back' plants can withstand lower

temperatures than large leafy plants, although likely eventually to succumb to prolonged severe, wet weather. In polytunnels may survive winter and resprout again rapidly in spring. Number of cuts from CCA seedlings depends on time of year; early spring sowings may bolt rapidly – even so spring cuts very valuable. Later sowings may give two or three cuts.

### Cultivars
Broad-leaved – reliable cultivars include 'Golda', 'Casco d'oro', 'Cornet de Bordeaux' (probably hardiest). Fine-leaved – some cultivars only suitable for certain sowings. Be guided by current information for new cultivars. Flexible established cultivars: 'Ione', 'Pancalière', 'Très fin maraîchère Nina'; hardiest – 'Ruffec', 'Wallonne'.

### Use in Salads and Cooking
Shred large broad-leaved types finely if unblanched; otherwise use as lettuce. Use fine-leaved types whole, in pieces or shredded to add beautiful texture/shapes to salads. Endive also cooked, for example braised, served in *bagna calda* (finely shredded and dressed with hot crushed garlic, anchovy, olive oil and butter), cooked *aux lardons* (dressed with the hot fat from fried bacon, blended with wine).

French: Broad-leaved – *chicorée scarole, escarole*; curled – *chicorée frisée*. Italian: broad-leaved – *indivia scarola*; curled – *indivia riccia*.

### FENNEL, FLORENCE Sweet fennel, finocchio *Foeniculum vulgare* var. *azoricum*
Annual plant with finely-cut feathery foliage, growing 30–60cm (12–24in) high. Edible part is base of leaf stalks, which overlap and swell to form succulent 'bulb' just above ground. Withstands only light frost. Closely related to the perennial common or wild fennel grown as a herb.

### Soil and Situation
Prefers light, sandy, fertile, well-drained soils, rich in organic matter, though will grow on any fertile, well-drained soil. Mediterranean marsh plant in origin, and needs plenty of moisture when growing and continuously warm weather. Pretty foliage and contrasting white stems make fennel an attractive plant, suitable for decorative beds.

### Cultivation
Bolting problem: Florence fennel has tendency to bolt prematurely

rather than develop a bulb if cool conditions encountered, especially from early sowings. (Bolting may also be related to day length.) Some modern hybrid cultivars have improved bolting resistance. To minimize bolting delay sowing until early summer when day length becoming shorter; protect if cold weather threatened; do not grow in windswept, draughty situation; do not allow to dry out once established. Also inadvisable to transplant fennel unless unavoidable, so if not sown *in situ*, best to sow in modules, or in seedtrays pricking out when no more than three-to four-leaf stage. Watch out for slug damage in early stages; otherwise usually healthy crop.

Sow late spring to mid–summer for main summer/autumn crop. Use bolt resistant cultivars for early sowings. Plant them out under cover in cool areas. Sow mid- to late summer for late autumn/early winter crop, which can be covered or transplanted under cover for late crop lasting into winter. Thin or plant 30cm (12in) apart. If continuous supply required sow at three week intervals throughout growing season. Growth normally fairly rapid. Keep plants watered and mulched. Feeding with seaweed-based fertilizer beneficial. Traditionally the base was earthed up when it started to swell, to make it whiter and sweeter – but not essential. Plants normally ready for use fifteen to twenty days later.

### Harvesting
Plants can be uprooted when ready; alternatively cut just above ground level, leaving stump in the ground. Small shoots develop from the stump; can be used in salad for flavouring. Cut back plants prove much hardier than large leafy plants.

### Cultivars
'Zefa Fino' recommended for early sowings – but not infallible! Improved hybrid cultivars likely to be introduced.

### Use in Salads and Cooking
Bulbs have delicious, fresh, aniseed flavour. Exquisite salad when sliced finely. Also cooked in soups; braised; served with mornay sauce. Leaves can be chopped finely in salads. Flowers are also edible. Seeds used for flavouring.

### FENUGREEK *Trigonella foenum-graecum*
Fairly hardy Mediterranean legume, grown in past for fodder and today, as green manure. Seeds widely used in cooking curries. Seed popular for

sprouting; normally ready in three to four days. Eat when about 1.3cm (½in) long. Fairly spicy flavour. Can also grow as seedling sprouts; eat at two tiny seed leaves stage when curry flavour is only very faint. I recently discovered can also be grown as CCA seedling crop: young leaf tips have delightful fresh pea flavour, though soon become coarser. Can probably sow from early spring to late summer as recommended for use as green manure (see Manures and Fertilizers p.35). For use as salad personally have only tried mid-autumn and late winter sowings under cover for unusual winter salad, as leaves rapidly coarsen in open. Mice appear magnetized by the seed: set mouse traps after sowing if likely problem in your garden. Tom Stobart in *Herbs, Spices and Flavourings* says older leaves can be cooked in curries, but bitter if cooked like spinach.

### GARLIC *Allium sativum*
Uniquely flavoured, hardy bulb of ancient medicinal and culinary use. Bulbs consisting of up to 30 individual cloves develop underground. Many strains exist, adapted to different climates (see Cultivars p.164). Young garlic leaves eaten as 'garlic greens'. (See also Rocambole p.195.)

### Soil and Situation
Needs open, sunny position. Best bulbs produced in rich, light, well-drained soil. Where grown on heavy soil work a little sand or ashes into bottom of drill, or grow on ridge at least 10cm (4in) high. Commercial growers have found garlic responds to potash. Work in fresh wood ash before planting; otherwise grow in soil manured for previous crop. Bulbs liable to rot in wet soils or if overwatered, but do need some moisture during summer.

### Cultivation
Some strains will not sprout unless subjected to temperatures below zero for four to six weeks. Wherever feasible, especially in temperate climates, plant early to mid-autumn; this gives plants time to become established before winter. Will be ready early summer, so can be thoroughly dried for winter storage. Otherwise plant as early in year as soil conditions allow, from late winter to mid-spring. This crop will mature later and in cool areas/poor summers may not ripen well. Alternatively plant in modules in late autumn, and plant sprouted cloves outside in spring. Good method where soils heavy or poorly drained.

Essential to plant healthy, disease free stock. Plant cloves split off from mature garlic bulb. Select firm, plump cloves, preferably from the outer layers of bulb. Ideal size for planting 1.3cm (½in) diameter. Push into soil, flat base downwards, so at least 2.5cm (1in) below surface. On lighter soils can plant up to 10cm (4in) deep. For highest yields space 18cm (7in) apart each way. Keep well weeded during summer months.

For 'garlic greens' plant small cloves about 4cm (1½in) apart under cover (cold frames ideal situation) in autumn.

## Harvesting and Storage

Unlike onions garlic is ready for harvesting when outer leaves turning yellow, inner leaves still green, generally mid-summer. Wait until dry spell; dig out bulbs carefully. Very important to dry thoroughly in sun. In prolonged sunny weather dry outside, raised off ground. Otherwise dry in greenhouse, polytunnel or somewhere similar, hanging or laid on trays. Dry off for up to two weeks until bulbs blanched really white. Remove loose rotten leaves and other debris. Store for winter in dry, frost-free, airy place, hanging in bunches, laid loosely on trays, or plaited. (Plaiting easier if leaves moistened first.) Ideal storage temperature 5–10°C (41-50°F). Garlic prone to rot if bulbs become damp. Always handle bulbs very gently to minimize bruising and risk of rotting. A French lady whose family had grown garlic for sale for thirty years told me to handle it 'like fruit'. It 'hurt her' to see people throw it about! (This applies to all the onion family.) Garlic keeps six to twelve months depending on strain.

Cut 'garlic greens' in spring, leaving to resprout for second cut.

## Cultivars

Many strains have evolved which are adapted to different climates. Grow what is recommended for your area. Some evidence that homegrown garlic becomes adapted to local conditions after several seasons. White- and pink-skinned types exist; pink generally considered better flavoured and better keepers.

## Use in Salads and Cooking

Available all year round, either freshly lifted or stored for later use. Strong but unique flavour, use sparingly. Salads can be improved immeasurably if the salad bowl is rubbed first with a clove of garlic. Invaluable in cooking. Chinese make delicious pickle from whole garlic. Use 'garlic greens' like spring onions.

## GHERKIN (*see* Cucumber)

**GOOD KING HENRY (*see* Wild Plants and Weeds)**

**HAMBURG PARSLEY (*see* Herbs; Parsley, Hamburg p.228)**

**HORSE RADISH (*see* Wild Plants and Weeds)**

**ICEPLANT *Mesembryanthemum crystallinum***
Naturally perennial, but grown as annual in temperate and cold climates. Attractive sprawling plant with thick fleshy leaves and stems covered in tiny membranous bladders which make it sparkle, especially in the sun. Small white flowers develop on mature stems. Unique, refreshing salad plant – wonderful conversation stopper. Used as spinach substitute in hot climates where spinach runs to seed.

**Soil and Situation**
Maritime plant in origin; tolerates ordinary or fairly poor soil, provided good drainage. Prefers full sun; thrives in hot sunny weather. Can be grown in pots or hanging baskets, or ordinary beds.

**Cultivation**
Not frost hardy, so sow mid-spring indoors, transplanting outside after all risk of frost or *in situ* outdoors in late spring or after the last frost. Thin or plant 30cm (12in) apart. In cool climates can be grown under cover all summer. In early stages outdoor plants may need protection in cold weather; watch for slugs. Established plants more robust and can survive light frost in autumn, though quality impaired. Cover remaining outdoor plants in early autumn to prolong season. Stem cuttings can be taken during summer; they root rapidly supplying a follow on crop.

**Harvesting**
Once plants growing well pick individual leaves, or small 'branches' of leaves and stems. More shoots will develop from main stem. Keep picking regularly. Remove any flowers that appear to prolong the season: plants become tougher after flowering.

**Use in Salads and Cooking**
A plant you love or loathe. Raw leaves have fleshy but crisp texture, refreshing, sometimes salty flavour. Use young stems and leaves, either whole or cut into pieces. Leaves can be cooked like spinach, but I personally think them unappetizing when cooked.

**JAPANESE PARSLEY** (*see* **Herbs; Mitsuba p.228**)

**KALE, CURLED** *Brassica oleracea* (**Acephala group**)
Young leaves can be used raw in salad. For cultivation see standard gardening books in Further Reading p.251.

**KALE, ORNAMENTAL** *Brassica oleracea* (**Acephala group**) **and**
**CABBAGE, ORNAMENTAL** *Brassica oleracea* (**Capitata group**)
Variegated forms of common cabbage and kale; in practice seed catalogues rarely distinguish between them, classing both as kales. For centuries used in Europe, primarily grown for decorative purposes; today very popular in Japan, where many high quality hybrid cultivars being developed. Plants are notable for their wonderful colours – reds, whites, purples, yellows – and very decorative deeply serrated, frilled or wavy foliage. Plants never make tight heads, but often form very striking, almost unreal looking rosettes. Leaf types: Rounded, but gently waved or slightly frilled (probably mainly cabbages); very finely frilled or crinkled, like curly kale; deeply serrated, giving a slashed or feathery look. (These last two types are usually kales.) In all types there are dwarf, intermediate and tall forms.

Grow best in cool weather. Colours intensify when night temperatures fall to 10–15°C (50–59°F) usually in late summer/early autumn. Most cultivars can withstand light frost and some snow, but prolonged cold and wet winter weather often fatal. Cabbages least hardy. Kales hardiest – serrated-leaved forms probably hardiest of all. In my experience survive to about –10°C (14°F).

**Soil and Situation**
Tolerate poorer soil than most brassicas; in rich soil may become too lush and fail to colour up well, but soil must be well-drained and moisture-retentive. Open situation. Late autumn/early winter crop can be protected or grown under cover. Highly decorative plants; ideal for decorative vegetable potager. Hybrid cultivars very uniform; often used as late summer/autumn bedding plants. Dwarf types can be potted up for winter use in conservatories or cool situation indoors.

**Cultivation**
Best results obtained by sowing in modules, or sowing in seedtrays and potting up in 8–10cm (3½–4in) pots before planting out in ground. Sow late spring/early summer (and into mid-summer in frost-free areas). For

very early crops sow early spring at 20°C (68°F). Plant out 30-40cm (12-16in) apart, depending on cultivar. Unless in larger pots (see below) plant out at five- to seven-leaf stage. Plant firmly and upright, with lowest leaves a few centimetres above soil level.

For a late crop under cover plants can be potted on into larger pots, then planted out in polytunnels or in some other protection in early autumn. For winter conservatory use pot dwarf cultivars into 13-15cm (5-6in) pots, medium cultivars into 20-25cm (8-10in) pots. Alternatively plant two or three plants closely in 35cm (14in) pots, at least 30cm (12in) deep. Use good quality potting compost. Once planted be sure to keep a constant watch for cabbage white caterpillars which are a particular nuisance. Note: Cuttings can be taken of young shoots to perpetuate a particularly well-coloured cultivar.

**Harvesting**
Old cultivars mature in four to five months, newer hybrids in about three months. Unless entire head wanted for decorative purposes, pick individual leaves as required. Plants resprout over many months; in some cases almost become perennial, lasting a couple of seasons, though appearance rather straggly. Older plants may become branched, or develop side shoots, or develop rosettes of small secondary leaves, sometimes on the main stem. All useable for garnishing or salads. Pick leaves shortly before required, as they wilt fairly rapidly. If heavy frost is threatened plants can be pulled up by the roots and hung in a frost-free shed for a short period.

**Cultivars**
Many now available: be guided by current catalogues. $F_1$ hybrids generally best value. Good round-leaved cultivars include 'Osaka' series and 'Pink Beauty'; decorative frilled types include 'Chidori' and 'Wave' series; serrated types include 'Feather' and 'Peacock' series.

**Use in Salads and Cooking**
Colourful, beautifully shaped leaves marvellous addition to salad dishes or for garnish, especially in autumn and winter. Use small leaves whole, larger leaves shredded. How palatable they are raw is debatable. Can be coarse, but blanching for a minute in boiling water softens them. Can cook like cabbage, though not highly flavoured.

**KOHL RABI (*see* Secondary Salad Vegetables)**

## KOMATSUNA Mustard spinach *Brassica rapa* (Perviridis group)

A large, diverse group of Japanese vegetables, closely related to turnips but including types formed by crossing various brassicas/crucifers. Notable for vigour, and tolerance to high and low temperatures; some forms are among the hardiest of all leafy greens. Reputedly very nutritious. Mainly grown for cooked greens, but tender mature leaves, young leaves, tender young stems and flowering shoots are all suitable for use raw in salads. Flavour varies with cultivars and maturity of plants: cabbage flavour tends to predominate but also has undertones of spinach and mustard flavourings.

Although very hardy, in temperate and cold climates worth having some plants under cover in winter to get very tender growth. Can be exceptionally productive.

### Soil and Situation

Requires open site, and fertile, moisture-retentive soil.

### Cultivation

Versatile plant. Can be grown as large individual plants, as CCA plants at mature and semi-mature stages, or as CCA seedlings. As single plants most useful as autumn/winter crop. Sow mid-summer for outdoor crop, late summer for plants to be transplanted under cover. Sow *in situ* outdoors, or in seedtrays or modules for transplanting. Spacing can be very flexible, varying from about 10cm (4in) apart for small plants harvested young, to 30cm (12in) apart or more for very large plants to be harvested over a long period.

For CCA seedlings sow *in situ* from late winter to early autumn, in temperate climates making first and last sowings under cover. These will grow very rapidly, providing a good and almost continuous supply of fresh 'salading' in the winter months.

Plants normally healthy, but can be attacked by common brassica/crucifer pests and diseases. Benefit from being grown under fine nets in the summer months to protect against the various flying pests, for example flea beetles or pollen beetles which can cause extensive damage (see Pests and Diseases p.53).

### Harvesting

Cut whole heads of young plants, or single leaves of larger plants, leaving plants to resprout. They normally remain productive over many months, eventually running to seed in late spring. The young flowering shoots are normally tasty raw in salads, but try them first, as some may be more peppery than others.

**Cultivars**
New cultivars are continually being introduced to the west. Reliable cultivars currently available include 'Komatsuna', 'Tendergreen', and 'Green Boy'.

**Use in Salads and Cooking**
Very useful, especially in late winter, early spring to bulk up the various winter salads; some cultivars have exceptionally glossy, appetizing looking leaves. Use the young leaves and flowering shoots whole and the larger leaves shredded. Can be cooked by any of the methods suitable for greens or kales.

**KYONA** (*see* **Mizuna Greens**)

**LAMB'S LETTUCE** (*see* **Corn Salad**)

**LAND CRESS** (*see* **Cress, American Land**)

**LEEKS, MINI** (*see* **Secondary Salad Vegetables**)

**LENTILS** *Lens esculenta*
One of the easiest legumes to sprout. Use *whole* not split lentils: they can be yellow, red, brown or grey–green lentils. Normally ready within about four days. Eat when 6mm–1.3cm (¼–½in) long.

**LETTUCE** *Lactuca sativa*
Probably the best loved and most widely grown of all salad plants. Essentially a cool climate crop, growing best at temperatures between 10-20°C (50-68°F). Tendency to bolt prematurely or become bitter at higher temperatures. The many types have varying leaf form, texture and 'heartiness'. Leaves usually green, but some attractive red- and bronze-leaved forms. For stem lettuce, cultivated for its thick stem, see Lettuce, stem, p.175.

Main types: lettuce divided broadly into 'hearted' and 'loose-leaved' types. Hearted: (note: 'Cabbage' lettuce is general term covering both 'butterheads' and 'crispheads'.) Butterhead/round leaf – round-headed, flattish lettuce with soft, buttery leaves. Can be tasty but tendency to flop soon after picking. Generally faster maturing than crispheads, but more likely to bolt prematurely. Mainly grown in summer, though some cultivars now developed for winter cultivation under cover. Crisphead –

round-headed, flattish lettuce with crisp leaves. Compared to butter-heads slower to mature, but slower to bolt, and remain crisp longer after cutting. Some crisphead cultivars well-flavoured; with others, for example 'Iceberg' types, main asset is crisp texture. 'Iceberg' has come to denote large crisphead, sold with outer leaves trimmed off leaving only crisp white heart. American 'Iceberg' types adapted to warm summer conditions. 'Batavian' is a term loosely applied to a group of European crispheads, often with reddish tinge, which are relatively hardy and considered very well-flavoured. Crispheads mainly grown in summer months, but some suited to winter cultivation under cover. These include 'Parella' – unique type forming ground level rosette with tiny heart; notable for exceptional hardiness. Cos/romaine – tall, thicker-leaved, upright lettuces, with somewhat loose heart, crisp texture, distinct flavour. Keeps well when cut. In past sometimes tied to assist blanching. Slower growing than cabbage types, but more tolerant of low temperatures. Can also be grown in summer. Some types of cos can be grown at close spacing for 'leaf lettuce' (see p.173). Semi-cos – smaller forms of cos, with excellent, sweet flavour. Best known is the exceptionally sweet and crisp 'Little Gem'.

Loose-leaved (often called 'Salad Bowl' type after a well-known cultivar): characterized by only rudimentary hearts, leaves often dissected or frilly. Often slower to bolt than standard hearting lettuce; less prone to mildew. Bolting resistance coupled with ability to regenerate after being cut, means they can be picked over many weeks. Group includes cultivars adapted to hot and cold weather. Colours of bronze and red cultivars deepen in cold weather. Some cultivars soft-leaved; liable to be damaged by hail and severe weather. 'Salad Bowl' – the original cultivar, highly productive, indented leaves; many other cultivars now available. 'Oak-leaved' – form of 'Salad Bowl', with darker, probably tougher leaves with deeply rounded indentations like oak leaves; 'Lollo' – deeply curled, frilled, Italian loose-headed types, introduced within the last 20 years. All these 'Salad Bowl' types have green and red forms; among the prettiest, most decorative lettuces available. 'Marvel-of-Four-Seasons' – traditional, relatively hardy southern European cultivar with reddish leaves; performs like 'Salad Bowl' but forms more substantial heart. 'Cutting lettuce' – traditional European cultivars selected for sowing thickly as CCA seedlings. There are smooth, crisp and red-leaved forms. Red forms best sown early spring or in shady position to obtain deepest colourings; liable to bolt in hot weather. See also 'leaf lettuce' p.173.

**Soil and Situation**
Open site; best on light, well-drained, moisture-retentive, fertile soil. Should be rich in organic matter, preferably manured for previous crop, and limed if acid. Rotate where possible to avoid build up of root aphid and fungus diseases. Small-growing types, for example 'Tom Thumb', 'Little Gem' and cutting lettuce are useful for intercropping, intersowing, and containers. Most loose-leaf types very decorative grown in patches or to give decorative edge to vegetable or flower beds.

**Cultivation**
Lettuce can be sown *in situ*, or in a seedbed and transplanted, or in seedtrays or in modules (see Raising Plants 'Indoors' pp.77–84). Transplanting inadvisable in hot weather, so unless sown in modules, make mid-summer sowings *in situ*. By sowing in succession with appropriate cultivars can have almost all year round supply in temperate climates, apart from short mid-winter period when heated greenhouses may be necessary. (In my view most winter greenhouse lettuces are poorly flavoured, and broad-leaved endive far better value in winter.)

Protect young seedlings and plants against birds and slugs. Once mature, lettuces tend to bolt or deteriorate fairly rapidly. Will bolt prematurely in dry conditions. To minimize risk of premature bolting, especially in summer, never allow lettuce to dry out. Regular watering beneficial when growing. Where water is scarce, water heavily seven to ten days before harvesting. Crop responds well to being kept mulched.

For a continuous supply make small successive sowings throughout growing season, using cultivars suited to the season (see Main Sowings p.172). Thin early, in stages, to prevent seedlings becoming overcrowded. Use thinnings in salads or transplant to get a slightly later crop. Plant shallowly with seed leaves just above soil surface; cos lettuce can be planted slightly deeper. Lettuces grow well at equidistant spacing. Spacing varies with cultivars: space very small types 12–15cm (4½ –6in) apart; semi–cos types 18–20cm (7–8in) apart; standard butterheads and crispheads up to 30cm (12in) apart; cos, large crispheads, and 'Salad Bowl' types 35cm (14in) apart.

Germination Temperatures
Lettuce germinates at very low temperatures, but sometimes affected by *high temperature dormancy* ie it fails to germinate when soil temperature over 25°C (77°F). Results in poor, erratic germination. Most critical period a few hours after sowing. If germination problems are being

encountered and soil temperature high (occurs in late spring, summer, even autumn) take one of following measures: put seeds in fridge for week to ten days before sowing to break their dormancy; water soil immediately after sowing to lower its temperature; sow between 14.00 and 16.00 hours so critical period occurs during the night; cover seedbed or seedtray with white reflective material after sowing; sow in seedtrays or modules put in a cool place to germinate.

Main Sowings
Note: The following sowings apply to headed and loose-headed lettuce, and to lettuce grown as CCA seedlings.

Early sowings under cover (in temperate climates) – sow late winter/early spring for late spring/early summer crop. Either sow *in situ* to crop in cold greenhouse, frames or under cloches, or sow in seedtrays or modules to transplant outdoors mid-spring in sheltered position or under cloches, low tunnels or fleecy films (see Protected Cropping p.123). Suitable types: cos, 'Salad Bowl', butterheads recommended for early crops. For very early spring CCA seedling crops use traditional European types of 'cutting lettuce' and 'Salad Bowl' types.

Main sowings in open – sow mid-spring to mid-summer for main summer to mid-autumn crop. Can sow *in situ* or transplant the seedlings. (See Germination Temperatures p.171.) In damp climates it is best to use mildew-resistant cultivars for later sowings. If necessary, protect plants in autumn with cloches, low tunnels, or by planting under film to improve the quality. Alternatively plant under cover for late autumn/early winter crop. Suitable types: all, *except* butterheads recommended only for very early sowings.

Outdoor over-wintered hardy lettuce (temperate climates) – sow late summer/early autumn to crop late spring/early summer following year. This is a gamble, depending on the weather, but worth trying. Either sow *in situ*, thin to 7.5cm (3in) apart in autumn and make final thinning following spring, or sow in seedtrays and modules, keep in cold frame, unheated greenhouse or sheltered position outdoors in winter, and transplant in spring. Crop will be two to three weeks earlier and better quality if covered with cloches in winter. Suitable types: most cos lettuce, 'Marvel-of-Four-Seasons', hardy butterheads, for example 'Valdor'. Sow very hardy 'Parella' lettuce *in situ* late summer/early autumn. Can be broadcast if this method is preferred.

Protected winter crop in unheated greenhouse/polytunnels/frames – sow from very late summer to mid-autumn for cropping in late autumn/early winter or late winter/early spring. Make first sowings outdoors to transplant under cover. Make later sowings under cover. Try to keep plants well ventilated to prevent disease, especially in late spring. Remove cloches in warm weather if necessary. Suitable cultivars: a range of mainly butterhead cultivars exist, each suited to growing over fairly specific periods. Consult current catalogues for precise sowing dates for particular cultivars.

Protected winter crop in heated greenhouses – maintain a minimum night temperature of 2°C (36°F) and day temperature of 4.5°C (40°F). Sow from approximately early autumn to early winter, for crops from late autumn to late spring. Use currently available cultivars at recommended sowing dates.

'Leaf Lettuce'
'Leaf lettuce' is a sophisticated form of CCA seedling production which is geared to a continuous supply during the growing season of crisp lettuce leaves. It was developed at Horticulture Research International at Wellesbourne, UK, for the catering trade, to get particularly high yields of crisp individual lettuce leaves requiring minimum preparation. Very productive system for home gardeners. Yields from small areas several times higher than with conventional crop. Basic idea is to grow *cos lettuce* cultivars closely to encourage vigorous growth of upright leaves rather than hearts. First cut ready in about two-thirds the time of conventional-hearted lettuce.

Aim to have seedlings about 5cm (2in) apart; or twelve to fifteen seedlings per 30cm (12in) run in rows about 13cm (5in) apart. To achieve this either broadcast very thinly, or sow very thinly in drills (assuming about 80 per cent germination) or transplant to required distance apart. Cut leaves off 1.3–2.5cm (½–1in) above ground level when 8–13cm (3½–5in) high. Leave the plant to resprout at least once. Make sure ground fertile and weed free initially; keep the soil conditions moist throughout plant growth.

The Wellesbourne formula is for a continuous lettuce supply from late spring to mid-autumn in a temperate climate. To keep a family of four supplied sow approximately 0.8sq m (1sq yd) each time. Sowing timings vary as lettuce grows faster at some periods than others. (Months in brackets refer to UK conditions, for which the formula was developed.)
★ Sow weekly from mid- to late spring (mid–April to mid–May). These are ready on average seven and a half weeks after sowing, from late spring to early summer (late May to end June); after cutting will give second

crop about seven and a half weeks later, from mid- to late summer (early July-mid August).

* Sow weekly in late summer (first three weeks of August) to maintain continuity of yield; first cuts of salad leaves will be ready approximately three and a half weeks later in early autumn (September); and the second a further four and a half weeks later, in mid-autumn (first three weeks of October).

**Most Common Pests and Diseases**

Besides slugs, soil pests such as wireworm, cutworm, leatherjackets nibble off plants above or just below ground, especially in spring on newly-cultivated land. Lettuce root aphid may infest roots causing plants to wilt and die. Leaf aphids may attack in warm weather, colonizing underside of leaves and centre of plants, and possibly spreading virus diseases. Aluminium foil mulch may deter winged aphids from landing on plants.

Seedling damping off diseases, botrytis or grey mould, and downy mildew occur mainly in cold, damp weather from late summer to early spring. Lettuce mosaic virus stunts plants. Use any resistant cultivars. For other measures see Pests and Diseases p.51-62.

**Harvesting**

Headed lettuce: cut when hearts feel firm. Many cultivars will resprout from base after cutting, giving second crop of small leaves, occasionally even forming a second heart. In some cases leaves are bitter, but worth trying to avoid resowing. Most successful with spring maturing lettuce grown under protection. May give second reasonable cut within five to six weeks.

Loose-leaved 'Salad Bowl' types: pick leaves individually once useful size, or cut across plant 2.5cm (1in) above neck and leave to resprout, which may occur two or three times. If flower spikes cut off when bolting, may get new growth from base. Red-leaved forms left to run to seed make decorative spires; can be used for garnish. For harvesting CCA seedling lettuce see Salad Techniques p.86.

**Cultivars**

Improved cultivars are continually being developed. Consult catalogues for new introductions. The following are a selection of recommended cultivars available at the time of writing:

*Butterheads*: for under cover in winter – 'Novita', 'Columbus', 'Cynthia' and 'Magnet'; for over-wintering outdoors – 'Valdor'; for spring and summer sowing – 'Avondefiance', 'Musette', 'Marvel-of-Four-Seasons', 'Tom Thumb'.

*Crispheads*: for under cover in winter – 'Marbello', 'Kelly's'; for spring and summer sowing – 'Minetto', 'Malika', 'Saladin' ('Iceberg'), 'Warpath', 'Webb's Wonderful'.

*Batavian* – 'Rouge Grenobloise', 'Regina dei Ghiacci' ('Reine des Glaces'/'Frisée de Beauregard'), 'Dorée de Printemps', 'Rossia'.

*Cos and semi-cos*: for sowing spring to late summer – 'Little Gem', 'Lobjoit's Cos'; for sowing spring and autumn – 'Winter Density'.

*Salad Bowl types*: green – 'Green Salad Bowl', 'Lollo Bionda', 'Catalogna', 'Black Seeded Simpson', 'Grand Rapids'; red – 'Red Salad Bowl', 'Lollo Rossa', 'Valeria' (Lollo type).

*Cutting lettuce*: green – 'Lattuga bionda riccio da taglio' (curled), 'Lattuga liscia da taglio' (smooth), numerous local varieties in Italy; red – 'Biscia rossa', 'Rossa friulana'. Also red and green 'Salad Bowl' types.

*Cultivars suitable for leaf lettuce*: 'Paris White Cos' ('Blonde marâichère'), 'Lobjoit's Cos', 'Valmaine'.

## Use in Salads and Cooking

Mainly used raw. Can be braised and used in soup (useful means of utilizing bolted lettuce).

## LETTUCE, STEM Asparagus lettuce, Chinese lettuce, celtuce *Lactuca sativa* var. *angustana*

Very tall Asiatic lettuce, grown primarily for thick succulent stem which can be up to 7.5cm (3in) thick and 45cm (18in) high. Stem has lettuce flavour and very pleasant crunchy texture. Tolerates higher temperatures than western lettuce though may bolt prematurely in very hot weather; stands light frost.

## Soil and Situation

See Lettuce.

## Cultivation

In temperate climates grow as a summer to autumn crop. Either sow *in situ*, or sow in modules and transplant, as strong transplants required. Make main sowings late spring. For earlier crop sow mid-spring under cover; for late crop sow early summer, and transplant under cover. In very hot climates grow as a winter crop, sowing in early autumn.

Space plants 30cm (12in) apart each way. Thin seedlings when about 5cm (2in) high; plant transplants no later than three- to four-leaf stage or they fail to develop well. Plants require plenty of moisture in early leafy stage, but only moderate watering later when stems start to develop. Liquid feeding every few weeks beneficial. Don't worry if leaves look diseased; in most cases the stem will not be affected.

## Harvesting and Storage
Stems generally ready three to four months after sowing, when at least 2.5cm (1in) thick and 30cm (12in) high. Can then leave until just before flowering, but may become hollow at that stage. Pull out of ground and trim off root and remaining leaves except for the 'topknot' of leaves, which is only removed just before use. The stems keep for several weeks in cool conditions. In northern China they are transplanted close together in cold frames in late autumn, protected from frost, and used over several months.

## Cultivars
Few cultivars available in the west. 'Zulu' probably the best for temperate climates at the time of writing.

## Use in Salads and Cooking
Peel the slightly tough outer skin which can be bitter. Cut the stem into thin slices or matchsticks, and use raw in salads. Can also be cooked lightly, generally for no more than four or five minutes.

## LUCERNE (*see* Alfalfa)

## MIBUNA GREENS
Attractive, very productive oriental brassica/crucifer producing masses of narrow, strap-like leaves. Only recently introduced from Japan. Very closely related to mizuna greens, but somewhat less tolerant of very high and very low temperatures. In my experience survives winter temperatures of about -6°C (21°F) in the open. Very pleasant flavour, probably slightly stronger than mizuna. 'Green Spray' main cultivar available. For Latin name, cultivation and use see Mizuna Greens below.

## MIZUNA GREENS Kyona, Potherb Mustard *Brassica rapa* var. *Nipposinica* or var. *Japonica*
Unique, beautiful brassica/crucifer, cultivated for centuries in Japan.

Mature plants form clumps up to 23cm (9in) high and often over 30cm (12in) across, of finely dissected, dark green, glossy leaves with narrow white stalks. Easily grown plant, notable for natural vigour, and for tolerating very high and very low temperatures. Plants kept cut back in my garden have survived -16°C (3°F). Less likely to bolt prematurely from early spring sowings than many oriental greens, but may bolt in very dry conditions.

### Soil and Situation
Does best in fertile soil; it tolerates wide range of soils and conditions. For lush growth in summer must have reasonable moisture. Useful for intercropping and undercropping, either as seedlings or with plants kept compact by constant cutting. Very decorative in flower beds/vegetable beds, either grown in patches or as edging.

### Cultivation
Versatile plant: grow as single plants, or for CCA at any stage, or as CCA seedlings. Sow *in situ* or in seedtrays and transplant. For headed plants sow from late spring to early autumn. For CCA seedlings make additional sowings in late winter/early spring and then again in late autumn. These can be grown under cover in temperate and cold climates. Similarly plants that are sown in early autumn can be transplanted under cover, for a fast growing winter crop.

Space plants 10cm (4in) apart for small plants, 20-23cm (8-9in) apart for medium plants, 30-45cm (12-18in) apart for large plants for cutting over many months. Thinnings can be used in salads. Protect from flea beetle in the early stages (see Pest and Diseases pp.51-62).

Although plants withstand very cold weather, wet winter conditions and heavy snow lying on large plants cause rotting. In cold areas it is advisable to protect plants in open with low tunnels or cloches. They will cease growing in mid-winter, but will survive and start growing again in early spring.

### Harvesting
First cut can often be made within a month of sowing. Cut single leaves or cut across whole plant about 5cm (2in) above ground level and leave to resprout. Can be cut frequently. (A crop planted under sweet corn in late spring one year was cut five times before the majority of plants showed signs of flowering and becoming tougher, in spite of dry conditions. When flower spikes were cut off, many plants started growing from base again.)

## Cultivars

Most cultivars sold are selections of old cultivars with deeply serrated leaves. Where they are available grow hardier, less serrated cultivars such as 'Tokyo Beau' and 'Tokyo Belle', especially for winter use in cold climates.

## Use in Salads and Cooking

Very decorative in salads; deep green glossy leaves have a 'healthy' look. Use small leaves whole; larger leaves in pieces. Mild, fresh taste; juicy texture. Especially valuable in winter months, blending well with other salad plants. Can be cooked like any oriental greens; excellent in mixed stir-fries. Cooked flavour quite different from fresh – very 'Chinese'. In Japan very popular pickling vegetable. Flowering shoots and flowers can be used cooked or raw while still tender; but toughen on maturity.

## MUSTARDS, ORIENTAL Brown mustards *Brassica juncea*

The many types of oriental mustard being introduced to the west are characterized by fairly coarse leaves and strong, 'hot' flavours. Some have beautiful crepe-like textures and red colouring. Mostly grown for use cooked or pickled, but young seedlings and shredded mature leaves can be excellent raw. Some flowering shoots good raw if picked young, but very strong flavours may develop later. All mustards probably best used in small quantities, mixed with milder salad plants. Oriental mustards still relatively unknown, but worth experimenting to add zing to your salads.

Some mustards exceptionally hardy; most grow best in cooler seasons, with tendency to bolt prematurely in very hot weather or if sown early in the year. However, CCA seedlings may succeed under these conditions. Need reasonably fertile soil and plenty of moisture throughout growth period.

Some Suggestions For Salad Mustards
(See Further Reading p.251.)
Purple mustards – Generally very hardy, with beautiful coloured foliage, becoming darker in winter months. Grown successfully as summer seedling crop in Napa Valley, USA, harvesting when leaves about 2.5cm (1in) in diameter. Add colour and spiciness to salads. Sow in mid-summer for large plants for winter use. Space plants at least 30cm (12in) apart. Cultivars include 'Osaka Purple', 'Red Giant', 'Miike Giant'.

Wrapped heart and headed mustards – Group with variable hardiness, primarily grown in orient for pickling. Leaves and stems have very distinct flavour which tends to develop with maturity, often when small, tight, incurved hearts form. Excellent raw. Some develop into very large plants. Main sowing mid- to late summer for autumn use. Space up to 45cm (18in) apart for large plants, but can grow closer for smaller plants. (I have no experience of their performance as seedling crops.) Cultivars include 'Bao Xin' (wrapped heart), 'Amsoi'.

Curled mustards– Group with decorative deeply curled leaves. Often very hardy, but also tolerate high temperatures. Flavour ranges from very peppery to relatively mild, depending on cultivar, maturity and season. Sow spring to early summer to harvest young, or in mid- to late summer for winter use. Cultivars include 'Art Green', 'Green Wave'.

'Green-in-the-Snow' (Serifong) – Exceptionally hardy mustard, generally sown in late summer for a late autumn to winter crop. Sow as a CCA seedling crop, or space plants anything from 10-30cm (4-12in) apart, for plants ranging from small to large in size. Only pick young leaves for use raw in salads: they have a wonderful spiciness. Older leaves are generally too hot for most tastes, and should be cooked.

**MUSTARD, WHITE** *Sinapsis alba,* **MUSTARD, BLACK** *Brassica nigra*
Very rapidly-growing annuals, used for many centuries as salad seedlings. Seed of both types used in making mustard. Milder flavoured white mustard often used in 'mustard and cress'; but hotter, more 'mustardy' flavoured black mustard can also be used. Grow as CCA seedlings in the ground, or as seedling sprouts indoors. For cultivation, harvesting and use as CCA seedlings see Cress, Garden p.151. Mustard tends to run to seed faster than cress, so in hot weather fewer cuttings can be made before stems toughen and plants become unappetizing. Mustard is also used as a green manure (see Manures and Fertilizers p.33).

'Mustard and Cress' Seedling Sprouts Indoors
For growing indoors, traditional method of growing mustard and cress on a dish certainly the best. (For sowing method and harvesting see Seed Sprouting and Seedling Sprouts pp.98-104.) If grown in a jar, cress goes into an evil-smelling, stagnant, gelatinous mass!

Mustard normally grows faster than cress; if both required together, sow mustard three days later, in the same or separate dish. (Some new cress cultivars very fast growing. Do small preliminary trials to assess ideal timing of sowing.) Though normally grown on a windowsill, can start in the dark to draw up the seedlings, and move into the light when about 2.5cm (1in) high. Never allow seedlings to dry out while growing. In winter cress generally ready ten days after sowing, mustard seven days after sowing, if day temperature of 15-18°C (59-64°F) maintained, and night temperatures no lower than 5°C (41°F). If kept moist, mature seedlings will stand up to two weeks in good condition. The more substantial the base used, the longer they stand.

Note: In commercial 'mustard and cress' punnets salad rape is often substituted in place of cress, it has a larger leaf and slightly milder taste.

## THE ONION FAMILY *Allium cepa* and other spp.

Large family of narrow-leaved, strongly-flavoured, biennial and perennial plants. 'Bulb' onions develop large solid swollen bulbs, used fresh or stored. 'Salad' or 'spring' onions, are used immature, when leaves young and bulbs small or rudimentary. Rugged 'Welsh onion' grown primarily for its green leaves, as are various perennial forms of onion. 'Oriental bunching onion' grown for leaf and sometimes thick white stem. Bulbs, leaves and stems of all types used raw in salads.

### BULB ONIONS *Allium cepa*

Bulbs mainly brown, yellow or white skinned with white flesh. Some red-skinned cultivars with rose-tinted flesh are especially attractive in salads. (For cultivation see general vegetable books p.251.)

### SALAD ONIONS Spring onions, bunching onions, scallions *Allium cepa*

General term for onions used immature, when little more than leaves and slender white shank or tiny bulbs. Either use thinnings from maincrop bulb onions, or grow special cultivars. Some are straight stemmed; some have slightly swollen bulbs.

## Soil and Situation

Open site; fertile, thoroughly-dug and well-prepared soil. Good drainage essential. Onions sensitive to acidity, so lime if soil acid. Advisable to rotate onions over minimum four year cycle if possible to prevent build up of eelworm (nematodes) and various soil borne diseases.

## Cultivation

In mild areas sow *in situ* outdoors as soon as the soil is workable in spring. Rake seedbed beforehand to very fine tilth. Never sow when the soil is cold or wet; warm with cloches beforehand if necessary or sow under cloches. For a regular supply throughout summer and autumn months sow thinly *in situ* every two or three weeks from early spring to early summer. Sow in mid- and late summer for overwintered crop for use following spring. In cold areas use very hardy cultivars, or sow under cover.

Ideal spacing for salad onions approximately 30 plants per 30cm sq (12in sq). Can obtain by sowing 2-2.5cm (¾-1in) apart, in rows 10cm (4in) apart. Can also sow in wide drills spacing plants about 2.5cm (1in) apart. No need to thin; pull as required.

Water if soil becomes dry. Cloche protection beneficial from early autumn onwards in cold areas. Overwintered crop may suffer from botrytis and white rot disease in cold damp conditions; if so, use hardy evergreen oriental bunching onions (see p.182).

### Cultivars
Reliable hardy cultivar – 'White Lisbon Winter Hardy'.

WELSH ONION **Ciboule *Allium fistulosum***
Hollow-leaved, relatively hardy, perennial onion, growing 30-45cm (12-18in) high. Leaves up to 1.3cm (½in) wide. Base of leaf stems thickened, but not forming true bulb. Grown all over world; widely cultivated in the East. All-year-round substitute for spring onions as leaves remain green all winter in temperate climates.

### Soil and Situation
Does best in full sun, fertile, well-prepared soil, but tolerates ordinary soil. Useful edging for kitchen garden.

### Cultivation
Normally raised by dividing established clumps in spring or autumn. Pull plants apart and replant younger outer pieces about 23cm (9in) apart. In severe climates often grown as annual or biennial as seed–raised plants said to be hardier than those raised by division.

To raise from seed sow in seedtrays and transplant, or sow *in situ* in spring or late summer. Plant out, or thin in stages to about 23cm (9in) apart. Plant grows into clumps which thicken every year. Divide clumps every two or three years in spring or autumn, replanting young parts.

### Harvesting
Pick green leaves as required; flavour is fairly strong. If thicker onion required, pull off a few basal growths, leaving rest of clump to multiply.

ORIENTAL BUNCHING ONION **Japanese bunching onion** *Allium fistulosum*

Forms of perennial Welsh onion, selected over centuries in Asia and Japan so cultivars suited to wide range of temperatures. Different cultivars used at every stage from small seedlings to thick stemmed, large-leaved onions grown like western leeks. Main types: Multi-stem – generally form clumps of up to 20 leaves. Used as green leaves. Single stem – characterized by single main stem, but wide range of cultivars, from small types grown like salad onions to tall cultivars with white shaft up to 45cm (18in) tall and up to 2.5cm (1in) diameter. These can be blanched by earthing up. Some red-stemmed forms exist. Also cultivars which die back in winter, but regenerate in spring. For general salad use leafy forms most practical. (For cultivation of large stem types see *Oriental Vegetables* in Further Reading. p.251.)

**Soil and Situation**
See Salad Onions. High fertility essential for top quality crop. Avoid very heavy clay soils. Quite suitable for intercropping as habit upright, and can be harvested at any stage.

**Cultivation and Harvesting**
Although perennial, normally grown as annuals or biennials to get more tender leaves and keep stocks healthy. Can propagate by dividing mature clumps, but only do so if very healthy.

Either sow *in situ*, or sow indoors in seedtrays and transplant the seedlings. Germinate fastest in warmth (see bulb onions). Seedlings transplant well: in China often transplanted over a period of several weeks to give succession of crops. Plant shallowly; can plant in small groups of two or three seedlings.

Cultivation for Young Leaves
Use multi-stemmed types, or single-stem types recommended for use young. Sow thinly *in situ* in wide drills or patches throughout growing season. Make early and late sowings under cover. Pull for use at any stage from 5-15cm (2-6in), normally within five weeks of sowing. For larger plants with a little stem thin to 4cm (1½in) apart, and pull when 30cm (12in) high, usually within three months of sowing.

Cultivation for Larger Leaves and Winter Crop
Use single-stem cultivars, selecting the hardiest cultivars for the over-

wintering crop. Sow spring to early summer *in situ* or in seedtrays or modules. Thin or plant into small groups of up to three seedlings. Either grow in rows 38cm (15in) apart, spacing groups about 10cm (4in) apart, or space them about 20cm (8in) apart each way. Leaves will be ready for use within about four months of sowing. Pick individual leaves or uproot the entire plant. Hardy cultivars can be left in the ground and used during the winter and the following spring. Even after flowering leaves are normally still useable. The larger leaved types tend to be coarser; mainly used in cooking, but can be cut finely into salads.

## Cultivars

At the time of writing only a few cultivars available in the west. Watch out for new introductions. Best known are 'Kyoto Market' (multi-stem) and 'Ishikuro' and 'White Evergreen' (hardy single stems).

### PICKLING ONIONS *Allium cepa*

Tiny bulbs grown specially for pickling, used about thumb nail size. Most cultivars white-skinned, but some reddish brown.

## Soil, Cultivation and Harvesting

Tolerate fairly poor and dry soil, but grow best in fertile soil. Sow spring, *in situ* outdoors. Ideally want 30 plants per 30cm sq (4.7in sq). Either sow in rows 30cm (12in) apart, thinning to 6mm (¼in) apart, or sow in wide drills, allowing about 2cm (¾in) between plants. Generally no need to thin; competition keeps the bulbs small. Normally sown about 1.3cm (½in) deep, but in Holland commercial pickling onions sown 4–5cm (1½–2in) deep to keep them white.

   Allow foliage to die down and harvest as for bulb onions. Do not leave too long in soil or may resprout. Lift and store in a dry place until needed for pickling.

## Cultivars

Traditional cultivars include 'Paris Silver Skin', 'Barletta', 'Brunswick' (reddish brown), 'Purplette' (purple).

### TREE ONION Egyptian, bulb–bearing onion *Allium cepa* (Proliferum group)

Extremely hardy, perennial onion, growing up to 1.2m (4ft) high. Curious in that clusters of tiny, hazel–nut–like aerial bulbs or bulblets are formed on flower stems instead of seed. Main stem then grows higher, producing another tier or tiers of aerial bulblets. Plant eventually bends over to ground level where bulblets root of their own accord – unless they have been picked!

**Soil and Cultivation**
Prefers rich, well-drained soil, but succeeds in almost any soil. Plant large bulbs, single bulblets, or cluster of bulblets about 23cm (9in) apart in spring or autumn. (Bulblets often develop green shoots when still in the air attached to the plant; can be picked off and planted.) Protect against birds with black cotton. Planting whole clusters said to prevent some bird damage. Plants may need staking in exposed situations.

**Harvesting and Use**
Yields generally low. Large bulbs produce bulblets in first season, or second season if autumn planted. Bulblets usually produce large basal bulb in first year; aerial bulblets in second year. Leave plants in ground for further season so they become stronger and more prolific. A patch will perpetuate itself, but thin out when becoming overcrowded. Bulblets can be picked virtually all year, even in snow. Best used when fully grown before skins harden. Use fresh whole or chopped finely in salads, or pickled. Use young shoots like green onions. Use large basal bulbs when thinning out.

EVERLASTING ONION *Allium perutile*
Hardy onion, forming clumps rather like chives, 15–20cm (6–8in) high. Leaves remain green all winter in temperate climate. Grow and use like Welsh onion; propagation must be by division as plant does not produce seed. Milder flavour than Welsh onion.

**ORACHE (*see* Herbs)**

**PAK CHOI *Brassica rapa* (Chinensis group)**
Very closely related to Chinese cabbage, but leaves smoother, heads less compact. Leaves often characterized by broad midribs, swelling at lower end to give plant a typically rounded butt. Leaf stalks and midribs usually white, but in some cultivars very pretty light green. Many forms, ranging from small stocky cultivars 8–10cm (3½–4in) high, to tall types up to 45cm (18in) high. Important to select suitable cultivars for your climate and requirements. All pak chois have mild refreshing flavour and juiciness. For 'Rosette pak' see p.186.

For soil, situation, and general notes on methods of cultivation see Chinese Cabbage pp.136-8.

**Sowings**

Pak choi exceptionally versatile: can use at any stage from small seedlings to flowering shoots. Responds well to CCA treatment as seedlings, semi-mature and mature plants.

For CCA seedlings sow *in situ* outdoors from spring to early autumn. For spring and early sowings use bolt-resistant cultivars where available (though usually possible to get at least one cut from standard cultivars before plants run to seed). Make very early sowings under cover in late winter; very late sowings under cover in mid-autumn. These will prove very useful for winter and early spring crops. Sow closely in rows or in wide drills (see Seed, Sowing Outdoors and Planting pp.70-1).

For mature and semi-mature plants sow from mid-spring to early autumn, making last sowing about six weeks before first frost expected. Sow in seedtrays or modules to transplant, or *in situ*. For a very early crop sow under cover in early to mid-spring, transplanting outside in late spring. Use slow bolting cultivar. For late protected crop in temperate climates sow in late summer/early autumn, transplanting under cover during autumn. Use green-stemmed types, or the hardy cultivars with good cold resistance.

Spacing depends on cultivar and stage being harvested. Average spacing 13-15cm (5-6in) apart for small plants and squat types, 18-23cm (7-9in) apart for medium sized plants, up to 45cm (18in) apart for large plants. Thinnings can be used in salads, or transplanted in cool conditions for another crop.

**Harvesting**

Always use pak choi at its peak, when leaves are really crisp. For CCA seedlings cut at any stage from 4-13cm (1½-5in) high. In good growing conditions the first cut may be made within three weeks of sowing. Two or three successive cuts can often be made. For mature and semi-mature plants either cut individual leaves as needed, or cut across head about 2.5cm (1in) above ground level leaving it to resprout, or pull up entire plant. With CCA treatment semi-mature and mature heads may remain productive over a long period. Especially useful for plants under cover in autumn/early winter, as cut back plants have more resistance to frost. Plants eventually run to seed. Young and mature flowering shoots have a wonderful mild flavour and look very colourful raw in salads.

**Cultivars**
New cultivars are continually being introduced. Reliable ones available
at the time of writing include: 'Chingensai' (slow bolting, green-
stemmed); 'F₁ Joi Choi' (reasonably frost resistant; white-stem); 'Mei
Qing Choi' (reasonably good heat and cold tolerance; green stems).

**Use in Salads and Cooking**
Pak choi is said to be more nutritious than Chinese cabbage. Has a pleasant, mild flavour and a crisp texture. Young leaves and leaf stalks of
white-stemmed types are especially juicy. Green-stemmed types may
have more flavour. Use all parts raw in salads at any stage. Young leaves
are crisp and attractive looking.. Older leaves can be cut or shredded, or
cooked gently, by steaming or stir-frying them.

ROSETTE PAK CHOI **Tatsoi** *Brassica rapa* **var.** *rosularis*
Distinct type of pak choi with rounded, dark green, crepe-like leaves.
Leaves fairly upright in hot weather, but lie flat in winter to form beautiful ground level rosette. Makes beautiful edge to vegetable bed. Cool
weather crop. In well-drained soil can survive -10°C (14°F). Grow either
as CCA seedlings or as mature plants. Main sowing mid- to late summer
for autumn crop. Can sow throughout growing season but early sowings
may bolt in hot weather. Characteristic flavour, stronger than most pak
chois. Leaves very decorative in salads. Use small leaves whole; larger
leaves lightly cooked.

**PARSNIP (***see* **Secondary Salad Vegetables)**

**PEAS Mangetout and Pea Shoots(***see* **Secondary Salad Vegetables)**

**PEPPER, SWEET (***see* **Secondary Salad Vegetables)**

**PLANTAIN Buckshorn** *Plantago coronopus*
Virtually evergreen, European native plant, forming low rosette of nar-
row, jagged leaves. Easily cultivated, especially for use in winter to spring.
(See also Wild Plants and Weeds p.248.)

**Soil and Situation**
Natural habitat light, well-drained, gravelly or sandy soil, but doesn't
appear to be fussy. Grows larger and more succulently in fertile soil.
Makes attractive edging, especially in winter and spring.

## Cultivation
Grow either as single plants or as CCA seedlings. For single plants sow spring for summer to autumn crop, late summer for autumn to spring crop. Sow *in situ* or in seedtrays for transplanting, spacing plants about 18cm (7in) apart. For CCA seedlings sow from spring to late summer outdoors. For especially tender winter crop, make late sowing early autumn under cover.

## Harvesting and Storage
Pick off individual leaves as required. Cut seedlings at any stage from about 5cm (2in) high. Although spike-like seed heads are attractive, it is best to remove them to encourage continual cropping. In practice plants will seed themselves, and seedlings can easily be transplanted to wherever they are required.

## Use in Salads and Cooking
Use leaves raw when young and tender. Fairly strong flavour and become tough early, but refreshing green colour and pretty shape in winter salads. Can blanch older leaves in hot water to tenderize. (See also Wild Plants and Weeds p.248.)

Italian names: *Herba stella*, *minutina*; German name: *Krähenfuß-Wegerich*.

### PUMPKIN *Curcurbita maxima* and other species
Seeds can be sprouted, but it is a must to use the particular cultivars which produce unhulled seed, such as 'Triple Treat' and 'Lady Godiva'. Seeds may need rinsing three times a day. Eat when the sprouts have reached about 2cm (¾in) long.

### PURSLANE, SUMMER *Portulaca oleracea*
Low-growing, half-hardy, succulent plant with rounded fleshy leaves and juicy stems. Flourishes in mild climates all over the world. Two distinct forms. Green – thinner leaved, possibly better flavoured, possibly hardiest and more robust. Gold – thicker leaved, more succulent, very attractive in salads and when growing. In some situations green more prolific; in others gold. Worth experimenting.

## Soil and Situation
Prefers well-drained, light, sandy soil, but will grow on heavier soil provided good drainage. In temperate and cool climate sunny, sheltered position advisable or grow under cover. Good subject for odd corners in

greenhouses, frames, or under cloches. Grows profusely in warm and favourable conditions.

### Cultivation

Can be grown as single plants or, if preferred, as CCA seedlings. For single plants either sow *in situ* outdoors after all risk of frost has passed, or sow in seedtrays or modules in a gentle heat indoors in late spring, harden-off, and plant out after all risk of frost has passed. Never sow in cold soil as the seedlings are fragile initially and prone to the various damping off diseases (see Raising Plants 'Indoors' p.77 and Pests and Diseases p.61). Space single plants about 15cm (6in) apart each way. For CCA seedlings sow in wide drills or patches (see Seed, Sowing Outdoors and Planting p.71). Sow outdoors, after risk of frost has passed, continuing until mid-summer. Very useful CCA seedling sowings can be made under cover in mid-spring and in late summer, for welcome early summer and autumn crops.

In cold summers plants can look dejected, leaves drop off, and slug attacks become likely. Cloche or film protection serves as 'pick-me-up'! In warm weather keep the plants well watered to encourage their rapid growth. Gold varieties reputedly keep a brighter colour if they are watered in full sunshine.

### Harvesting

First leaves of single plants ready to pick within two months of sowing. Keep picking young leaves, shoot tips and young stems; Evelyn recommended 'leaves of middling size'. Always leave two leaves at base of stem for regrowth. CCA seedlings ready within four or five weeks, and may give two or three cuts before running to seed. Pick regularly and remove flower buds, which become very knobbly. Plants become coarser once allowed to flower, but may regenerate if cut right back to within roughly 4cm (1¾in) of ground.

French name: *Pourpier vert* (green), *à large feuille dorée* (golden).

### Use in Salads and Cooking

Use leaves and stems raw in salads. Crunchy succulent texture, rather 'cooling'. Glossiness of yellow form very pretty in salads. Pleasant rather bland flavour. (William Cobbett of 'Rural Rides' in chauvinist vein described purslane as 'fit only for pigs and Frenchmen'!) Blandness makes it popular with children. Leaves and stems can be pickled successfully. Leaves also used in soup, or cooked like spinach.

**PURSLANE, WINTER Claytonia, miner's lettuce, Indian lettuce**
*Montia perfoliata* (Previously *Claytonia perfoliata*)
Hardy annual with succulent leaves; early leaves simple, heart-shaped;
later leaves curious rounded shape, wrapped around the stem as if pierced
by it. We 'discovered' it in Belgium as *Claytone perfolie de Cuba*, but it was
introduced into Britain from the American continent in the nineteenth
century, and has become a naturalized weed. Closely related to North
American 'Spring Beauty'. Pretty salad plant, at best in cooler months.

**Soil and Situation**
Not fussy! Loudon's *Encyclopedia* (1860) says 'it has no pretensions to
supersede spinach . . . but in very poor soils, under trees, or in other pecu-
liar circumstances it may be found an useful resource'. Romps on light
soils, but can grow well on heavy soil.Good drainage essential.

**Cultivation**
Can grow as single plants or CCA seedlings. Sow mid- to late spring for
summer crop. Sow mid- to late summer for main winter to spring crop.
Make final sowing early autumn under cover for very early, top quality
winter crop. Seedlings can be transplanted into cold greenhouse as late as
early winter for a spring crop. In temperate climates advisable to have
some in open and some under cover to give a succession. As covered
crop runs to seed in spring, outdoor crop will be maturing.

Sow in modules for transplanting or sow very thinly in rows or wide
drills, thinning to 15-20cm (6-8in) apart. Can also broadcast thinly. Seeds
are black, tiny and slippery so sowing thinly not easy, but necessary as
seedlings become very entangled with each other and are difficult to thin.

Winter purslane normally very hardy, but may be advisable to protect
outdoor crops in severe winters, for example with film or light straw. If
roots get very wet in severe weather outdoor plants sometimes turn
'blue' and die. Outdoor plants normally run to seed and die in early to
mid-summer. In most conditions they self-seed abundantly, and start
reappearing in autumn, and then again in spring. If transplanting make
that the sure tiny roots don't dry out. Abundant self-seeding means you
may only need to buy one packet of seed in a lifetime. If plants start to
overrun garden (especially in spring) treat as green manure and dig in or
use as a mulch!

**Harvesting**
If plants well-established by autumn, will give several cuts during winter.

From late winter onwards plants vivid green; grow with extraordinary rapidity, quickly producing flowers on long stalks. Leaves, stalks and flowers all edible; cut carefully, leaving basal tuft intact for resprouting, or treat as CCA seedlings. Be careful not to uproot plants, which are very shallow rooting. Leaves become coarser once plants start to seed.

## Use in Salads and Cooking

Can be available all the year round if sown in spring and summer. Has become indispensable ingredient in my early spring salads, often substituting for lettuce. Notable for fresh appearance, cool, succulent texture. Some find flavour bland, but perfect accompaniment to sharpness of chicories, endives, cresses and mustards. Children love it. Leaves can be cooked like spinach – but seems a waste!

Note: I personally find leaves of the pink-flowered winter purslane, *Montia sibirica*, have an unpleasant aftertaste, so are unsuitable for salads. Not everyone agrees!

### RADISH *Raphanus sativus*

Diverse group of fast-growing salad vegetables of ancient culinary use, characterized by hot flavour and crunchy texture. Grown mainly for swollen roots, which range from 2cm (¾in) diameter to giant oriental types over 40cm (16in) across. Shape and skin colour very diverse; flesh normally white but rose-pink or green in oriental 'Beauty Heart' types. In certain cultivar's seedlings, mature leaves and seed pods also edible, raw or cooked. Some types can be stored. By growing different types usually possible to have year round supply.

Main types: Small radishes – the classical western radish. Either round or long, but rarely much more than 5-7.5cm (2-3in)long; skin colour most commonly white, pink, red or bicoloured but more rarely purplish, brownish or yellow. Mainly grown for summer use, but some small-leaved cultivars suitable for growing under cover in winter in northern latitudes. Large hardy winter radishes – round or long in shape, generally 500-1000g (1-2lb) in weight. Outer skin is white, black, red or violet. The texture is fairly coarse. Capable of surviving temperatures as low as -10°C (14°F). Sown mid- to late summer for use fresh during the winter, or, in areas with severe climate, lifted and stored. Large white 'mooli' ('daikon') radishes – range of mostly very long white or part green-skinned oriental radishes. Those best known in west are smooth skinned, anything from 10-60cm (4-24in) long, and are grown for summer and autumn use. However many types exist, suited to wide range of climates and soil conditions, including huge round cultivars. 'Beauty Heart' radishes – very striking oriental types originating in Manchuria in north China. Pink-fleshed 'Xin Li Mei' (pronounced 'shin lee may' which means 'heart inside beautiful') has green skin, is round or rectangular in form, sweet flavoured. Green-fleshed types generally long, also fairly sweet flavour. All types radish used raw in salads. Some large radishes are also cooked like turnips.

## Soil and Situation
Most radishes naturally cool season crops, tending to run to seed rapidly in hot weather. In general grow best in warm, light, fertile soils, manured for previous crop. Rich sandy soils ideal. Essential to have adequate supplies of water during growing period. In very poor or dry soils radishes become very hot flavoured. Small, fast growing types very useful for intersowing or intercropping. For example can be broadcast with early carrots; sown on the surface above early-planted potatoes; sown between widely-spaced brassicas, rows of peas, beans or lettuce; used as row markers between slow-growing crops. In all these cases radishes ready to pull before the main crop would be disturbed.

## Cultivation
Small Radishes: Spring to Autumn
Must be grown fast or they become woody outside, puffy inside. For continuous supply sow little and often at about ten day intervals. Normally ready within four weeks of sowing. Sow *in situ* outdoors as soon as soil workable in early spring until early autumn. Make very early sowings under cover in late winter for the first crop, and sow in mid- to late autumn under cover for late crop.

Sow thinly and shallowly, broadcast, or in rows about 15cm (6in) apart, or in wide drills (see Seed, Sowing Outdoors and Planting pp.69-71). Thin early to 2.5cm (1in) apart. (It sounds absurd, but if possible *sow* seeds 2.5cm (1in) apart; countless failures stem from thick sowing, then failing to thin soon enough.) Overcrowded seedlings become leggy, entangled, and never form useful size radishes.

Summer sowings may run to seed rapidly in hot weather. Use bolt-resistant cultivars where available. Water drills thoroughly before sowing (see Seed, Sowing Outdoors and Planting p.73). Sow in lightly shaded situation, but not too shaded or plants become drawn.

Watch out for flea beetle nibbling holes in seedling leaves. (For control see Pests and Diseases p.54.) Water only if necessary to prevent soil drying out. Pull for use as soon as ready; some modern cultivars stand much longer than older cultivars without deteriorating. For cultivars see p.194.

### Small Radishes: Winter Under Cover

Can be very useful crop in temperate climates in cold or slightly heated greenhouses or polytunnels. Sow suitable cultivars only from mid-autumn to late winter. Thin to 5cm (2in) apart. Slower maturing than summer radishes. Do not overwater, but if leaves look very dark, some watering necessary. For cultivars see p.194.

### Large Hardy Winter Radishes

This group is a valuable source of radish from mid-autumn to mid-spring. Do best in light, well-drained soil, but tolerate heavier soil than ordinary radish. Sow mid- to late summer; may take up to three months to develop. Normally sown *in situ*, but can sow in modules and transplant before tap root starts to develop. Important to sow thinly, or thin early to 15–23cm (6–9in) apart each way. Water sufficiently to prevent soil drying out during growing season. Control flea beetle in early stages. Flavour best if left in ground over-winter protected with straw or litter; probably advisable to lift if soil very wet, or roots being severely damaged by slugs or mice, or temperatures likely to fall below about -8°C (17°F). Store in boxes of sand under cover, or in piles or clamps outdoors covered by about 10cm (4in) of straw. If roots too large to use in one go, cut roots can be wrapped and kept in fridge or cool place for week or so.

### Large White 'Mooli' Radishes

Strong tendency for many 'mooli' radishes to bolt if sown early in the year, or if temperatures drop suddenly. Main sowing early to late summer; for late spring sowings use bolt-resistant cultivars. Sow in modules, as for hardy winter radish, or sow *in situ* 1.3–2cm (½–¾in) deep, or in 4cm (1¾in) deep drills, pulling soil around stems as radishes develop for extra support. Spacing depends on cultivar and stage of harvesting. Space small types and any being pulled young about 10cm (4in) apart; large types up to 25cm (10in) apart or further for exceptionally large cultivars. Most currently available cultivars mature within two months. 'Mooli' radishes subject to common brassica/crucifer pests (see Cabbage, Chinese p.136). Where pest damage serious consider growing under fine nets (see Pests and Disease p.53). Harvest when mature or at intermediate stages. Cultivars vary in ability to stand without becoming coarse. (See *Oriental Vegetables*, Further Reading p.251.)

Note: Traditional European 'Bavarian' radishes, generally about 20cm (8in) long, sometimes cultivated like the 'mooli' radish, but can be sown earlier without premature bolting. Probably coarser in texture.

### 'Beauty Heart' Radish

Pink-fleshed types – sow as for 'mooli' radish from mid- to late summer *in situ* or in modules for transplanting. Transplant at three- to five-leaf stage. In areas where autumn weather unpredictable cover, or transplant under cover, in late summer/early autumn. Space plants 20cm (8in) apart each way. Keep soil reasonably moist. Roots liable to crack if subjected to alternating dry and wet conditions. Normally ready ten to twelve weeks after sowing. Roots remain in good condition for several weeks when mature. Can lift and store as winter radishes if required.

Green-fleshed types – more tolerant of cold weather than pink-fleshed types. Sow as 'mooli' radish mid- to late summer, or early autumn under cover. Space 13-20cm (5-8in) apart depending on cultivar. Normally mature within two months of sowing. Roots should be lifted before the advent of severe frost.

### Radish Seed Pods

Immature radish seed pods widely used in East and, in the past, in Europe, both fresh and pickled. Excellent flavour and texture; many people find preferable to radishes. Either grow types cultivated for the purpose, such as traditional 'Rat's Tail Radish' (*Raphanus caudatus*) which can be 30cm (12in) long or German radish 'München Bier'; or allow a few plants of ordinary radish to go to seed. In my experience, the larger the radish, the more succulent the pods are likely to be. Large hardy winter radishes produce abundant pods if left to overwinter and run to seed following spring. Many oriental types, and longer types of western summer radish, also develop good pods. Depending on cultivar, flavour ranges from very pleasant mildness to overpoweringly hot. In the absence of systematic research, experiment with whatever you are growing. Always pick pods while green and tender enough to snap cleanly in half. Sow 'Rat's Tail' and 'München Bier' spring to summer, thinning to 30cm (12in) apart. Plants can grow very large if allowed to seed. Watch out for pollen beetle attacks (for control see Pests and Disease p.59).

### Seedling Sprouts

Little punnets of radish seedlings with a pair of seed leaves and 7.5-10cm (3-4in) long white, green or pink stems widely sold in Japan as 'kaiware'.

Very easily grown and excellent for quick winter crops. (For cultivation see Seed Sprouting and Seedling Sprouts pp.98-104.) Any radish cultivars can be used, but specially fast growing cultivars with fairly large seed recommended for purpose. For cultivars see below.

Leaf Radish
Young radish leaves, at stage beyond seedling leaves, often tasty and tender enough to use raw in salads. In past in Europe were forced on hotbeds for winter 'salading'. Radish thinnings at two- to three- true leaf stage (known in China as 'wa wa cai' or baby vegetables) can be used similarly. In theory any radish cultivar can be used for leaf, but most suitable types have smooth leaves and bulk up rapidly. (Young leaves often unpleasantly coarse and hairy.) Worth experimenting with available spare seed. Excellent cultivar for purpose is 'Bisai' which is both heat and cold tolerant. Sow *in situ* outdoors, in wide drills or broadcast (see Seed, Sowing Outdoors and Planting pp.69-71) throughout growing season, or under cover in late winter, early spring, and again in late autumn. First cut may be ready within two weeks of sowing. Treat as CCA seedlings. Eat young leaves raw, older leaves cooked. If a few plants remain they may eventually develop medium sized 'mooli' type radishes. Radish stems also used as cooked vegetable in China.

**Cultivars**
Small spring to autumn crop – numerous cultivars available, some especially adapted to sowing at certain seasons. Be guided by current catalogues. Best known: 'French Breakfast'; recommended for very early sowings: Saxa (Red Forcing); long-standing in summer: 'Red Prince'. Small winter crop under cover – 'Helro', 'Robino', 'Saxa'. Hardy winter radish – 'Cherokee', 'China Rose', 'Violet de Gournay', 'Black Spanish'. Large white 'mooli' radish – $F_1$ hybrids generally recommended, for example 'April Cross' (slow bolting), 'Minowase Summer' (slow bolting and mild flavoured). 'Beauty Heart' radish – 'Man Tang Hong' best red cultivar available at the time of writing; watch out for green cultivars becoming available in future. Established green Japanese cultivars include 'Green Flesh', 'Shantung Green Skin', 'Green Meat Chinese'. Seedling radish – '40 days', 'Bisai'. Leaf radish – 'Bisai'.

**Use in Salads and Cooking**
Small radishes – use raw, whole or sliced. Hardy winter and 'mooli' radishes – use sliced or grated in salads. Sharpest flavour in skin, so use

peeled if it seems too strong. Can be cooked, generally like turnips, for example boiled, in stews, soups or curries, or roasted under a joint. Can be pickled. Leafy tops can be cooked like greens. 'Beauty Heart' – use red types grated, sliced, or cut into matchsticks *unpeeled* so green skin forms attractive outer edge. Sometimes served sprinkled with sugar. Chinese carve pink types into beautiful flowers, or even insects like dragonflies. Green-fleshed types used like ordinary radishes. Radish pods – excellent raw in salads; recommended in finely-sliced brown bread and butter sandwiches. Can be steamed or mixed in stir-fries. Popular pickle world wide. Seedling sprouts – mainly used raw or as a garnish, but can be incorporated into soups and sauces. Leaf radish – use raw in salads when young, steam or stir-fry when larger and becoming coarse.

### RAPE, SALAD *Brassica napus*
Salad rape is one of the most useful and productive salad seedlings. Often used as mustard substitute in mustard and cress mixtures. Much milder flavoured (does not become unpleasantly hot when mature), and much slower to run to seed. For cultivation for CCA seedlings and seedling sprouts see Cress p.151 and Mustard, white, p.179. In temperate climates can sow outdoors throughout growing season as CCA seedling crop, often cutting three or four times. When plants 20cm (8in) or more in height pick small leaves for salads, larger leaves for cooked greens. Very useful for winter to early spring salad crop, sown late autumn or late winter, either under cover, or in sheltered place. Germinates at low temperatures, and can survive -10°C (14°F). Where grown in mixtures with cress sow three days after cress so both ready at same time.

### RICE *Oryza sativa*
Rice grains easily sprouted. Use unpolished brown rice, round or long grained. Mild flavour; normally ready in three to five days. Eat 1.3cm (½in) long.

### ROCAMBOLE Sand leek *Allium scorodoprasum*
Type of garlic originally from Eastern Europe which forms small bulbs, but most useful for fine chive-like leaves which appear very early in spring and again in autumn. Often forms tiny bulbils in flower stems, which emerge quaintly coiled.

### Soil, Situation and Cultivation
Little information exists on cultivation. In my experience tolerates most

well-drained soils and light shade. Sow seed in spring, or plant bulbs or small aerial bulblets from spring to autumn. Plant bulbs 2-2.5cm (¾-1in) deep, spaced approximately 7.5cm (3in) apart. Once established rocambole seeds itself freely and reappears throughout garden. Some risk of it becoming a weed.

## Use in Salads
Leaves have a delicate texture and pleasant chive flavour with a hint of garlic. Use in salads like chives. Where there is an adequate supply of bulbs lift and use like garlic.

## ROCKET, SALAD Arugula, rucola, Mediterranean rocket/cress, Italian cress *Eruca sativa, E. vesicaria*
Fairly hardy, annual Mediterranean plant, often overwintering in temperate climates. Young leaves have unique spicy flavour to which salad lovers become addicted! Grows best in coolish weather and is then apt to run to seed rapidly in hot dry conditions. Low-growing until seeding, when shoots up to over 60cm (2ft) high. Naturalized in parts of Europe and elsewhere.

## Soil and Situation
Tolerates most soils and situations. Mid-summer crop best in light shade. In cold areas sheltered position advisable for winter crop. Grown under-cropping brassicas in parts of Europe; seedling crop is also very useful for intercropping.

## Cultivation
Very easy crop to grow either as single plants or as CCA seedlings. Responds particularly well to CCA treatment at all stages. Sow outdoors throughout the growing season, from late spring as soon as soil becomes workable until early autumn. Germinates at fairly low temperatures; can make very early sowings under cover in mid- to late winter, and again from mid-autumn to early winter.

Normally sow this plant *in situ*, in rows or in wide drills or broadcast (see Seed, Sowing Outdoors and Planting pp.69-71). In cool weather can also be sown in seedtrays and then transplanted. Space single plants 15cm (6in) apart. Flea beetle may cause a problem here in the early stages of plant growth. (For control see Pests and Diseases p.54.) Can also be grown as seedling sprouts indoors (see Seed Sprouting and Seedling Sprouts p.98). Frequent watering are advisable in summer to keep plants tender, and to moderate flavour, which becomes stronger with mature plants and under dry conditions. Very easy to save seed; leave a few of best plants in late spring, and collect seed pods when dry. Small plants more likely to survive cold winter than large; cloche protection beneficial in winter to improve quality.

## Harvesting
Seedlings can be ready for cutting within three to four weeks of sowing. Start cutting when about 5cm (2in) high, cutting about 2cm (¾in) above ground level. Plants may resprout as many as five times in favourable conditions. Pick individual leaves from single plants, or cut across whole plant leaving it to resprout. In summer cut flower spikes back to basal tuft to revitalize growth. Leaves can be stripped off stems of mature plants for use. Flowers are edible in salads.

French: *Roquette*. Italian: *Rucola*.

## Use in Salads and Cooking
In most climates can be available fresh all year round if several sowings made and winter crop protected. Delicious spicy flavour; leaves and flowers edible. Leaves also used in sauces and cooked like spinach; in France cooked with peas.

Note: Not to be confused with garden rocket *Hesperis matrionalis*.

### RYE *Secale cereale*
For sprouting see Barley p.135. Sprouts eaten either when very tiny or when 2-2.5cm (¾-1in) long.

### 'SALADINI'
The name often now given to seed mixtures of salad plants, based on the traditional European salad mixes, known in France as *mesclun/mesclum*. Typical modern 'saladini' mixture might include cos lettuce, red and green 'cutting' lettuce, salad rocket, red and sugar loaf chicory, curly endive and corn salad. Numerous other salad plants and herbs can be included. (For cultivation see Salad Techniques p.85.)

### 'SALADINI, ORIENTAL'
This is a seed mixture of oriental greens, originally devised in 1991 to acquaint western gardeners with some of the wonderful, leafy oriental vegetables. The original mix was komatsuna, white-stemmed pak choi, loose-headed Chinese cabbage, mizuna, mibuna and purple mustard.

Young leaves are used raw to create flavoursome salads; older leaves can be cooked like greens.

## Cultivation

Normally sown *in situ* in wide drills for CCA seedlings in salads. Sow outdoors spring and early summer; avoid mid-summer sowings in hot weather as liable to bolt rapidly, and continue sowing late summer/early autumn. Extend season by sowing under cover late autumn, and mid-winter/early spring. Can also sow in seedtrays in good cutting compost to get at least one cut, or in used growing bags.

Several weeks after mixture has germinated can distinguish different seedlings in mixture; if some large plants wanted prick out into seedtrays or transplant 30-38cm (12-15in) apart in permanent position in open or under cover. (For details, see individual plants.) Protect from common brassica pests (see Cabbage, Chinese p.136). For long productive period plenty of moisture and fertile soil essential.

## Harvesting

Normally treat as CCA seedling crop (See Salad Techniques p.85). Number of cuts possible before plants start to bolt varies with season: most productive sowing probably late summer, but early sowings very useful. Even when plants growing taller, can continue harvesting some leaves, often over long period. When plants eventually start bolting young flowering shoots useable, raw or cooked.

### SALSIFY Salsafy, oyster plant, vegetable oyster *Tragopogon porrifolius*

Hardy biennial plant, growing over 90cm (3ft) high, with long tapering roots, narrow leaves and purple daisy-like flowers. Roots, leafy shoots (known as chards), buds and flowers can all be used in salads. (For Flowers and Wild Salsify see p.239.)

## Soil and Situation

Any position. Roots develop best on deep, light, stone-free soil, manured well for previous crop. Seed heads beautiful translucent 'powder puff', so in second season plants very pretty in decorative potager. Salsify has welcome tendency to self-seed.

## Cultivation

Sow early to late spring *in situ*. If growing primarily for roots, thin to 10cm (4in) apart. If growing for shoots or flowers can sow groups of three to four seeds at about 15cm (6in) intervals, leaving plants unthinned. Germination tends to be erratic. (Use fresh seed as viability deteriorates fairly rapidly.) Keep plants well weeded and watered during summer; mulching beneficial.

**Harvesting and Storage**
Roots ready for use mid-autumn to late spring. In very cold areas, or for convenience, lift and store for winter in boxes of sand. Otherwise leave in soil, covering with straw or bracken to facilitate lifting when ground is frosty. Leave a few roots to flower in following spring/early summer. Flowering season may continue into autumn. For cooking pick buds just before opening with about 10cm (4in) of stem (which is delicious). Otherwise use open flowers raw in salads.

Production of Chards
Two alternative methods used:
Firstly, in autumn cut off old leaves about 2.5cm (1in) above ground; mound up stems with 12-15cm (4½-6in) of light soil. Well-blanched chards push their way through in early spring.

Secondly, when growth starts in spring cover plants with at least 10cm (4in) straw or dry leaves. Resulting chards will be less blanched but very clean and tasty in salads. Probably the better method in heavy soils.

With either method plants can also be covered with darkened flower pots or upturned buckets, as for 'Witloof' forcing (see p.92).

Cut leaves when about 10-12cm (4-4½in) long. They are most tender at the base. Stumps will resprout several times, giving several cuts. During late spring and early summer the green leaves are tender enough to be used in salads. Allow some of the plants to flower and use the cooked buds/flowers in salads.

**Cultivars**
Little choice available, but look out for more productive introductions.

**Use in Salads and Cooking**
Delicate flavour of roots reminiscent of oysters. Cook scrubbed but unpeeled, and peel after cooking. Serve hot or cold with dressing. Chards ready late winter to late spring. Use raw in salads or lightly cooked. Use flowers raw or pickled. Cook buds and attached stems lightly, boiled or steamed. Serve hot or cold with melted butter or vinaigrette dressing.

### SCORZONERA Viper's grass *Scorzonera hispanica*

Hardy perennial, in gardening books perpetually twinned with salsify. Similar in appearance and use except leaves broader, roots black-skinned, flowers yellow.

### Soil and Situation

As for salsify.

### Cultivation

As for salsify, except that being perennial it can be left in the soil for second season. Lift one or two sample roots in autumn; if only finger thickness leave in ground until following autumn; they will thicken without toughening. Can also sow in late summer for use following autumn.

Besides raising from seed, old gardening books suggest propagation from roots. Cut or break roots into pieces, or plant cut-off tops of roots in good moist ground when roots are lifted.

### Cultivars

'Lang Jan' among best of improved modern cultivars.

### Use in Salads and Cooking

As for salsify, except that according to Jan Blüm of Blüm Seeds roots should *not* be peeled as distinct flavour is mainly in the skin. Flower buds form fair-sized clusters and, with some the tops of stalks (see salsify) are exceptionally tasty and succulent, almost like asparagus. Boil lightly and eat hot or cold.

### SCORZONERA, FRENCH *Scorzonera picroides*

Annual form growing in rosette-shape, mentioned in old gardening books. Was sown in drills like chives and cut several times during season, the young leaves being used raw in salads. Has, unfortunately, disappeared from modern catalogues.

### SEAKALE *Crambe maritima*

Perennial seashore plant of ancient usage, grown for blanched young leaf stalks in spring. Large attractive plant with broad, frilled and twisted, glaucous blue-green leaves, which are sometimes tinged pink when young. Grows up to 60cm (2ft) high. This was not cultivated until early nineteenth century. Does best in cool maritime climates. (For wild plant see Wild Plants and Weeds p.249.)

**Soil and Situation**

Thrives in sunny situation. Grows in wide range of soil provided well-drained; deep rich sandy soils ideal. Although requires moisture when growing, tolerates summer drought well. Plantation may last eight to ten years, so dig ground very thoroughly before planting. Work in plenty of well-rotted manure or compost. Lime to bring pH to 6.5. Seakale is closely related to brassicas; never plant in clubroot infested soil.

**Cultivation**

Normally raised from seed or by root cuttings ('thongs'), but to increase stock can also lift mature plants in autumn and spring and divide rootstock carefully. For top quality plants space plants 45-60cm (18-24in) apart. Closer spacing is possible in small gardens, but you must expect smaller shoots.

Raising from Seed

Cheapest method, but resulting plants may be variable. Use fresh seed, as viability falls off in second year. Seed has hard outer coat, which gives floating seed its buoyancy, and may take a long time to break down and germinate, perhaps as long as two to three years. Ensure ground kept moist during germination period. (Some people have had improved results by scraping off outer shell.) Sow in seedtrays or seedbed and transplant or sow *in situ*. Sow early to mid-spring, or even during winter months. Transplant or thin to final spacing. Seedlings may be attacked by flea beetle. (For control see Pests and Diseases p.54.)

Keep weed free, water if drying out in early stages, remove any flowering stems, and apply seaweed fertilizer occasionally during the growing season. If many feeble shoots are produced, thin out to encourage strong ones. Best to build up plants and defer blanching until plants are in third season. Propagate from the best plants in future years, discarding weakest.

Raising from Thongs

More reliable method, giving earlier results. Purchase thongs when available for autumn or spring planting, or prepare your own as follows. Lift established plant (at least two years old) in autumn. Select roots of finger thickness, and cut into pieces 10-15cm (4-6in) long. Trim flat across top end, diagonally across lower end, to avoid planting upside down! Store upright in moist sand until early spring, when buds form on thongs. Rub out all but central bud. Plant outdoors in spring. Plant upright with bud covered by 5cm (2in) soil. Cultivate as for seed-raised plants. Can force *in situ* in autumn if plants seem robust, or delay forcing for a year.

### Forcing and Harvesting
Plants either forced *in situ*, (which can be repeated every year), or lifted and forced indoors for an earlier crop. This exhausts plants which must then be discarded. The following methods are relatively simple.

*In situ* – when plants die down in autumn remove all decaying foliage. In mid-winter cover crowns with 7.5cm (3in) of dry leaves to raise temperature, then exclude light and force into growth by covering completely with traditional clay seakale pots if available, or large boxes or pots, or any structure covered with black polythene film. Allow space for growth 45cm (18in) high. Complete darkness essential to prevent bitterness in young growths and develop best flavour. Can pile additional straw, manure, or leaves over the structure to raise temperature. Young blanched shoots normally ready about twelve weeks later in early to late spring. Use sharp knife to cut young shoots 10-20cm (4-8in) long, cutting below soil level with small portion of root attached. Cut just before use, as shoots toughen on exposure to light. Leave small shoots to come into leaf during the summer. Remove cover after cutting; allow plant to grow again, and blanch again following year. If crowns of old plants become exposed, cover with a little soil to protect them.

Forcing indoors – widely practised in past to get earlier crop. Wait until crowns at least three years old. Lift plants after they have been exposed to frost. Trim off side roots, and pot close together in boxes, pots or in soil in a darkened area under the greenhouse staging, as for 'Witloof' chicory (see p.148). Ideal temperature: 15-21°C (59-70°F). Shoots ready within a few weeks. Harvest as for plants forced outdoors.

### Cultivars
Little choice in practice. 'Common' – slightly pink tinge when young, 'Lily-white' – purer white.

### Use in Salads and Cooking
Forced young stems have unique, delicate, nutty flavour; crisp texture. Slice into salads. Very young leaves can be used during spring and summer while still tender. Well-known gardener Beth Chatto chops young, pink leaves with chives and tarragon for spring salad. Seakale also cooked like asparagus, served with melted butter, grated cheese or sauces.

### SENPOSAI HYBRIDS *Brassica hybrids*

Japanese brassica/crucifer hybrids, developed by various cabbage and komatsuna crosses. Naturally vigorous, healthy crops, with good tolerance to heat, cold and disease . . . hence Japanese name meaning 'thousand jewel vegetable'. Mainly grown as source of cooked greens when young, but seedlings and young leaves also excellent raw in salads. Pleasant flavour with cabbage and spinach hues.

### Soil, Situation and Cultivation

See Komatsuna p.168. Can be sown throughout growing season. Suggest that the most productive use is to sow in wide drills (see Sowing Outdoors p.71), cutting when 5-10cm (2-4in) high for use as CCA salad seedlings. Then thin to about 5cm (2in) apart, and cut for use as young greens when 15-20cm (6-8in) high, roughly six to eight weeks after sowing. Very useful winter crop – under cover in severe climates; outdoors in mild areas. Can also be sprouted or used for seedling sprouts (see Seed Sprouting and Seedling Sprouts pp.98-104).

### Cultivars

Various cultivars have appeared. At the time of writing 'Senposai No.2' probably best flavoured and most attractive leaf.

### SHALLOT Multiplier onions *Allium cepa* (Aggregatum Group)

Reasonably hardy, distinctly flavoured onion-like bulb which rapidly multiplies into cluster of individual bulbs. Good substitute for onions as easily grown and fast maturing; most cultivars store for exceptionally long time – much longer than onions. Grows well where temperatures too high for bulb onions, over 30°C (86°F). Normally roundish in shape, but some long and banana-shaped forms. Flesh reddish or creamy (technically, often described as yellow). Reds considered better flavoured, but smaller, slower growing, and may not store as well.

### Soil and Situation

Open site; deeply-worked, well-drained, light soils best. Rotate as for onions; do not plant on freshly-manured soil.

### Cultivation

Traditionally grown from bulbs or 'sets', but stock often diseased, and susceptible to bolting. New, very healthy, seed-raised cultivars are now being introduced, with good bolting resistance. Use where available.

Raising from Sets

Always start with healthy stock; some shallot strains are virused. Be suspicious of very cheap offers! Ideal size for planting about 2cm (¾in) diameter, as small sets less likely to bolt than larger sets – which do not necessarily produce larger shallots. In temperate climates plant most cultivars late winter, early spring. Where winters very mild plant late winter. (Note: Some cultivars, for example 'Santé', only suitable for late spring planting or they bolt prematurely. Be guided by suppliers' directions.) Where winter soil conditions poor can also start in seedtrays indoors in winter and transplant in early spring.

Remove loose scales before planting. Plant in shallow drills, pushing sets into ground to at least half their depth so only tips above ground. For maximum yields plant 18cm (7in) apart each way. Protect against birds with black cotton (see Pests and Diseases p.54). If any sets are uprooted *lift* and replant carefully. Young roots are damaged if simply pushed back in. Keep weed free. Little further attention required.

Raising from Seed

Sow indoors in seedtrays as for bulb onions, or sow *in situ* outdoors as soon as soil is workable. *Sowing* shallots is quite new and information on ideal spacing varies and is still scant. Aim to space seedlings about 5cm (2in) apart each way. Each seedling will develop into one shallot rather than a cluster. At wider spacing shallots will start to develop into clumps.

Note: Small sets or seedlings can be planted 2.5cm (1in) apart each way to give green shoots for harvesting very early like green onions. They can be started under cover for even earlier crop.

**Harvesting and Storage**

Shallots are normally ready from mid-summer onwards. Harvest and store as for bulb onions. Sets may keep for ten to sixteen months, depending on cultivar and conditions. Provided sets are perfectly healthy, reserve a few small ones to plant following season.

**Cultivars**

Traditional: 'Long Keeping Yellow', 'Long Keeping Red', 'Hative de Niort'; new yellows: 'Santé', 'Atlantic', 'Creation', (grown from seed); new reds: 'Pikant' and 'Delicato'.

**Use in Salads and Cooking**

Use as bulb onions; superb pickled.

**SHEPHERD'S PURSE** *Capsella bursa-pastoris*
Common annual weed. (For description, harvesting and use see Wild Plants and Weeds p.249.) When cultivated plants grow much larger than in wild.

## Soil, Situation and Cultivation
Not fussy about soil. Grows best in cool weather. Sow outdoors throughout growing season except in particularly hot weather. Extend season by sowing under cover late autumn and early spring. Either sow broadcast or in wide drills (see Seed, Sowing Outdoors and Planting pp.69-71), treating as CCA seedlings crop (see Salad Techniques pp.85-7), or space plants 10-15cm (4-6in) apart for larger plants. Generally runs to seed fairly quickly. Seed is quite difficult to obtain, so it is really worth saving any of your own from good large-leaved strain.

## SORREL, COMMON/BROAD-LEAVED *Rumex acetosa*, Buckler-Leaved/French Sorrel *Rumex scutatus* (Confusingly, *R. acetosa* is also sometimes called 'French sorrel')
Vigorous, hardy, perennial plants, with arrow-shaped leaves characterized by superb sharp, lemon flavour. Common sorrel generally 30-45cm (12-18in) high but up to 90cm (3ft) in some cultivars; long relatively broad leaves. Buckler-leaved sorrel dwarfer and somewhat sprawling. Leaves small, heart-shaped, very sharply flavoured. Both species found wild in Europe.

## Soil and Situation
Common sorrel prefers moist soil, tolerates some shade. Buckler-leaved needs good drainage and open situation; useful as path or bed edge. Both easily grown, excellent ground-cover plants.

## Cultivation
Grow as annual or perennial. As annual, sow *in situ* early spring, thin to 10cm (4in) apart. Pull whole plant for use.

To start perennial patch sow in spring in seedtray or *in situ*. Thin or plant 25-30cm (10-12in) apart. Alternatively divide mature roots in autumn or early spring, preferably when still dormant. Or leave a few plants to seed, and shake the seeds on to new, moist ground when ripe, or allow to seed naturally and transplant the seedlings to wherever they are required.

Water plants in very dry conditions, and top dress in spring with well-rotted manure or compost. Cut off flowering shoots as they develop to prolong season. Renew beds every three or five years if plants start to decline in vigour.

Sorrel is one of the last plants to die back in the autumn, reappearing very early in spring or late winter. If it is protected with cloches or fleecy film it may give pickings all winter, especially in mild areas or if placed in a very sheltered position. Giving the plant cloche protection in late winter will bring on early growth dramatically, at a time when salad is extremely scarce.

Where winters severe can lift several roots in late autumn, plant in boxes, and move into greenhouse for winter; or even plant direct in greenhouse soil. Alternatively, sow the seed in pots in mid-summer for winter use indoors.

### Harvesting
Can usually start picking two to three months after sowing, when two to three leaves on plant. Pick small individual leaves initially. Once plant well-established can cut across neck, treating as CCA crop. In hot summers leaves may become hard and extremely bitter if grown in exposed position; worth having a few plants in a shadier site to maintain a good-quality supply.

### Cultivars
Named cultivars fairly rare; 'Large de Belleville (Chambourcy)' – large broad-leaved form, pink-tinged leaf stalks. Popular in France.

French: *oseille*.

### Use in Salads and Cooking
Young leaves delicious used sparingly in salad, whole or chopped. Also used in green mayonnaise. Cooked in many ways, for example soup, sauces, cooked like spinach (often mixed with spinach to moderate the acidity) and in stews.

### SPINACH *Spinacia oleracea* and Spinach Beet (Perpetual spinach – a form of Swiss chard) *Beta vulgaris* subsp. *cicla*
True spinach and spinach beet (which has large spinach-like leaves but technically in beetroot family) mainly used cooked but popular in salads in United States. In Europe grown as CCA salad seedlings in the past. Tradition well worth reviving. Personally feel that CCA seedlings most productive and satisfactory way of growing spinach for salads, though mature leaves can be used raw, especially if shredded.

**Soil and Situation**
Requires fertile, moisture-retentive soil; tolerates light shade.

**Cultivation**
True spinach essentially cool weather crop and prone to rapid bolting at high temperatures and in dry conditions. Spinach beet more tolerant of high and low temperatures, probably most reliable type for all-the-year-round supply, though leaves coarser, probably less delicately flavoured than spinach.

Sow *in situ* outside from early spring to late summer. Sow as CCA seedlings in wide drills (see Seed, Sowing Outdoors and Planting p.71), or thin to about 15cm (6in) apart for small plants for CCA treatment. Late summer sowings will often stand until late following spring, especially if protected during winter. Also worth making early spring and late summer/early autumn sowings under cover. If using *ordinary* spinach most satisfactory sowings generally early spring under cover, late spring outside, late summer outside, and early autumn under cover. May run to seed rapidly, but worth experimenting to see what works best in your conditions. Although hardier types widely recommended for late sowings, in practice summer spinach cultivars often prove hardier than reputed. In cool areas protect late summer sowings, if necessary, to preserve quality. Can often cut CCA spinach seedlings over many months before the plants begin running to seed.

Note: Standard Swiss chard cultivars could be used for CCA seedlings, but in my opinion they are rather too coarse and 'heavy' flavoured for use in salads.

### SUNFLOWER *Helianthus annuus*
Use unhulled seed for sprouting. Seeds sprout slowly, so rinse thoroughly to keep fresh (see Seed Sprouting and Seedling Sprouts pp.98–104). Generally ready in five to eight days. Use when no more than 6mm (¼in) long or they become bitter.

### TEXSEL GREENS Ethiopian or Abyssinian mustard/cabbage *Brassica carinata*
Recently introduced brassica/crucifer, developed from an Ethiopian mustard, which may be natural hybrid between cabbage and mustard. Its many virtues include being highly nutritious, fast growing, reasonably hardy (has survived -7°C (20°F) in my garden) and versatile. Attractive glossy leaves with pleasant 'spinachy' flavour.

## Soil and Situation

Prefers open position, but tolerates light shade in mid–summer. Grows best in fertile, well-drained, moisture-retentive soil. Apt to bolt prematurely in dry conditions; grows fastest in cool weather. Because fast growing useful for intercropping and catch cropping; can be sown after main summer crops lifted, both outdoors and under cover. Also grown in soils where clubroot rules out growing most brassicas, as Texsel greens ready for harvesting before the plant becomes infected.

## Cultivation

Can be grown as 'greens', harvesting fairly small plants when about 20-30cm (8-12in) high; or as CCA seedling crop; or as seedling sprouts (see Seed Sprouting and Seedling Sprouts pp.98-104 and Harvesting, below).

Generally sown *in situ*. For continuous supply sow outdoors from early spring to early autumn at two to three week intervals. Mid-summer sowings less successful in hot conditions. Make very early sowing for CCA seedlings late winter/early spring under cover, and last sowing under cover in mid-autumn for winter crop. In soils infected by clubroot successive sowings can be made if plants pulled up by roots when harvested, and a three week gap left before re-sowing.

For CCA seedlings sow broadcast or in wide drills (see Seed, Sowing Outdoors and Planting pp.69-71). For highest yields of small plants either sow in rows 15cm (6in) apart, thinning to 5cm (2in) apart; or in rows 30cm (12in) apart, thinning to 2.5cm (1in) apart. Can also space plants about 8-10cm (3½-4in) apart for smaller plants; 15cm (6in) apart each way for medium sized plants; 25-30cm (10-12in) apart for large plants.

Take precautions against flea beetle in early stages of plant growth. Although Texsel green can be affected by most brassica pests, generally seems to be healthy crop. Can grow under fine nets if necessary (see Pests and Diseases p.53).

## Harvesting

In temperate climates can be available all the year round from successive sowings; probably best value in early spring and late autumn. My personal view is that the younger the leaves, the tastier. Use seedling sprouts when about 2.5cm (1in) high, generally within 10 days of sowing. In spring and autumn CCA seedlings may be ready three weeks after sowing. Cut about 1.3cm (½in) above ground. Will usually resprout once more, though occasionally bitterness develops with second cut. Young plants ready on average seven weeks after sowing. Either pull whole plant when 20-30cm (8-12in) high, or pick off individual leaves as required. They will remain productive over several weeks, until they run to seed. Even when plants seeding some small leaves can usually be picked from flower stems.

### Cultivars
'Texsel greens' has now superseded 'Karate' – the original Ethiopian mustard cultivar developed.

### Use in Salads and Cooking
Seedlings, young leaves and young stems have refreshing, mild but 'interesting' flavour. Use raw in salads. Larger leaves can be broken into pieces about 5cm (2in) long. Cook older leaves like greens, boiling or steaming, whole or in small pieces, for no more than three to four minutes.

### TOMATO *Lycopersicon esculentum*
Tender South American plant with red, yellow, orange, pink and occasionally white fruits, originally introduced to Europe as ornamental greenhouse climber. Grows poorly at temperatures below 10°C (50°F) and above 32°C (90°F). In cool climates it is often necessary to grow under cover. To grow outdoors requires at least eight frost-free weeks after planting. Tomatoes also need high light intensity. Shop bought fruits usually picked immature so much of the flavour is lost. For salad use, growing your own is very rewarding in terms of both quality and flavour.

Plant types: 'Indeterminate climbing' – main shoot can grow almost *ad infinitum*, over 3.6m (12ft) in suitable conditions; side shoots can develop into very long 'branches'. Usually grown as cordons, tied to canes or twisted around string, with side shoots nipped out regularly and growing point 'stopped' when sufficiently tall. Can be trained skilfully in many forms. 'Semi-determinate climbing' – main shoot stops growing early, often before reaching 1m (3½ft) high. Many 'Marmande' cultivars in this group. 'Bush' or 'determinate' – side branches develop instead of main shoot so plant remains bushy and sprawls on ground. The side shoots do not have to be cut back. Often early maturing. Useful for culture outdoors as no supports required for the plants, or where space limited, as can grow under cloches or low tunnels, or even in hanging baskets in the greenhouse or outdoors. 'Dwarf' – very small, compact types, often no more than 20cm (8in) high. Ideal for container growing. All types can be grown indoors or outside.

Fruit types: Several distinct types exist besides the well-known standard smooth, round, red tomato. Beefsteak – very large, smooth, fleshy; Marmande – large, irregular shape often ribbed, fleshy, well-flavoured; Oxheart – conical, fleshy, well-flavoured; Pear – 'waisted', pretty, but rarely well-flavoured; Plum – rectangular, solid, traditional Italian canning type; Cherry – small, round fruits averaging less than 2.5cm (1in) diameter, often, but not invariably, sweet or distinctly flavoured. Currant – very decorative, tiny finger-nail sized fruits. There are red and yellow forms of all fruit types.

## Soil and Situation

Requires fertile, well-drained soil, limed if acid. Work in plenty of well-rotted manure, compost/wilted comfrey before planting. Can prepare ground by digging a 30cm (12in) deep trench and working in manure. In warm climates sunny, open situation ideal. In temperate climates outdoor crop needs sunny, warm site sheltered from cold winds. Against sunny wall suitable provided plenty of soil moisture. Otherwise grow under cover, either in the ground or in containers. Dwarf cultivars can be grown as bed edgings.

Member of potato family, so rotate as potatoes over four or five year period if possible; however in blight-prone areas avoid growing *alongside* potatoes as easily infected with potato blight.

Soil Sickness

Where tomatoes grown for more than two or three years consecutively in same soil, especially in greenhouses, 'soil sickness' may start to develop due to build up of soil pests and diseases and fertilizer salts. Crops become progressively poorer. Solutions include: soil sterilization, replacing soil completely, growing in containers or growing bags, adopting soilless systems such as 'ring culture', and grafting tomatoes onto rootstocks with good pest and disease resistance (see Further Reading p.251).

Note: Polytunnels excellent solution to soil sickness (see Pests and Diseases p.62).

## Cultivation

Where climate allows it is usually more preferable to grow tomatoes outdoors, as fewer pest, disease, feeding and watering problems, and flavour usually better. In temperate climates must start plants under cover to get long enough growing season. Can then plant outdoors; or in unheated greenhouses or polytunnels; or outdoors under cloches, or in frames, low polytunnels, or under perforated or fleece films (see p.212). Growing in *heated* greenhouses for very early crop requires a considerable amount of specialist skill. Most 'outdoor' cultivars can be grown successfully indoors, but some modern 'greenhouse' cultivars are unsuitable for out-door cultivation.

Tomatoes can be grown in the soil or in rich potting compost in con-tainers such as pots, boxes, or 'growing bags'. The larger the container the better: 20cm (8in) pot minimum satisfactory size.

Sowing
Sow indoors in gentle heat early to mid-spring, allowing six to eight weeks from sowing to planting. Sow seeds 2cm (¾in) deep in seedtrays, modules, or small pots (see Raising Plants 'Indoors' pp.77–82). Ideal ger-mination temperature 20°C (68°F), though seedlings withstand consid-erably lower temperatures once small roots develop. Plant up in 5–8cm (2–3½in) pots at three-leaf stage. Where plants are bought, choose short sturdy plants, grown in individual pots rather than boxes.

Space out plants as they grow so individual plants are not touching. Keep them well ventilated and in good light. Do not coddle: the stur-dier and hardier they are the better! Plant late spring (under cover), early summer (outdoors). Harden-off well before planting outside. Never plant if soil temperature below 10°C (50°F), or if further frost expected. Best stage for planting when 18–20cm (7–8in) high, with first flowers showing. With outdoor bush crops, research has shown plant-ing when first truss just visible gives the best combination of earliness and high yield. Outdoor crops can be protected in the early stages with cloches, frames or low polytunnels. (For growing under perforated films, see p.212.) Planting through black, or white and black mulching films or permeable fabrics will conserve moisture and keep fruits clean (see Mulching pp.47–9).

Plant dwarf types 25–30cm (10–12in) apart; bush types 45–60 (18–24in) apart; climbing types 38–45cm (15–18in) apart. Tomatoes often planted in rows of staggered pairs to save space. When planting in pots leave at least 7.5cm (3in) space at top to allow for top dressing in late stages.

For tall types erect supports when planting, for example strong individual posts 1.2–1.5m (4–5ft) high. Alternatively, run two or three parallel wires between posts as supports. In greenhouses can suspend strings from overhead wire, either attached to hook in ground or tied to lowest branch on plant, allowing some slack. Twist plants around the string as they grow.

Outdoor Crop Under Perforated/Fleecy Films

System developed for outdoor crop in temperate/cool areas where no greenhouse available. Use bush cultivars. Raise plants indoors, plant out as soon as risk of frost is passed, planting through mulching film if wanted. Cover with perforated or fleecy films either laid directly over plants or laid over low hoops (see Protected Cropping, pp.115–125). Leave intact until flowers start to press against film. At this stage must cut film to allow insects to pollinate, but must be done in stages to 'wean' plants. Initially make intermittent cuts roughly 90cm (3ft) long down centre of row (see diagram p.117). Roughly a week later cut remaining gaps. Don't remove cut film: allow it to lie bunched up on either side of plants to act as additional windbreak.

Note: Ordinary polythene film is unsuitable for this method, as lack of ventilation leads to high temperatures and high humidity which cause a variety of problems.

Training, Feeding, Watering, Plant Health

Training: with cordon cultivars nip out side shoots which form on main stem. Remove shoots which arise from the base. As plants grow tie the main stem to the supports or twist around the string, allowing room for stem to thicken. Eventually plants have to be 'stopped' by nipping out the top growing point two leaves above a truss. Stop outdoor plants in mid- to late summer, so that remaining fruits have time to mature and ripen. Stop indoor plants when they reach the top of the supports, *or* in late summer as for outdoor plants. No side shooting or stopping is required for bush cultivars. In all cases remove any yellowing and diseased leaves that appear.

Watering: tomatoes require plenty of water, but many problems stem from faulty watering, especially under cover. Plants should neither be overwatered nor allowed to dry out. My personal view that under cover flavour probably maximized by watering heavily when soil on verge of becoming dry. Outdoors probably unnecessary to water (except in very dry conditions), until flowering starts. Plants in containers need regular watering. Keep all plants mulched to minimize need for watering. Under cover regular sprinkling on bright sunny days encourages fruit to set.

Feeding: outdoor crop planted in ground normally requires no feeding unless plants appear starved after second truss has set. If so feed weekly with tomato feed or diluted liquid comfrey. Plants in containers and plants grown indoors need regular feeding once or twice weekly once bottom trusses start swelling. As the plants grow top dress plants in containers with fresh potting compost, to cover surface roots. This can also be done with greenhouse tomatoes.

Plant health: most serious problem on outdoor plants is blight, especially in wet humid conditions in 'blight prone' areas. Can spray with Bordeaux mixture when infected leaves first noticed in mid- to late summer. Indoor plants prone to range of fungus diseases. Good growing conditions and maximum ventilation best preventive measures (see also Pests and Diseases pp.51-2). Whitefly often serious pest. Interplanting with French marigolds may help prevent; damp down frequently in warm weather to lower temperature and maintain humidity. Use biological control once attack evident (see Pests and Diseases p.55).

Harvesting

Number of fruit trusses varies widely from three to four outdoors in cool climates to up to twelve or more under cover.

Where outdoor fruits unlikely to ripen in open, cut plants down from supports in late summer (leaving roots in ground), lay on straw or plastic, and cover with cloches to ripen. Alternatively pull up by roots and hang in greenhouse or indoors. Immature fruits will also ripen slowly in dark cupboards, though much of flavour lost. In greenhouses plants can similarly be cut down if frost imminent, and covered with fleece film to prolong season.

Thoughts on Flavour

For maximum flavour pick fruits when firm and ripe. Flavour often a balance of acid and sweet elements. Influenced by cultivar (very subjective), enhanced by sunlight and *not* overwatering and overfeeding. Note also that flavour varies during season. My personal view that cherry types lose flavour once cold temperatures experienced, but solid fleshed types retain flavour much better after cold.

**Cultivars**

There is a huge choice. Many modern cultivars are bred primarily for glasshouse use, and have considerable disease resistance and yield highly. Flavour sometimes sacrificed. Experiment under your conditions and for your taste. The following are among the cultivars that I find well-flavoured. 'Ailsa Craig', 'Alfresco', 'Britain's Breakfast', '$F_1$ Counter', '$F_1$ Dombello', '$F_1$ Dona', 'Gardeners' Delight', '$F_1$ Kon Tiki', 'Marmande', 'Nepal', '$F_1$ Ostona', 'Oxheart', '$F_1$ Prisca', '$F_1$ Sungold', '$F_1$ Supermarmande', and 'Whippersnapper'.

## Use in Salads and Cooking

Fresh tomatoes excellent raw. Also widely used cooked by baking, in casseroles, or made into purées, sauces, juice, chutney. Can preserve by bottling, freezing and drying.

**TURNIP (*see* Secondary Salad Vegetables)**

**WATERCRESS** *Nasturtium officinale* **(Rorippa nasturtium-aquaticum)**
Hardy perennial aquatic plant, native of Europe. Long stems creep or float on surface, readily producing roots. Leaves have spicy, pungent flavour, very rich in vitamins and minerals. Cool season crop; in temperate climates grows best in spring and autumn. In warm climates mainly cultivated during winter months.

## Soil and Situation

Grows naturally in springs or fresh-running streams in chalk or limestone situations. Prefers constant water temperature of about 10°C (50°F). Requires fairly sheltered situation, and bright light but not full sun. Typical 'stream' conditions are ideal.

## Cultivation and Harvesting

Not easy to cultivate in typical garden, unless have flowing stream with running, uncontaminated, slightly alkaline water, enriched through decayed organic matter. Where these conditions exist plant rooted cuttings about 15cm (6in) apart along the stream bank in spring. Simplest way to obtain rooted cuttings is to buy shop watercress and put in a jar of water. Roots develop very rapidly.

Garden Bed Methods
I have no first-hand experience of either of the following methods, but I am informed they are well worth trying. Trench method – dig a 30cm (12in) deep trench, working about 15cm (6in) of compost or manure into the bottom before replacing soil. Plant rooted cuttings in the spring.

Sunken bed method – mark out an area say 0.8m sq (1yd sq). Prepare the ground deeply, digging in plenty of organic matter and little ground limestone. Make the bed 2.5cm (1in) below the level of the ground. Firm the surface, flood the bed. In spring broadcast seed thinly on the surface. Gently water the bed daily to flood it. Keep weed free. When shoots large enough cut with scissors. Do not cut too far down the stem if plants being over-wintered.

Cultivation in Pots
Practical method for small quantities. Stand pots outdoors, or in window, not in direct sunlight, in winter. Put a layer of gravel or moss in the bottom of a 20cm (8in) pot, to prevent soil being washed out. Cover with rich potting soil or potting compost, to which a little ground limestone is added. Stand pot in pan of fresh cool water. Plant several rooted cuttings in pot. Change the water regularly to prevent it becoming stagnant, possibly daily in hot summer weather. Feed occasionally with liquid fertilizer. Top dress the pot from time to time with well-rotted garden compost. Pick shoots as available. If plants start to deteriorate take cuttings and start again.

With all systems keep crops very well watered. Pinch out top growths to encourage branching and remove all flower heads. Feed occasionally with liquid seaweed. Pick lightly in first season until plants well-established. Once established most crops can be cut two or three times in the season. Protect outdoor winter crops from strong winds and frost with cloches, a frame or fleecy films. Or make a bed in a greenhouse for winter use, or plant up pots for winter use indoors.

## Use in Salads and Cooking
Use young shoots and leaves raw but sparingly as strong flavour. Also cooked like spinach, and in soups, in many parts of the world.

### WHEAT *Triticum vulgare*
For sprouting see Barley p.135. Sprouts normally ready after four to five days. Eat when very tiny.

# Chapter 13
## Secondary Salad Vegetables

A number of popular and some less known vegetables, which are normally cooked, can be used as salad vegetables. They are sometimes eaten raw, but are more frequently cooked and allowed to cool. Brief notes are given here on their use in salads, and, where relevant, on suitable cultivars and specialized growing methods. For standard cultivation consult the selection of general books on vegetable growing (see Further Reading p.251).

Tropical and semi-tropical plants (marked T) must normally be grown under cover in temperate climates. CCA = cut-and-come-again (see Salad Techniques p.85).

**AMARANTHUS** *Amaranthus* **sp. (T)**
Grow as CCA seedlings or plants spaced about 15cm (6in) apart. Use young leaves raw in salads.

**ARTICHOKE, GLOBE** *Cynara scolymus*
Eat the central 'chokes' of very small heads raw or pickled; use larger chokes cooked and cold.

**ARTICHOKE, JERUSALEM** *Helianthus tuberosus*
Grate the tubers raw into salads or eat cooked and cool. The flavour of raw tubers is quite different from those that are cooked.

**ASPARAGUS** *Asparagus officinalis*
Use spears cooked and cooled.

**ASPARAGUS PEA** *Tetragonolobus purpureus*
Use pods cooked and cold.

**AUBERGINE** *Solanum melongena* **(T)**
Fruits superb in salads, cooked and cold.

**BASELLA** *Basella* **sp. (T)**
Eat glossy young leaves and stems raw in salads.

**BEANS**
As there are toxins in almost all raw beans, beans should only be used in salads cooked and cold. Young bean pods, immature bean seeds (flageolets) and mature bean seeds (fresh or dried) make excellent salad dishes after cooking. For dried beans leave pods unpicked until turning brown; then pull up plants, hang in airy shed, shell when perfectly dry.

**Bean, Asparagus (Yard Long)** *Vigna sesquipedalis* **(T)**
Eat slender pods boiled then cooled. Steam leaves and young stems for adding to salads.

**Bean, Broad (Fava)** *Vicia faba*
Young leaf tips excellent raw; use shelled beans cooked – the younger the better. Pink-seeded cultivars best flavoured.

**Bean, French (Kidney, Snap)** *Phaseolus vulgaris* **(T)**
For flavour grow slender *filet* types, yellow 'waxpods' and purple-podded cultivars. 'Chevrier Vert' recommended for flageolets and drying; 'Dutch Brown' for drying.

**Bean, Lablab (Hyacinth bean)** *Lablab niger/Dolichos lablab* **(T)**
Excellent flavour, especially purple-podded cultivars. Boil or steam then cool for salads. Young leaves edible raw.

**Bean, Runner (Scarlet)** *Phaseolus coccineus* **(T)**
Sliced, cooked, green pods are good in salads.

**BEETROOT** *Beta vulgaris*
Either grate the roots of beet raw into salads, or cook whole until tender in boiling water or baked in foil then use whole, diced or sliced in salads. Small early beet probably best flavoured. Yellow and white cultivars, and 'Chioggia' (pink with white rings when cooked) very decorative contrasted with red beets. Use young leaves raw. Deep red leaves of 'Bull's Blood' especially colourful. Sugar beet is edible and sweetly flavoured; can use in salads like red beet, though rather colourless.

**BROCCOLI, CHINESE (CHINESE KALE, GAI LAAN)** *Brassica oleracea* **var.** *alboglabra*
Young stems and flower buds excellent flavour and texture raw, or steamed and cold.

**BROCCOLI, PURPLE SPROUTING** *Brassica oleracea* **(Italica Group)**
Eat shoots raw or cooked and cold, according to taste.

**CABBAGE** *Brassica oleracea* **(Capitata Group)**
Primarily a cooked vegetable, but can use all year round as coleslaw and in mixed salad. Some people find flavour strong, but sliced finely, most cultivars can be used raw. Spring cabbage probably sweetest; crinkly-leaved savoy types good flavour; 'Dutch winter white' types bland but quite crisp and can be stored for winter; red-leaved types add superb colour to salads and can be pickled (also excellent cooked and cold); some red cultivars can be stored for winter. Ornamental types barely edible but highly decorative, especially in winter salads.

**CALABRESE (GREEN BROCCOLI)** *Brassica oleracea* **(Italica Group)**
Use florets raw or cooked and cold, according to taste.

**CARDOON** *Cynara cardunculus*
Use stems of young plants after blanching in the garden; unusual, subtle flavour cooked and cold.

**CARROTS** *Daucus carota*
Mainly used cooked, but some people (not me!) enjoy grated raw carrot in salad. Year round supply feasible using fresh and stored carrots. Early 'Amsterdam' and 'Nantes' types probably sweetest and most tender. Can use thinnings of maincrop cultivars in salads.

**CAULIFLOWER** *Brassica oleracea* **(Botrytis Group)**
For salad use see Calabrese (above). Green curded 'Romanesco' types, red curded cultivars, and 'mini-cauliflowers', obtained by close spacing of early types, recommended for salads.

**CELERIAC (TURNIP ROOTED CELERY)** *Apium graveolens*
**var.** *rapaceum*
Valuable winter vegetable. Use bulbous stem grated raw into salads just before use. Squeeze lemon juice over gratings to prevent discoloration. Also excellent cooked and cold. Leaves can be chopped fresh into salad, or dried as celery substitute.

**CHICORY, CATALOGNA (ASPARAGUS)** *Cichorium intybus*
Striking tall growing chicory from southern Italy, with long narrow

leaves, grown for the flowering shoots which normally develop in second season. Shoots bitter raw, but excellent, distinct flavour cooked and cold. Needs warmer climate than other chicories. Sow summer, spacing plants 20cm (8in) apart. In temperate climates transplant under cover in late summer. Shoots form following spring.

### CHOY SUM *Brassica rapa* var. *parachinensis* and other spp.

Use young flowering shoots when in the bud stage, either lightly cooked and cooled, or simply raw. They are tender, decorative and tasty in salads. Especially recommended for salads: purple-flowered choy sum/'hon cai tai' *Brassica rapa* var. *purpurea*, flowering rape $F_1$ hybrid 'Bouquet' *Brassica rapa* var. *oleifera*.

### CHRYSANTHEMUM GREENS (SHUNGIKU, CHOP SUEY GREENS, GARLAND CHRYSANTHEMUM) *Chrysanthemum coronarium*

Raw leaves have aromatic, fairly strong, chrysanthemum flavour. Use moderate quantities in salads, mixed with other leaves. Japanese blanch them in boiling water for a few seconds then plunge them into cold water before using in salads. Flower petals edible but discard flower centre which is bitter.

### COURGETTES (ZUCCHINI) *Cucurbita pepo*

Use very young fruits of long marrows/summer squash sliced raw in salads when 5-7.5cm (2-3in) long; use flat 'Patty Pan' types no larger than 5cm (2in) diameter. Use larger courgettes cooked and cold. (See also Flowers in Salad, Squash Family p.240.)

### HORSE RADISH *Armoracia rusticana*

Small quantities of grated roots can be used fresh in salad or as garnish for meat. Young leaves have mild horse radish flavour; excellent in salads.

### KOHL RABI *Brassica oleracea* (Gongylodes Group)

Grate or slice raw into salads, or use cooked and cold. Use older cultivars when no larger than tennis ball; but modern hybrids stand better and can be used larger.

### LEEK *Allium porrum*

Standard leeks good both cooked and cold. Slender 'mini-leeks' very tender; can be used raw as a more unusual and tasty ingredient in salads.

Flavour varies from very mild to almost piquant, probably depending on cultivar and growing conditions. To grow mini-leeks sow early spring to mid-summer in shallow wide drills (see Seeds, Sowing Outdoors and Planting p.67). Space seeds 6mm-1.3cm (¼-½in) apart. Harvest when the plants are 15-20cm (6-8in) tall, after about thirteen weeks. Can leave standing for many weeks. Most suitable cultivars long stemmed, early types, for example 'King Richard'. Later types inclined to develop tiny bulbs instead of straight stems when they are grown close.

**PARSNIP** *Pastinaca sativa*
Large roots have excellent, sweet flavour which can be appreciated better when they are cooked and served cold. Smaller 'mini-parsnips' can be grated raw and served in salads. Grow by sowing in drills and thinning to about 5cm (2in) apart. Smooth skinned 'Lancer' particularly recommended for 'mini-parsnips'.

**PEAS, MANGETOUT (SUGAR PEAS, SNOW PEAS)** *Pisum sativum* var. *macrocarpon*
Standard garden peas are normally cooked (though sweet, wrinkle seeded types are pleasant in salads) but edible podded types are excellent raw in salads. Pick traditional flat podded mangetouts when the tiny peas are just visible beneath skin. Pick exceptionally sweet 'Sugar Snap' type, characterized by rounded fleshy walled pods almost 'welded' to the peas, when pleasantly plump and still tender. Use both types of mangetout whole or sliced raw in salads. When more mature can cook lightly and use cooled, but may need to remove tougher strings from pods before serving.

**PEA SHOOTS** *Pisum sativum*
Oriental delicacy with wonderful pea flavour when used as a raw salad ingredient. 'Shoots' are young tendrils and top pairs of leaves on pea stems harvested when they are about 5-10cm (2-4in) long. You can either pick a few tips from ordinary pea crop without harming them, or grow the 'semi-leafless' cultivars, which develop masses of tendrils instead of leaves, making them ideal for the salad-lover; pick tendrils while still very green and tender.

**PEPPER, SWEET (CAPSICUM)** *Capsicum annuum* (Grossum Group)(T)
Immature and fully ripened sweet peppers excellent raw, sliced thinly in salads. Superb cold dishes made from cooked peppers. Use different coloured peppers to create beautiful effects.

**POTATOES** *Solanum tuberosum*

Texture of cooked potatoes ranges from dry and floury to moist and 'waxy'. Waxy potatoes generally most suitable for salads as stay firm after cooking and often notable flavour when cold. Some yellow fleshed cultivars and various long, narrow, European cultivars renowned for good salad quality. Where these are unavailable, early and mid-season potatoes, which are the faster growing types, seem closer textured and better in salads than main season, slower maturing types. Some potatoes waxy in early stages but become more floury on maturity. Cultivars recommended for salads and normally available in Europe include: 'Belle de Fontenay', 'Linzer Delikatess', 'Charlotte', 'Eigenheimer', 'Ratte', ' Pink Fir Apple'. Fairly rare blue fleshed species potato, *Solanum ajanhuri* var. *peruviana* has waxy texture and looks striking in salads.

**TURNIP** *Brassica campestris* **(Rapifera Group)**

Small turnips good grated raw into salads. Fast maturing, round white Japanese cultivars such as 'Presto' and 'F₁ Tokyo Cross' sweetest and most suitable. Most turnips very hardy in leafy stages; grow as CCA seedling crop for use raw. For cultivation see Rape, Salad p.195.

# Chapter 14
# Herbs

There was a time when all salad plants were considered herbs – quaintly dubbed 'sallet herbs' – yet today salads and herbs are divorced in our minds, and the use of herbs in salads is perfunctory. But what a difference the skilled, discreet use of herbs can make to a salad! This was brought home to me many years ago in Ireland, when by chance I spent a night in a house where the overgrown garden had, until recently, been tended by a herbalist. Our hostess went out in the dusk to collect a few herbs to enliven our tired supper lettuce. The result was superb – a medley of subtle freshness I have never forgotten. Most of the herbs were unknown to me then, but the lesson was never lost.

On how to use herbs in salads I can do no better than quote that versatile gardening writer Eleanour Sinclair Rohde: 'It is just the suspicion of flavouring all through the salad that is required, not a salad entirely dominated by herbs.' Her method was to mix into the salad a piled tablespoon of very finely chopped herbs; she listed about twenty.

An infinite number of herbs can be used in salads to give infinite variety. The only rule to follow is that the stronger the herb, the more sparingly it should be used. To my mind, fresh herbs are always preferable to herbs that have been dried or otherwise preserved, which poses a challenge in the winter months, when only a handful naturally remain green. Quite a number, however, lend themselves to being cut down in late summer, potted up in good, light, well-drained soil or compost, and brought into a cool greenhouse or an indoor windowsill to provide fresh herbs during the winter.

Many of the more succulent herbs, such as chives, parsley and basil, can be frozen fairly successfully, either in sprigs, or chopped into water in ice cube trays. (Thaw the cube in a strainer when needed.) Many herbs can be dried. Pick them in their prime, usually just before flowering, dry them slowly in a very cool oven or hung indoors covered with muslin to keep off the dust, then store them in airtight jars.

The following brief notes cover some of the herbs most suitable for salads. I have omitted alecost and tansy, which were in the original edition, as they now seem to me obnoxiously strong. Their place has been taken by caraway and perilla (shiso) – two much subtler flavours.

**ANGELICA** *Angelica archangelica*
Beautiful vigorous biennial growing up to 2m (6½ft) high. Likes rich, fairly moist soil. Sow *fresh* seed autumn, planting following spring or autumn 1.5m (5ft) apart. Plants left to flower will seed themselves; the seedlings can be transplanted. Use young stems and leaves sparingly in salads. Very decorative at back of borders.

**ANISE** *Pimpinella anisum*
Annual, 30cm (1ft) high, delicate foliage. Likes warm position, well-drained soil. Sow *in situ* spring, thinning to 15cm (6in) apart. Traditionally grown for seeds, but aniseed-flavoured leaves pleasant chopped into salads.

**BALM, LEMON** *Melissa officinalis*
Perennial, about 60cm (2ft) high. Tolerates any soil from dry to moist; excellent ground-cover plant. Raise by dividing plants in autumn, or sow in seed boxes in spring, finally spacing 60cm (2ft) apart. Delicate lemon scent; chop leaves into salad.

**BASIL** *Ocinum basilicum*
Tender, annual, Mediterranean herb, height varies from ground hugging to about 45cm (18in). Many types: lettuce leaved or Neapolitan (very large leaves); common, sweet or Geneva (medium sized leaves); bush, dwarf, and compact types with small leaves. Miniature 'Greek' basil has tiny leaves and an excellent flavour. Red-leaved forms are very decorative, however generally less flavour. For distinct flavours try anise, cinnamon and the superb lemon basil. In temperate and cool climates grow under cover or in sheltered, sunny position outdoors. Sow in spring indoors, plant under cover late spring; plant outdoors after risk of frost has passed, about 13cm (5in) apart. For winter use indoors make late sowing in mid-summer and plant in pot, or trim back few plants (bush basil responds well) late summer, pot up, bring indoors. May provide leaf until Christmas. Basil flavour unique, strong, clove-like. Chop leaves sparingly into salads; wide use in salad dishes, especially with tomatoes, and to flavour oils and vinegars.

**BORAGE** *Borago officinalis*
Young leaves traditionally used in salads; texture rather hairy so best finely chopped. Blue flowers also edible. Plants remain green until fairly heavy frost, so useful for winter salads if grown under cover. Where

grown mainly for leaves, chop off flower stalks to encourage bushiness. (See Flowers in Salad p.233.)

## BURNET, SALAD *Sanguisorba minor*
Low-growing, exceptionally hardy perennial plant, sometimes found wild. Feathery leaves remain green all winter. Attractive winter edging; also pretty when seeding. Sow spring or summer *in situ*, thinning to 15cm (6in) apart. Leaves produced more abundantly if flower spikes cut off. Use young leaves raw; flavour reminiscent of cucumber. Japanese boil leaves lightly and then dip in cold water for salads.

## CARAWAY *Carum carvi*
Hardy biennial, up to 60cm (2ft) high when seeding, feathery foliage. Cultivated mainly for aromatic seeds produced in year after sown; mild flavoured young leaves often remain green in winter, can use in salads. Roots also edible. Likes reasonably fertile soil, fairly open position. Sow outside late spring or summer, *in situ* in shallow drills. Thin to 20cm (8in) apart. (Don't transplant unless sown in modules.) Once established may self-seed. Can plant a few under cover in autumn for winter herb.

## CHERVIL *Anthriscus cerefolium*
Hardy, rapidly-growing biennial herb, delicate fern-like leaves, up to 60cm (2ft) high. Refreshing aniseed flavour; especially valuable as winter herb. Grow in slightly shady position, summer; sunny position, winter. Sow spring *in situ* for summer use; late summer *in situ* outdoors, or in modules to transplant under cover, for winter/early spring use. (Leaves better quality in winter if protected.) Thin or plant to 10cm (4in) apart. If few plants allowed to flower self-seeds readily. (Sometimes too readily.) Young seedlings can be transplanted in moist conditions. Decorative edging plant if *not* allowed to seed.

## CHIVES *Allium schoenoprasum*
Hardy, widely grown perennial, generally about 25cm (10in) high, giant form up to 45cm (18in) high. Does best on fertile, moisture-retentive soil. Excellent edging plant. Stands constant cutting. Sow spring, planting three or four seedlings together in a clump, spacing clumps 23cm (9in) apart. Cut off flower stalks to encourage foliage, unless flowers wanted (see Flowers in Salad p.234). Divide plants, in spring or autumn, every three or four years if vigour declining. Replant in fresh site. Plants generally die back in mid-winter; cloche a few for very early supplies in

spring. Delightful mild onion flavour; used finely chopped in salads and salad dishes.

## CHINESE CHIVES (GARLIC CHIVES) *Allium tuberosum*

Very hardy, perennial, slow-growing flat-leaved chives forming neat clumps 25-30cm (10-12in) high. Widely grown in China and Japan where fresh and blanched leaves, flowers, flower buds, and young flower stalks all eaten, raw and cooked. Delightful, subtle garlic flavour. Flowering plants very decorative (see Flowers in Salad p.234). Tolerates wide range of climatic conditions and soil, provided good drainage, reasonable fertility. Sow fresh seed spring to early summer. Best to sow in seedtrays or seedbed as seedlings fragile. Plant in permanent position summer to early autumn, when seedlings about 10cm (4in) high. Plant up to six seedlings in clump, with clumps 20cm (8in) apart. In first season only cut leaves sparingly and remove flower buds to encourage strong growth. Can pot up plants in late summer for use indoors in winter. Apply manure to established plants in spring. Plants long-lived, so no need to lift and divide unless growth is weak: in this case lift and replant younger outer sections. Can also lift and divide to increase your stock. Plants can be blanched to get yellow, subtler flavoured leaves. Use dark buckets or blanching pots at least 25cm (10in) deep. Either cover newly sprouting clump in spring, or recently cut clump in summer. Blanched leaves ready three to four weeks later. Leaves *must* be dry before blanching operation starts.

## CORIANDER *Coriandrum sativum*

Hardy annual 13cm (5in) high in leafy stage, over 45cm (18in) when seeding. Universal culinary use of leaves and seed. Distinctive curry flavour. Does best in light soil. For leaves grow small seeded types; for seed grow large-seeded types. For continuous supply make successive sowings *in situ* from spring to late summer, thinning to 15cm (6in) apart. Runs to seed rapidly in hot weather. Can make late autumn sowing under cover for winter supply. Can also sow in wide drills as cut-and-come-again seedling crop (see Salad Techniques p.85). Leaves can be frozen but not dried; seeds used mainly in curries.

## DILL *Anethum graveolens*

Feathery, fairly hardy annual 13cm (5in) high in leafy stage, over 1.2m (4ft) when seeding. Unique, delicate flavour; leaves used in salads and cooking, seeds and seedheads in pickling vinegars, especially for gherkins.

Needs reasonably fertile, moist, weed free soil or seedlings may be over-whelmed in early stages. Sow thinly *in situ* from spring to mid-summer. For leaf grow as cut-and-come-again seedling crop; for seed thin to 10-15cm (4-6in) apart. Very decorative both in young and seeding stages. Often self-seeds. For leaf production use cultivars selected for leafiness.

### FENNEL, COMMON *Foeniculum vulgare*

Fairly hardy perennial with feathery foliage up to 1.5m (5ft) tall. Green and bronze forms, the latter highly decorative. Tolerates most well-drained soils. Sow in spring *in situ* or in modules for transplanting. Thin or plant 45cm (18in) apart. Can also propagate by dividing rootstocks in spring. For a constant supply of foliage keep plants cut to within 30cm (1ft) of ground and remove flower spikes. Chopped leaves and chopped and peeled young stalks used in salads and in cooking; aniseed flavour. Plants often self-seed. (For cultivation of Florence Fennel see p.161.)

### GOOD KING HENRY *Chenopodium bonus-henricus*

Hardy perennial, growing into bushy plant about 50cm (20in) high. Tolerates light shade and most soils. Raise by dividing old plants, or by sowing seed in spring *in situ*, or in a seedbed, or indoors, preferably in gentle heat. Plant in humus-rich soil mid- to late spring, 38cm (15in) apart. The more fertile the soil, the thicker the 'spears'. Use leaves first season; shoots from second season onwards, cutting just below soil level. Cover plants with litter in spring to bring on shoots. Renew clumps every five to six years. Use young leaves and tasty asparagus-like shoots or 'spears' raw in salads.

### HYSSOP *Hyssopus officinalis*

Relatively short-lived perennial, shrubby plant, reasonably hardy, about 45cm (18in) tall. Lovely blue, pink, purple or white flowers which attract bees. Likes light, well-drained soil; makes pretty low hedge if trimmed. Propagated by soft cuttings taken spring/early summer; or sow spring, thinning or planting 60cm (2ft) apart. Pinch back shoot tips to keep bushy. Leaves remain green until fairly late in winter. Strong minty flavour; use sparingly in salad. Flowers also edible. Compact, low grow-ing blue-flowered cultivar 'Mountain hyssop' especially decorative.

### LAVENDER *Lavandula* sp.

Leaves can be used very sparingly, finely chopped, in salads, but mainly grown for flowers.

**LOVAGE** *Levisticum officinale*
Stately, decorative, hardy perennial growing up to 2.4m (8ft) tall. Prefers rich, moist soil; tolerates light shade. One of the earliest plants to appear in spring. Easily raised by sowing seed in spring or autumn, eventually planting 60cm (2ft) apart, or by dividing roots. Plants also seed themselves and seedlings can be transplanted. Can cut stems right back during growing season to encourage fresh young growths. Leaves have distinct, strong celery flavour; chop into salads or rub leaf around the salad bowl. Leaf stalks used to be blanched and eaten like celery.

**MARJORAM** *Origanum* sp.
Low-growing Mediterranean herbs, of varying hardiness. Some forms annual in cold climates but otherwise perennial. Height varies from dwarf to 30-60cm (1-2ft) high. Leaves have gentle, pleasant, characteristic flavour – one of my favourites in salads and cooking. Variegated forms, with gold or gold tipped leaves, probably less flavour but very decorative in salads. Near evergreen forms very useful for winter. Marjorams like reasonably fertile, well-drained soil and full sun – though golden forms can stand some shade as scorched by full sun. Annual forms raised from seed sown in spring, preferably indoors as gemination often slow. Plant 10-15cm (4-6in) apart. Perennial forms raised by division or stem cuttings taken from spring to summer. Bushier marjorams benefit by being trimmed back regularly to discourage straggliness. Can pot up late summer to bring indoors for winter use. Marjorams retain flavour well when dried. Much confusion exists over marjoram names. If you acquire a particularly decorative, hardy or useful form, hang on to it!

**MINTS** *Mentha* sp.
(Another herb suffering from much confusion over names.) Many types cultivated: garden or spearmint up to 45cm (18in) high; rounder-leaved apple and Bowles mints, up to 1.3m (4¼ft) high; pennyroyal, excellent ground-cover mint. Variegated golden and white forms especially decorative in salads. Most mints rampant growers requiring rich, moist soil; advisable to move every few years as they exhaust soil. Propagate by division, or lift in spring or autumn, replanting 5cm (2in) long pieces of root, or young shoots with roots attached. Lay roots horizontally 5cm (2in) deep, about 23cm (9in) apart. Can lift plants in autumn, plant in boxes, and bring indoors for fresh winter leaf. Mints display considerable variation in flavour: experiment to find your preferences and use sparingly. Most dry well for winter use.

### MITSUBA Japanese parsley *Cryptotaenia japonica*

Hardy, evergreen, perennial woodland plant, with a trifoliate leaf on a long leaf stalk, growing up to 45cm (18in) high when flowering. It is closely related to the North American honewort or wild chervil *Cryptotaenia canadensis*. It grows wild in Japan, where the plants are often blanched to make the stems whiter, longer and that much sweeter. The seeds can be sprouted. Young leaves and stems are used raw in salads. Unique angelica-like flavour. For cultivation see *Oriental Vegetables*, Further Reading p.251.

### ORACHE (MOUNTAIN SPINACH) *Atriplex hortensis*

Tall, handsome plants growing over 1.5m (5ft) high, once widely grown in Europe as spinach substitute. Pale (known as white), green and red forms exist; red form very decorative in garden and salads. Orache runs to seed fast in hot weather; best grown as spring and autumn crop. Sow *in situ* spring to early summer for spring/summer crop or late summer for autumn crop. Preferably sow in rich, moisture-retentive soil. Sow as CCA seedlings (see Salad Techniques p.85) or thin to about 30cm (12in) apart. Use first at seedling stage; then keep pinching out growing points to make plants bushy and delay running to seed. Use tender young tops and young leaves in salad. Cook older leaves like spinach. A few plants left to flower will seed themselves. Start cutting young seedlings as soon as they appear in spring.

### PARSLEY *Petroselinum crispum*

Fairly hardy, biennial herb, growing 10cm (4in) to over 60cm (2ft) high in giant Italian forms; dwarfer curled leaf forms most widely grown, but plain or broad-leaved French and Italian types possibly easier to grow, and many consider better flavoured. Parsley needs good soil, plenty of moisture, tolerates light shade in summer. Sow in spring for summer to autumn use; summer for winter to early spring use. Plant these late sowings outdoors in mild areas, or under cover or in pots for winter use indoors in colder areas. Parsley germination is notoriously slow, so sowing in modules recommended. If sowing *in situ* water drills beforehand (see Seeds, Sowing Outdoors and Planting p.72) or keep ground moist while germinating. Thin or plant to 23cm (9in) apart. Cut off flowering heads as they develop to prolong useful life. Foliage dies back in severe winters but often remains green. Cover with cloches to maintain winter quality. Chopped foliage used in many types of salad and for garnishing many different dishes. Parsley often self-seeds.

**PARSLEY, HAMBURG** *Petroselinum crispum* **var.** *tuberosum*
This is a dual purpose, hardy type of parsley grown primarily for its parsnip-like root; but parsley-flavoured foliage remains green for the whole winter and can be used like parsley. Sow spring in modules or *in situ* in reasonably fertile, moisture-retentive soil. Tolerates light shade. Thin to 23cm (9in) apart. Except in severe climates it can be left in soil all winter. Roots are also good cooked and cold or grated raw into salads.

**PERILLA (SHISO)** *Perilla frutescens*
Decorative, tender Japanese herb growing 45–90cm (18–36in) tall. Green form most subtle flavour; use red form mainly to colour pickles or dressings. Use seedling sprouts raw in salads. Use leaves from large plants sparingly. For cultivation see *Oriental Vegetables*, Further Reading p.251.

**ROSEMARY, COMMON** *Rosmarinus officinalis*
Evergreen Mediterranean shrub, up to 90cm (3ft) tall. Moderately hardy in well-drained soil, sheltered position. Likes chalky soil. Normally propagated from soft cuttings taken in spring, or semi-hardwood cuttings or layering in summer. Can also raise common rosemary from seed sown spring in heat 21°C (70°F). Eventually space plants 60-90cm (2-3ft) apart. Seed-raised plants may be hardier. Trim back fresh growths in late summer to increase hardiness. In cold climates protect plants in winter, or grow in large pots and bring under cover before hard frost. Chop leaves sparingly in salads. Flowers also edible. Some rosemary cultivars are white-flowered (see Flowers in Salad p.238).

**SAGE, COMMON (***Salvia officinalis***)**
Relatively hardy, perennial bushes about 60cm (2ft) high. Thrive on light, well-drained soil. Red-leaved and variegated forms decorative, but less hardy. Easiest way to propagate is from tip or heel cuttings taken in spring; common sage can be raised from seed sown spring. Space bushes 45-60cm (18-24in) apart. Trim back young growths lightly after flowering in summer. Plants can become leggy and are best renewed every three or four years. Leaves strongly flavoured, so use sparingly in salads; young shoots of red sage widely used in past. Sage dries well, but fresh leaves useable much of winter. Flowers edible (see Flowers in Salad p.239).

**SAVORY, SUMMER AND WINTER** *Satureja hortenis* **and** *S. montana*
Summer savory: bushy annual up to 30cm (12in) high, Winter savory:

somewhat sprawly hardy, evergreen perennial. Both like sunny position, good, well-drained soil. Sow both in spring, *in situ* or in modules, spacing plants 15cm (6in) apart. Winter savory also propagated by heel cuttings taken in spring, or by division of old plants. Both can be potted up for use indoors in winter. Summer savory milder flavour, leaves more tender, traditionally used with beans. Winter savory coarser leaves, stronger flavour, but remains green outdoors in winter. Both useful in various salad dishes. Flowers also edible; attract bees.

### SWEET CICELY *Myrrhis odorata*

Very decorative, hardy, slow-growing perennial up to 1.5m (5ft) tall. Grows best in rich, moist soil, partial shade. Sow fresh seed autumn, thinning to 8cm (3½in) apart, planting in permanent position following autumn 60cm (2ft) apart; or divide roots carefully spring or autumn. Mature plants readily seed themselves; can transplant seedlings. Plants die down late and start growing early, so useable much of year. Leaves sweet aniseed taste; long use in salads and as sugar substitute. Roots boiled, cooked, and sliced in salads.

### TARRAGON, FRENCH AND RUSSIAN *Artemisia dracunculus*

Narrow-leaved reasonably hardy perennials. Main forms: 'French' tarragon – up to 75cm (30in) high, less robust, smoother, darker, shinier leaves, superior flavour; 'Russian': up to 1.4m (4½ft), more robust, coarser, poorer flavoured but reputed to improve with age. Like sunny position, well-drained, light soil. 'French' propagated by carefully dividing plants in spring, 'Russian' from seed sown in spring. Space plants 60cm (2ft) apart. Distinct, strong flavour, used to flavour vinegar and as an ingredient in salad dishes.

### THYME *Thymus* sp.

Large family of hardy, low-growing, perennial herbs, many with beautiful flowers. Popular culinary thymes include common *T. vulgaris*, lemon *T.* x *citriodorus*, caraway *T. herba barona*, creeping *T. pulegioides*. Like dry, well-drained soil, in a sunny position; many thrive on chalky soils. Decorative edging plants, especially variegated-leaved forms. Propagated by dividing old plants, by taking tip cuttings in spring, and by sowing seed in spring. Plant out about 15-30cm (6-12in) apart, depending on cultivar. Keep plants trimmed; renew beds every few years. Can pot up plants for winter use. Most thymes fairly strong flavour; use sparingly in salads, or to infuse salad dressings or vinegar. Flowers also edible.

# Chapter 15
# Flowers in Salad

Until the last few years the practice of using flowers in cookery and salads had almost died out. Recently it has staged a welcome comeback: nasturtiums garnishing salads and stuffed courgettes on the menu have become the hallmark of the enterprising cook. Perhaps it is strange that flowers ever fell from favour, for our ancestors made copious use of wild and cultivated flowers in their cuisine, and all over the world flowers of vegetables, herbaceous plants, shrubs and trees are still grown and sold for cooking and use in salads.

Long ago in Europe violets, primroses, cowslips and many other flowers were collected from the wild for salads. Today the need to preserve wild species is paramount, so wild flowers should only be collected where they are in abundance. In the British Isles it is now illegal to dig them up – unless they are scheduled weeds or on your private land. So if you want wild flowers in your salads, grow them in corners of the garden. Several companies now sell wild flower seed.

Flowers should be gathered when they are at their most fresh, early in the day when the dew has just dried on them. Always handle them gently, preferably cutting with a knife or scissors. Carry them in a flat basket to avoid squashing them. They can be gently washed if necessary and patted dry with paper towelling. If not required immediately keep them in a closed plastic bag in a fridge. Just before use the flowers or petals can be freshened by dipping in ice-cold water. Cut off the stems before use, and with large flowers, remove the green receptacle at the base of the flower.

Flowers are mainly added to salads for their lovely colours and textures, but in many cases their delicate scent and flavour contributes to the taste. Flavour can vary from one cultivar to the next, so if trying anything new from your garden, take a little nibble first to make sure it is going to enhance a salad.

It is mainly the petals of edible flowers that are eaten. With large flowers in particular, it is advisable to remove the pistil and/or stamens. With flowers with daisy-like heads pull the petals gently away from the centre and add them to the salad dish. Otherwise flowers can either be used whole or chopped into a confetti-like mixture and sprinkled over the top

of a salad. But take care not to completely *overwhelm* the salad with them
. . . it happens even in the best circles.

Always add flowers to a salad at the last minute, after it has been dressed
and just before serving. Otherwise they absorb the dressing and become
soggy and discoloured. Besides being used fresh, flowers are sometimes
dried or pickled for use in salads. Very many flowers are also used in cooking – but that is another story.

In some seasons flowers are invaded by insects, such as the pollen beetle. We have found that if you pick the flowers and leave them on a flat
dish for ten minutes or so, most of the insects will crawl away.

In the following brief notes I have limited myself mainly to those flowers I have used frequently. See the list at the end for further possibilities.
For many new ideas on salad flowers incorporated in this revised edition,
my thanks to Robin Stern for her notes written for Seattle 'Tilth' in 1988.
As common names vary and are unreliable, Latin names are also given as
an aid to accurate identification. (For further information on cultivation,
consult standard gardening books. See Further Reading p.251.)

## ALKANET, GREEN (EVERGREEN) (*see* Anchusa)

### ANCHUSA *Anchusa italica*
Perennial garden flower, 1.3m (4¼ft) high. Lovely bright blue flowers at
their best in early summer. Ordinary soil in sunny border. Plant autumn
or early spring, or treat as biennial, sowing spring, over-wintering small
plants in cold frame and planting out following spring. Cut down main
stem after flowering; smaller growths will prolong flowering season.
Flowers blend beautifully in salads with rose petals and rosemary flowers.
Flowers of the closely related wild form, Green or Evergreen Alkanet,
*Pentaglottis sempervirens*, are also edible.

### ANISE HYSSOP *Agastache foeniculum*
Fairly hardy perennial, 60cm (2ft) high. Excellent plant for attracting
bees. Purplish flower spikes, almost peppermint flavour. Prefers rich soil,
sunny position. Sow seed spring or divide established clumps in spring.

### BERGAMOT, SWEET *Monarda didyma*
Perennial, 30-60cm (1-2ft) high, spreading. Flowers scarlet, occasionally
purple, lavender, white, pink; flowering mid-summer to early autumn.
Traditionally dried for tea. Does best on moist, rich soil. Divide plants
every two to three years, replanting youngest parts. Flowers beautiful on

salads with borage. Some of the $F_1$ hybrids are bitter. Leaves also edible but they are bitter and therefore will not be to everyone's taste.

### BORAGE *Borago officinalis*
Annual, 1m (3½ft) high; bulky plants. Bright blue star-like petals contrast with black anthers. Flowers all summer until frost. Ordinary, well-drained soil. Self-seeds once established; just thin out seedlings. Otherwise sow early spring indoors; late spring *in situ* outdoors. Space plants 25-35cm (10-14in) apart. In temperate climates can sow in mid- to late summer for late crop or to transplant under cover for winter leaves, late flowers, and maybe very early flowers following year if greenhouse frost-free. Flowers sweet-flavoured; remove hairy sepals before eating. Young leaves edible finely chopped in salads or boiled. Freeze flowers into ice cubes for exotic touch. Some cultivars have white flowers.

### BRASSICAS/CRUCIFERS *Brassica* sp.
Young flowering shoots of many brassicas, especially oriental types such as Chinese cabbage, pak choi, choy sum, flowering rape and komatsuna are very sweet and tasty raw in salads. Flowers of oriental mustards become quite peppery. Leave plants to seed at end of their natural season. Flowering shoots especially tender when grown under cover. (For cultivation see individual crops.)

### BROOM, COMMON *Cytisus scoparius*
Hardy shrub, grows wild and can be cultivated. Thrives on poor soil, dry conditions. Buds appear mid- to late spring, followed by bright yellow flowers. Best transplanted young. Prune back nearly into old growth after flowering. Broom buds and flowers extensively used in the past in salads, fresh and pickled. Do not eat too many: excessive quantities are toxic!

### CARNATION (*see Dianthus*)

### CHICORY, WILD (SUCCORY) AND CULTIVATED TYPES
*Cichorium intybus*
Dandelion-like plants with striking flowering spikes 30cm-1.2m (1-4ft) high, flowering late spring to early autumn depending on which chicory. Flowers varying shades of blue, occasionally pink. Either collect wild chicory flowers (commonly found on chalk) or let a few plants of cultivated chicory flower. Pick flowers just before using as they close and fade very rapidly; use petals or whole flower. Flavour intriguing, can be

slightly bitter; reminiscent of chicory leaves, but milder. Flowers can be pickled. (For cultivation see Salad Plants pp.141-8.) Highly decorative plant for back of potager or border.

### CHIVES *Allium schoenoprasum*
Ordinary garden chives. Tiny individual flowers make up the ball-like flower heads. Colours stunning purples and occasionally pink, with delightful onion flavour. A favourite of mine in cooking and salads. (For cultivation see Herbs p.224.)

### CHIVES, CHINESE (GARLIC) *Allium tuberosum*
Slow-growing, hardy perennial. Beautiful star-like flower spikes, up to 60cm (2ft) high mid–summer to autumn. Use flowers fresh or dried in salads: sweet, mild, onion/garlic flavour. Chinese dress flower buds with sesame oil as a salad; flowers also ground and salted as spice. Very decorative plant. The stems and leaves of young flowers also edible. (For cultivation see Herbs p.225.)

### CHRYSANTHEMUM, FLORIST *Dendranthema* x *grandiflorum*
Florist chrysanthemum is main one used for culinary purposes in Japan and China, but petals of other chrysanthemums can be used in salads. Some more bitter than others: try them out first. Florist chrysanthemums half hardy perennials, 60cm-1.2m (2-4ft) high. Do best in cool weather. Ordinary garden soil. Feed regularly in growing season. Generally raised from cuttings taken in late winter and spring from young shoots growing from rootstocks. Can lift few plants in late autumn for cutting material. Before use raw can blanch flowers by dipping into boiling water for a second; or cover with cold water, bring to boil, drain, then dip in cold water. Flowers of the edible Chrysanthemum greens (Shungiku) *C. coronarium* also edible. (For cultivation see Secondary Salad Vegetables p.219.)

### COURGETTE (*see* Squash)

### COWSLIP *Primula veris*
Hardy perennial, 23cm (9in) tall. Beautiful clusters of yellow flowers in spring. Natural habitat chalky, clay and alkaline meadows. It is becoming rarer due to overpicking. Can be cultivated. It needs to have an open site, with well-drained, not over-rich soil. Best to sow in seedbed in spring, thin to 20cm (8in) apart, transplant into final position autumn. Once fully

established the plants can be divided. Use leaves and flowers in salads; flowers can be pickled.

## CUCUMBER (*see* Squash)

## DAISY (ENGLISH DAISY) *Bellis perennis*
Cultivated form of the common, little white-flowered hardy perennial daisy of lawn and field. Cultivars include large and small double flowered forms and attractive new introductions. Can be in flower much of year from very early spring onwards. Sow in seed boxes in spring for flowering the same year, or early to mid-summer for flowering early the following season. Use small flowers whole, petals only of larger forms; colour more notable than flavour. Leaves also edible (see Wild Plants and Weeds p.245). Small wild 'meadow daisy' flowers can be used. As far prettier open, pick directly before use if possible; otherwise pick when open, keep in closed plastic bag at room temperature until needed. Use whole. Warning! Leatherjackets – cranefly larvae – love to over-winter in daisy roots!

## DAISY, OX-EYE or MARGUERITE *Leucanthemum vulgare*
Very common wild white daisy, flowering throughout summer. Pick off petals for salads. Leaves also edible. (See Wild Plants and Weeds p.245.)

## DANDELION (*see* Wild Plants and Weeds)

## DAY LILY *Hemerocallis fulva*
I recently learnt, from an authoritative source in China, that *raw* day lilies can be toxic. So I will omit them – in spite of having used them raw in salads. (I did find some had a rather bitter aftertaste.) In oriental cuisine day lilies are picked in the bud stage, and then *dried* before cooking.

## *DIANTHUS* sp.
Popular garden *Dianthus* include carnations, pinks and sweet william, grown variously as annuals, biennials and perennials. The flowers are edible, with flavours varying from strong clove scent to mild 'pink' scent to musky. (For cultivation see Further Reading p.251.)

## ELDER *Sambucus nigra*
Shrubby tree of hedgerows, covered in early summer with bunches of sweet-smelling, creamy blossoms of thousands of tiny flowers. Tolerates

most soils. Easily grown in gardens. Can raise from 20-25cm (8-10in) hardwood cuttings taken in autumn; will be ready for planting within a year. When trees become too large cut back to stump, which will resprout. Never wash flowers or the attractive fragrance is lost completely. Shake heads gently over salad before serving; the tiny flowers drop off easily. Be sparing: too many impart a cat-like smell. North American Indians used leaves and flowers in salads. In England buds and flowers used to be pickled.

**GERANIUM** (*see Pelargonium*)

**HARDHEADS** (*see* **Knapweed, Lesser**)

**HERBS** (*see* **Culinary Herbs, p.240**)

**HOLLYHOCK** *Althaea rosea*
Popular tall perennial of cottage gardens, numerous colours. Old forms up to 2m (6½ft) high; some newer forms are semi-dwarf. Likes rich, moist soil. Tall ones need staking. Grow as biennial as old plants get rust disease. Sow spring to summer in seedbed, thin to 15cm (6in) apart, plant out autumn 1m (3½ft) apart. Keep watered and mulched in summer. (In cold areas over-winter in frames, plant out spring.) Petals and cooked buds used in salads.

**KNAPWEED, LESSER (HARDHEADS)** *Centaurea nigra*
Very common hedgerow plant up to 35cm (14in) high with thistle-like feathery purple flowers, early summer to early autumn. Petals used in salads in the past. Somewhat bitter.

**LAVENDER** *Lavandula spica; L. vera*
Half hardy perennial bushes with spikes of usually blue-purple flowers in the summer, though there are some white and pink forms. It needs a well-drained soil and a sheltered position. The easiest way to propagate is by cuttings in shaded frame in late summer, or rooted outdoors in the autumn. Trim back plants in spring to prevent any straggliness. It is advisable to replant every five years. Use chopped flowers and leaves sparingly in salads, desserts, jellies. In the past salads were served on sweet-smelling beds of lettuce and lavender sprigs. The hardiest lavenders are *L. angustifolia* (English lavender), *L. latifolia*, and *L.* x *intermedia* (hybrids between the two).

**MARIGOLD, POT (ENGLISH)** *Calendula officinalis*
(Traditionally *pot* marigold, rather than the African and French marigolds
(*Tagetes* sp.) used in salads, though all are edible.) Fairly hardy annual,
usually about 30cm (1ft) high, with flowers of lemon, orange and related
shades, from late spring to late autumn. Usually self-seeds readily. Prefers
loamy soil, sunny position. Sow spring onwards, in seedtrays indoors or
very thinly *in situ* outdoors. Must thin early to 25cm (10in) apart, or they
become floppy. In temperate climates can sow in open or cold greenhouse late summer/early autumn for very early flowers following year.
Remove dead flower heads to prolong flowering. May be attacked by
mildew in damp weather. Historically one of the most widely used medicinal and culinary flowers; saffron substitute. Use young leaves and petals
whole and chopped in salads; flowers can be dried and pickled.

**MARROW (*see* Squash)**

**NASTURTIUM (INDIAN CRESS)** *Tropaeolum majus*
Climbing, trailing and dwarf tender annuals. Spurred flowers available in
all shades of red to yellow, bloom early summer until frost. 'Alaska' cultivars: dainty, variegated leaves. 'Empress of India': pretty purplish leaves.
Thrive on poor soils, dry banks, and a sunny position. Sow spring *in situ*
or indoors. (In the seventeenth century raised early on hotbeds.) Thin or
plant to 23cm (9in) apart. Leaves (whole or chopped), flowers and buds
have long usage in salads because of their hot, peppery flavour. Seeds
pickled as caper substitute. Pick when green soon after flowers wither.
Where wanted primarily for leaves, grow in richer soil. Flowers of closely
related species, for example Canary Creeper *Tropaeolum peregrinum* and
yellow-flowered *T. minus* also edible. In some seasons nasturtiums devas-
tated by caterpillars and aphids.

**PANSY, GARDEN** *Viola wittrockiana* , **PANSY, WILD**
**(HEARTEASE, JOHNNY JUMP-UP)** *Viola tricolor*, **and other**
**VIOLAS, VIOLETTAS (MINIATURE VIOLAS), and** *Viola* **species.**
**For SWEET VIOLET** *Viola odorata* **see p.240.**
The flowers of these related low-growing annuals and perennials are edi-
ble raw in salads. Diverse colours and flower patterns – dainty single
colours at one extreme, multi-coloured pansy 'faces' at the other.
Appearance probably more valuable than flavour, which ranges from
sweet (generally in smallest types) to musky to nondescript. My personal
preference for salads is small, dainty types, but winter-flowering pansies

are a great standby for winter salads. In general pansies like well-worked soil, with open or partial shade. Best treated as biennials: stagger sowings for all year round flowers. Remove dead flowers to prolong flowering season. (For cultivation of all types consult general books see Further Reading p.251.)

### PELARGONIUM spp. (Popularly known as 'Geraniums')
Tender, colourful perennials, flowering prolifically over the summer months. Flowers are a wonderful range of colours from white to red. Many of them have distinctly flavoured leaves, for example Lemon geranium, *P. crispum*, which have long been used in cooking, and can be incorporated sparingly in salads. Flavour of most flowers delicate; flowers of scented-leaf types generally stronger. In temperate climates most types raised from stem cuttings taken in summer and over-wintered under cover; others from seed sown early in spring. (For detailed cultivation see general books in Further Reading p.251.)

### PINKS *(see Dianthus sp.)*

### PRIMROSE *Primula vulgaris*
Familiar wild perennial, up to 20cm (8in) high, yellow flowers in spring, easily cultivated. Prefers humus-rich soil, semi-shade. Sow in leafy compost in spring, in boxes indoors or in frame in cool position, planting autumn or early following spring 15cm (6in) apart. Mulch with well-rotted compost in spring. Remove lower leaves to protect from slugs and snails; keep weed free. Every three years divide mature plants, or leaves produced rather than flowers. Flowers and young leaves used in salads.

### PUMPKIN *(see* Squash)

### ROSE *Rosa sp.*
Any roses, wild or cultivated, can be used in salads. Select those with most fragrance. To avoid destroying flowers take only those with petals on the verge of falling. They add beautiful colour and fragrance to salads; sprinkle on top either alone or mixed with other flowers. Rose petals have long been used for culinary purposes.

### ROSEMARY *Rosmarinus officinalis*
Perennial evergreen Mediterranean shrub, normally violet-blue flowers but some forms have white flowers. Main flowering period spring/early

summer. Flowers delicate and attractive in salads. (For cultivation see Herbs p.229.)

### SAGE, CLARY *Salvia sclarea*
Hardy biennial garden flower up to 60cm (2ft) high with pretty mauve and white flowers and colourful purplish-pink bracts from mid-summer to early autumn. Sow summer, transplant in autumn about 45cm (18in) apart. Lovely potager plant. Flowers and bracts have curious and particularly appealing, flavour.

### SAGE, COMMON *Salvia officinalis*
Relatively hardy, perennial bushes about 60cm (2ft) high. Flowering forms include blue-flowered narrow-leaved common sage; white and pink forms of common sage; blue-flowered form of red sage. (Broad-leaved form of common sage rarely flowers in temperate/cool climates.) Flowering period normally late spring to summer. Flowers have pleasant mild sage flavour: add fragrance and colour to salads. (For cultivation see Herbs p.229.)

### SAGE, PAINTED *Salvia horminum*
Hardy annual, 30cm (1ft) high, having colourful purple, pink and white bracts in summer. Sow spring, or autumn as Clary sage above. Space 25cm (10in) apart. Bracts very colourful in salads, but they have a rather strong flavour.

### SALSIFY *Tragopogon porrifolius*
Normally grown as a root vegetable. (For cultivation see Salad Plants p.198.) Beautiful purple flowers, from early summer to early autumn. Raw flowers and cooked buds – hot or cold – can be successfully used in salad dishes. Unusual flavour. Flowers open for a relatively brief period in the morning; close and fade fast when picked. So pick just before use, or as soon as open and keep in closed bag in the refrigerator. For raw flowers use the petals only. Wild salsify (Goatsbeard) (*Tragopogon pratensis*) has yellow flowers which can be used similarly as an appealing and decorative salad ingredient.

### SCORZONERA *Scorzonera hispanica*
Normally grown for using as cooked root vegetable. (For cultivation see Salad Plants p.200.) Yellow flowers. Use flowers and buds as salsify for salad dishes.

## SQUASH FAMILY AND RELATED SPECIES *Cucumis, Cucurbita* and others

The flowers of cucumbers, summer squash (courgettes and marrows), winter squash (pumpkins), and various oriental gourds are all edible. If you want 'fruit' as well, only pick male flowers, but leave a few males on each plant for pollination. Female flowers recognized by tiny bump of embryonic fruit behind the petals. Flowers best picked when just about to open. Widely used in cooking (stuffed, fried, in soups), but can use raw, whole or sliced, in salads. Distinct flavour. (For cultivation see individual plants.)

## SWEET WILLIAM (*see Dianthus* sp.)

## SWEET VIOLET *Viola odorata*

Small violet, occasionally white, flowers in early spring. Easily cultivated in ordinary soil with plenty of humus, shaded position. Plant crowns in spring or autumn 23cm (9in) apart; or sow autumn in cold frame. Will germinate following spring for planting out, though germination erratic. Violets widely grown in past for cooking and as salad herb. In the fifteenth-century flowers eaten raw with onions and lettuce!

## CULINARY HERBS

The flowers of many culinary herbs have much the same flavour as the leaves. They are often tiny, and the flavour is surprisingly strong. They can be used in cooking or sprinkled sparingly in salads. Try basil, chervil, dill, bronze and green fennel, hyssop, lemon balm, lemon verbena, marjorams and oregano, mints (except pennyroyal), rosemary, perilla, sweet cicely, and thyme. (For cultivation see general books on herbs in Further Reading p.251.)

## OTHER EDIBLE FLOWERS

Acacia, *Acacia* sp.; Beans (Broad or Fava), *Vicia faba*; Beans (Runner), *Phaseolus coccineus*; Begonia, *Begonia Semperflorens-Cultorum* and *B. tuberhybrida* hybrids; Black locust, *Robinia pseudo-acacia*; Bladder campion, *Silene vulgaris*; Busy Lizzy, *Impatiens walleriana*; Calamint, *Calaminta neptoides*; Chamomile, *Matricaria recutita*; Chickweed, *Stellaria media*; Clover, *Trifolium pratense*; Corn salad, *Valerianella locusta*; Cresses (see Wild Plants and Weeds p.244), Cress, rock *Arabis* sp.; Dandelion, *Taraxacum officinalis*; Elder flower, *Sambucus canadensis* and *S. caerulea*; Feijoa sellowiana, (syn. *Acca sellowiana*); Forget-me-not, *Myosotis sylvatica*; Fuchsia, *Fuchsia* sp. (inner petals); Hawthorn, *Crataegus* sp.; Hibiscus, *Hibiscus* sp.; Jasmine, *Jasminum* sp.; Lemon blossom, *Citrus limon*; Honeysuckle, *Lonicera japonica*; Horse radish, *Armoracia rusticana*; Lilac, *Syringa vulgaris*; Malabar spinach, *Basella* sp.; Mallows, *Malva* sp.; Marigolds, African, French and citrus-scented, *Tagetes erecta*, *T. patula* and *T. tenuifolia*; Mignonette, *Reseda odorata*; Mulleins, *Verbascum* sp.; Onion, nodding, *Allium cernum*; Orange blossom, *Citrus sinensis*; Orchid tree, *Bauhinia variegata*; Passion flower, *Passiflora* sp.; Peas, *Pisum sativum*; Peppers, *Capsicum annuum* (soak flowers in cool water to make petals curl); Petunia hybrids, *Petunia* sp.; Pineapple mayweed, *Matricaria matricarioides*; Portulaca, *Portulaca grandiflora*; Purslane, winter (Miner's lettuce), *Montia* sp. (previously *Claytonia* sp.); Radish, *Raphanus sativus*; Red bud, *Cercis* sp.; Rocket, Sweet, *Hesperis matronalis*; Safflower, *Carthamus tinctorius*; Saffron, *Crocus sativum*; Salad rocket, *Eruca vesicaria* (cold brings out red pigments); Scotch heather, *Calluna vulgaris*; Shepherd's purse, *Capsella bursa-pastoris*; Snapdragon, *Antirrhinum majus*; Sunflower, *Helianthus annuus*; Sweet woodruff, *Galium odoratum*; Thistle, *Cirsium* sp.; Tulip, *Tulipa* sp.; Valerian, red, *Centranthus ruber*; Vetches, *Vicia* sp.; Yarrows, *Achillea* sp. (pink more bitter than others); Yuccas, *Yucca* sp.

# Chapter 16
# Wild Plants and Weeds

In his immense Victorian encyclopedia on gardening J C Loudon has a short but compact section on 'Edible wild plants, neglected or not in cultivation'. His main reason for including them was 'to enable the gentleman's gardener to point out resources to the poor in his neighbourhood in seasons of scarcity'. He adds rather ominously that 'all vegetables not absolutely poisonous may be rendered edible by proper preparation'.

In many parts of the world, however, the approach to the amazing storehouse of food in wild plants – from which all our cultivated vegetables derive – is far more enthusiastic. This enthusiasm is most noticeable in mountain areas, where, starved of fresh greenery during the long winter months, the spring tradition of gathering the first 'mountain herbs' for use in salads stretches from Europe to Japan.

I wouldn't normally advocate a salad made entirely from wild plants; but it is great fun and a source of satisfaction and variety to add a few leaves of this or that to a salad. They are an excellent source of vitamins and minerals, and many have 'healthy' properties as well.

The main problem with wild plants is identification. To paraphrase what the old salad sage Evelyn said three hundred years ago: they say that any fool can gather salads – you can hardly go wrong if you choose herbs which are young, tender and green – but many fatal mistakes have been made by those who mistook hemlock and aconites for garden parsley or parsnip; fine-leaved water dropwort for wild celery, and so on. One must be *absolutely* certain, basing identification on several parts of the plant, and consulting a good book on wild plants until one is familiar with the plants. Never base identification simply on one illustration in a book.

Here are brief notes on some weeds and wild plants which can be eaten raw. I have tried only a fraction of them, but since combing literature, past and present, to discover what was used, I have found myself eyeing corners of my own garden and neighbouring hedgerows with intense interest. As a result hardly a week goes by without using some weed or wild plant in a salad. As a general rule, the younger the leaves, the better they will taste. The leaves of most weeds and wild plants coarsen with age so pick early on.

This list is merely a starting point for those who want to pursue the matter further. Besides the common names, Latin names have been given for accurate identification. (Common names can be very misleading; the same name is sometimes applied to both an edible and a poisonous species!) It is illegal to dig up wild plants in the countryside – so take only a few leaves as you need them, or cultivate the plants in your garden.

### ALEXANDERS *Smyrnium olusatrum*
Biennial plant, up to 1.5m (5ft) high, common around coasts. One of earliest to appear in spring. Whole plant edible once cultivated. Buds and spicy young leaves used in salads; stems used to be blanched. Spicy seeds can be used as pepper substitute. Don't confuse with poisonous hemlock water dropwort (*Oenanthe crocata*) found in similar places at same time.

### BEECH *Fagus sylvatica*
Very young leaves, sweet–tasting.

### BROOKLIME *Veronica beccabunga*
Common in streams, marshes, wet places. Young tops used in salads. Opinions differ as to whether it is more or less bitter than watercress.

### BURDOCK, GREATER AND LESSER *Arctium lappa* and *A. minus*
Common, large–leaved rampant plant growing 1.5m (5ft) high, seeds protected by burs. Used all over the world, cooked and raw. Pick young leaf stems in spring, strip off peel, cut into small pieces for salad.

### BURNET, SALAD *Sanguisorba minor* or *Poterium sanguisorba*
Common, virtually evergreen weed of chalky grassland. Leaves cucumber–flavoured. Can dip into hot water momentarily before use to soften astringency. (For cultivation see Herbs p.224.)

### CAMPION, BLADDER *Silene vulgaris*
Widespread white-flowered roadside weed. Young mild-flavoured leaves and shoots eaten raw and cooked.

### CAT'S EAR *Hypochoeris radicata*
Very common perennial weed in countryside and garden. Leaves green all year round; can be picked for salads.

### CELERY, WILD (SMALLAGE) *Apium graveolens*
Found in damp places near the sea. Leaves and young stems chopped into salads. (Do not confuse with hemlock or hemlock water dropwort.)

**CHICKWEED** *Stellaria media*
Very common garden weed. Surprisingly tasty. I have used young growths and leaves in salads almost all year round. Grows more lushly in slightly moist, shaded positions, for example in my fruit cage. Worth 'nurturing' best patches. Chop with scissors; regrows rapidly.

**CHICORY, WILD** *Cichorium intybus*
Young leaves may be used whole in spring salads and older leaves shredded finely to relieve the tart flavour. It can be blanched and forced (see Dandelion opposite). (See Flowers in Salad p.233 and for cultivation see Salad Plants p.147.)

**CORN SALAD (Lamb's lettuce)** *Valerianella locusta*
Common plant on dry soils; very hardy, leaves remaining green all through the winter. Young leaves, young flower stalks, top of root and flowers all edible in salads. Often self-seeds. (See Salad Plants p.149.)

**COWSLIP** *Primula veris* **and PRIMROSE** *Primula vulgaris*
Young leaves and flowers used in salads.

**CRESSES**
Many of the not necessarily related wild plants widely known as 'cresses' are suitable for use in salads. Most have characteristic, pungent flavour. Many remain green all through the winter or appear very early in spring. Best to use young leaves. Easily cut with scissors; regrow rapidly.

**American Land Cress (Upland cress, land cress)** *Barbarea verna*
Biennial evergreen, common on waste ground. Formerly widely cultivated as salad plant and for oily seeds. (See Salad Plants p.152.)

**Field Penny Cress (Common cress)** *Thlaspi arvense*
Very common annual weed in waste places, arable fields and gardens. Young leaves spicy addition to salads.

**Hairy Bitter Cress** *Cardamine hirsuta*
Annual weed common on wasteland, bare ground in gardens. Small-leaved, ground-hugging plant until flowering spikes shoot up in spring. Seeds fired out of pods dramatically, resembling an attack of midges if pods touched. Extremely hardy; very useful in salads late into winter and early in spring. A patch will regenerate itself in a garden; thin out

seedlings to keep plants a reasonable size. Cloche a few plants in spring to make leaves more tender and larger. Wavy Bitter Cress very similar.

### Watercress *Rorippa nasturtium-aquaticum* or *Nasturtium officinale*
Confusingly sometimes called brooklime. Common in running water. Older leaves from top of plants have more flavour than young leaves. Never pick from stagnant water or where water contaminated by pastures, because of risk of liver fluke infection. For this reason, it is advisable to cultivate from shop-bought watercress or grow American land cress.

### Winter Cress (Yellow rocket) *Barbarea vulgaris*
Biennial or perennial evergreen cress with broad, deeply indented leaves, common on damp roadsides and waste places. Very similar to American land cress. Extremely hardy; can be used in salad all winter. Use basal leaves and leaves on flowering stems.

### DAISY, ENGLISH *Bellis perennis*
Ubiquitous daisy of garden lawns. The young leaves can be used in salads. Sometimes strong aftertaste. (See Flowers in Salad p.235.)

### DAISY, OX-EYE *Leucanthemum vulgare*
Young leaves used in salads in Italy. (See Flowers in Salad p.235.)

### DANDELION *Taraxacum officinale*
Ubiquitous weed, all parts edible. Can blanch *in situ* to make leaves more tender. Flowers used raw in salads and for making wine.

### DOCK, RED-VEINED *Rumex sanguineus*
Dramatic network of crimson veins on narrowish leaves. Decorative rather than edible as coarse texture. Blanch briefly in boiling water to soften. Easily cultivated but beware, self-seeds prolifically.

### EVENING PRIMROSE, LARGE AND COMMON *Oenothera erythrosepala* and *O. biennis*
Tall yellow-flowered biennial now found wild; introduced to Europe from America for cultivation of edible root. Young leaves eaten in salads.

### FAT HEN (Lamb's quarters) *Chenopodium album*
Common weed of cultivated ground and wasteland. Young leaves eaten raw in salads; also cooked like spinach.

## GARLIC

Several wild plants closely related to garlic can be used in salads; flavour varies from mild to strong. Useable parts include leaves, stems, bulbs, sometimes tiny aerial bulbs, flowers. Best known wild or wood garlic (ramsoms) (see below). Others include crow garlic (*Allium veneale*), field garlic (*A. oleraceum*), keeled garlic (*A. carinatum*); rocambole (sand leek) (*A. scorodoprasum*), notable for its earliness and very twisted leaves.

### Garlic, Wild (Wood, Ramsoms) *Allium ursinum*

Common in damp woods. Strong garlic flavour. Chop leaves into salads.

### Garlic Mustard (Jack by the hedge) *Alliaria petiolata*

Common hedgerow weed appearing very early in the year. Bruised leaves have faint garlic smell. Use finely chopped in salads, or cooked.

## GOAT'S RUE *Galega officinalis*

Vigorous legume, pretty pink and white flowers, lovely in flower border; young leaves quite strong taste in salads.

## GOLDEN SAXIFRAGE *Chrysosplenium oppositifolium*

Plants of shady mountains, streams and wet ground. Leaves gathered for salads; the *cresson des roches* of the Vosges.

## GOOD KING HENRY *Chenopodium bonus-henricus*

Wayside perennial, generally cooked like asparagus but young growths and asparagus-like shoots, which appear very early in spring, can be used raw in salads. Do not confuse with dog's mercury (*Mercurialis perennis*) – quite similar in appearance but poisonous. (See Herbs p.226.)

## GROUND ELDER *Aegopodium podagraria*

Pernicious weed! Distinct angelica flavour in young leaves. Regular picking may weaken plant. Also similar to dog's mercury, see above.

## HAWTHORN *Crataegus monogyna*

Very young leaves and flower buds chopped into salads. Nutty taste.

## LADY'S SMOCK (Cuckoo flower) *Cardamine pratensis*

Pretty pale purple flower found in damp meadows and streamsides. Leaves remain green late in winter; watercress spiciness. In spring, pick young leaves from lower rosette.

**LETTUCE, WALL** *Mycelis muralis*
Perennial growing 1m (3ft) high on chalky walls. Leaves eaten in salads.

**LIME** *Tilia europaea*
Use young leaves, before they roughen, with sprinkling of lemon juice.

**LUNGWORT** *Pulmonaria officinalis*
Perennial grown as garden plant and sometimes found wild as escape.
Young leaves chopped into spring salads.

**MUSTARD** *Sinapis alba*
'Mustard and cress' mustard; cultivated as green manure and also for
seeds from which mustard is extracted; often found wild. Young
seedlings may be eaten in salads, but it is difficult to identify them at this
stage in a field, so probably more practical to grow them at home. (For
cultivation see p.179.)

**NIPPLEWORT** *Lapsana communis*
Common weed and wayside plant. Leaves edible raw.

**OYSTER PLANT** *Mertensia maritima*
Attractive creeping plant native to north Scottish shores. Bright blue
flowers. Blue-green leaves said to have oyster flavour.

**PARSLEY PIERT** *Aphanes arvensis*
Small plant, pretty foliage, found mainly on dry soils. Old salad plant.

**PLANTAIN, BUCKSHORN** *Plantago coronopus*
Common plant on European coastal regions. French used to cultivate it,
sowing in spring and then thinning to 13cm (5in) apart. Cut flowers off
as they appear to maintain a steady supply of tender leaves for use in salads. Remains green late into winter. Self-seeds prolifically. Plunge older
leaves in boiling water to tenderize. (See Salad Plants p.186.)

**PLANTAIN, RAT'S TAIL** *Plantago major*
Very common countryside and garden weed famous for its ability to survive trampling. Eat central young leaves; pleasant slightly mustardy taste.

**POPPY, FIELD** *Papaver rhoeas*
Common red-flowered poppy. The young leaves are eaten raw in the

Mediterranean; seeds widely used in and on cakes. Do not confuse with Red Horned Poppy (*Glaucium corniculatum*).

### PURSLANE *Portulaca oleracea*
Succulent plant found on light soils. Used raw and pickled in salads; Cobbett said 'fit only for pigs and Frenchmen'! Refreshing but bland. (See Salad Plants p.187.)

### PURSLANE, SEA *Halimione portulacoides*
Succulent, grey- and silver-leaved plant of salt marshes. Leaves used in salads, but need careful washing.

### RAMPION *Campanula rapunculus*
Now uncommon plant, found on gravelly soils. Once widely cultivated for sweet, turnip-like roots, which were eaten cooked and raw in salads, and for young leaves, used raw. Evelyn also suggested earthing up stems to blanch, and eating seed leaves and young tops.

### RED SHANK *Polygonum persicaria*
Very common weed of arable land. Use leaves raw or cooked. Similar to very acrid Water pepper (*Polygonum hydropiper*) found in damp places.

### ROCKET, WALL (Wall mustard) *Diplotaxis muralis*
Found on rocks, walls and on waste ground. The leaves are eaten raw in the Mediterranean.

### SALSIFY, WILD (Goatsbeard) *Tragopogon pratensis*
Common in dry grassy places. Narrow-leaved weed with dandelion-like flowers. Flowers, buds, young leaves, shoots and roots used in salads. (For flowers see p.239; for cultivation see p.198.)

### SAMPHIRE, MARSH (Glasswort) *Salicornia europaea*
A strange, succulent plant that is found on salt marshes and on shingle beaches; its ashes were once used as a constituent in the making of glass. For salads, the young leaves and shoots are traditionally gathered in early/mid-summer. Refreshing, salty flavour. Older growths, gathered in late summer/early autumn were cooked. It can apparently be grown in gardens by sowing fresh-gathered seed in the autumn in a good, well-drained soil. Young growths can be pickled in vinegar. It is known as 'Roscano' in Italy. 'Salsola' is a closely related genera eaten in Asia.

## SAMPHIRE, ROCK *Crithmum maritimum*
Fleshy-leaved plant found on cliffs and shingle. Leaves and stems cooked, or pickled for salads.

## SCURVY GRASS *Cochlearia officinalis*
Shiny-leaved plant found on coastal cliffs. Leaves rich in vitamin C, eaten raw in salads. Used to be cultivated. My experience of cultivation: sown early summer, remained vivid green all winter. (Ideal winter edging plant.) I found the very strong flavour of mature leaves unpleasant. Not everyone agreed. Maybe seedling leaves, as advised by Evelyn, would be better. Self-seeds prolifically. (If obtainable thicker Danish scurvy grass, *C. danica*, considered better for cultivation; long-leaved scurvy grass, *C.angelica*, may be better flavoured.)

## SEAKALE *Crambe maritima*
Native perennial on European sand and shingle beaches, now becoming scarce: pick sparingly. Traditional practice was to cover plant with 45cm (18in) shingle, either in autumn when died down, or in early spring, and scrape away shingle to cut young shoots. (For cultivation see p.201.)

## SHEPHERD'S PURSE *Capsella bursa-pastoris*
Very common weed, green much of the year. Basal rosettes and stem leaves excellent raw in salads; distinctive flavour said to be due to sulphur. Cultivated and sold in China for use raw or cooked like spinach. Said to be richer in vitamin C than oranges. One snag – it harbours clubroot. (For cultivation see p.205.)

## SORREL, FRENCH *Rumex acetosa* and BUCKLER-LEAVED *R. scutatus* (though much confusion over naming!)
Found wild in grassland, woods, roadsides; appears very early in year. Leaves have sharp lemon taste. (For cultivation see p.205.)

## STONECROP, REFLEXED *Sedum reflexum*
Succulent-leaved perennial found wild on walls and rocks. Extensively used in salads in past. Easily grown in rock gardens and dry borders, sowing seed outdoors mid-spring, or dividing roots in spring. Other edible sedums: *Sedum acre* – used in small quantities as pepper substitute; *Sedum album* – used in salads or cooked; *Sedum rosea* – used in salads in Greenland. Evelyn recommended the seed leaves and young tops of the stonecrop 'Trip Madam', but which one was it?

### STRAWBERRY *Fragaria vesca*
Young leaves of wild and cultivated strawberries can be eaten raw. (Not personally impressed by the flavour!)

### THISTLE, MARSH *Cirsium palustre* or *Carduus palustris*
Use raw young shoots and stalks, after removing prickles and peeling.

### THISTLE, MILK *Silybum marianum*
Biennial thistle with beautiful white-veined foliage. Young leaves and stems (peeled and chopped) used in salads. Roots eaten raw and cooked. Easily grown in garden. Sow in spring, thin or plant 60cm (2ft) apart.

### THISTLE, SOW (Corn, perennial or field milk sow thistle) *Sonchus arvensis*
Common weed of damp places and arable land. Trim bristles off leaves before using raw.

### TOOTHACHE PLANT (Australian cress) *Spilanthes acmella*
Annual with attractive yellow flowers. Leaves eaten in salads.

### VALERIAN, RED *Centranthus/Kentranthus ruber*
Red- and white-flowered forms found on dry banks and walls. Very young leaves eaten in salads or cooked. Roots used in soup. Cultivated in gardens by sowing in spring and planting out about 60cm (2ft) apart; or by dividing old plants in spring or autumn. Flowers also edible.

### WINTERGREEN, COMMON *Pyrola minor*
Berried evergreen plant found in woods and on moors, rocks and dunes. Young tender leaves used in salads in North America.

### WOAD *Isatis tinctoria*
Striking, biennial dye plant. Young leaves used in salads.

### WOOD SORREL *Oxalis acetosella*
Delicate folded clover-like leaves appear in woods in early spring. Sharp sorrel flavour; long usage in salads. Old English name – Alleluia!

### YARROW (Milfoil) *Achillea millefolium*
Very common weed, green most of the year. Use feathery leaves in small quantities in salads; can also strip leaves from stems and cook.

# Further Reading

## VEGETABLE GROWING & TECHNIQUES
*Container Gardening*, Kenneth Beckett, David Carr and David Stevens (Frances Lincoln 1982)

*The Vegetable Garden*, Vilmorin-Andrieux (John Murray, 1885, reprinted 1977)

*The Complete Know and Grow Vegetables*, edited by J. K. A. Bleasdale, P. J. Salter and others (Oxford University Press, revised edition 1991).

*The Complete Manual of Organic Gardening*, edited by Basil Caplan (Headline Book Publishing, 1992)

*The Vegetable Garden Displayed*, Joy Larkcom (Royal Horticultural Society, completely revised edition 1992)

*Oriental Vegetables*, Joy Larkcom (John Murray, 1991)

*Vegetables for Small Gardens*, Joy Larkcom (Reed Illustrated Books, completely revised edition 1995)

*Worms Eat My Garbage*, Mary Appelhof (Flower Press, 1982)

*The Collingridge Handbook of Greenhouse Gardening*, A. C. Macself and Arthur Turner (Collingridge Books, 1982)

*The Organic Greenhouse*, Sue Stickland Search Press, 1993)

## HERBS, WILD PLANTS AND FLOWERS
*Annuals and Bedding Plants*, Graham Rice (Croom Helm London/ Timber Press Oregon, 1986)

*Culinary Herbs*, Mary Page and William T. Stearn (Royal Horticultural Society, 1974)

*Herb Gardening*, Claire Loewenfeld (Faber & Faber, 1964)

*Herbs, Spices and Flavourings*, Tom Stobart (Penguin Books, 1977)

*The Wild Flower Key*, Francis Rose (Frederic Warne,1981)

*Wild Flowers in Britain*, Roger Phillips (Pan Books & Ward Lock, 1977)

*Wild Food*, Roger Phillips (Pan Books 1983)

## LEAFLETS
**Horticulture Research International** publish guides for gardeners. Enquiries: The Librarian, HRI, Wellesbourne, Warwick, CV35 9EF

**HDRA** (Henry Doubleday Research Association) publish leaflets on many aspects of organic cultivation. Enquiries to HDRA, National Centre for Organic Gardening, Ryton on Dunsmore, Coventry CV8 3LG

# Glossary

**Annual** Plant which germinates, flowers and dies within twelve months

**Base dressing** Fertilizer worked into the soil prior to sowing or planting

**Biennial** Plant which germinates, flowers and dies within two years

**Blanching** (horticultural) Excluding light from plants to render them white and tender; (culinary) immersing briefly in boiling water

**Bolting** Flowering prematurely

**Brassica** Large genus of plants including cabbages, turnips, swedes, mustards. Known as crucifers in the USA

**Check** Growth being halted through adverse conditions such as drought and cold

**Chicons** The compact, pointed, bud-like growth which develops from the root when chicories are forced in the dark

**Clamp** Method of storing root crops to protect them from frost. Essentially roots are piled on a straw base and covered with straw and/or earth

**Cordon** Plant growing up single stem, either vertically or at an angle

**Cotyledon** The first tiny leaf or pair of leaves to emerge on germination. Also known as 'seed leaf'

**Cultivar** A variety raised in cultivation

**Dibber** A small hand tool with a sharp or rounded end for making holes in the ground for planting

**Drill** A shallow furrow in the soil into which seeds are sown

**Earthing up** Drawing up soil around the base and stem of a plant

**F₁ Hybrid Seed** see p.63

**Growing point** Tip of plant. If removed upward growth ceases, but side branches may develop instead making the plant bushier

**Half-hardy** Plant unable to survive normal UK winter conditions without protection

**Hardwood cuttings** Cutting taken from matured growth at end of growing season

**Hardy** Plant capable of surviving normal United Kingdom winter conditions without protection.

**Heart up** Leaves changing from a loose state to a dense, compact 'heart' or 'head'

*In situ* **sowing** Sowing where plant is to grow, so avoiding transplanting

**Lateral** A side shoot or branch which comes off a main stem. Sub-laterals are shoots which develop on the laterals

**Leaf axil** Angle between leaf and stem

**Legumes** Plants in *Leguminosae* family, which includes peas and beans, characterized by the production of pods and the ability of nodules on the roots to fix nitrogen in the soil

**Ley** A grass or green manure crop grown for a year or more to improve the soil condition

**Marinate** (Culinary) To leave soaking in oil and vinegar (and possibly herbs) for a few hours

**Off-set** Plant produced at base of parent plant

**Open-pollinated** When the seed is produced from natural, random pollination

**Perennial** Plant which lives for several years

**Seed leaves** see Cotyledon

**Short- and Long-day Plants** Plants in which flowering is governed by day length. In northern latitudes short-day plants naturally flower and seed in the shortening days after mid-summer, while long-day plants do so in the lengthening days from spring to mid-summer

**Softwood cuttings** Cuttings taken from young growths early in the season

**Species** Grouping of plants which differ only in minor details, and will freely cross with each other. Closely related species are grouped together in a genus. eg in *Lactuca sativa*, the Latin name for lettuce, *Lactuca* is the generic (genus) name, while *sativa* is the specific (species) name

**Spit** A spade's depth of soil

**Stopping** Removing the growing point of a plant

**Tap root** A large single root, as opposed to a fibrous root

**Tender** Plants which are injured by frost or cold weather

**Top dressing** Fertilizer application to growing plants

**Truss** A flower cluster or inflorescence

**Viable seed** Living seed, capable of germination

# Index